Over The Hill And Around The World

by Darby Roach

Copyright © 2016 by Darby Roach

All rights reserved. No part of this publication may be reproduced, distributed, or transmitted in any form or by any means, including photocopying, recording, or other electronic or mechanical methods, without the prior written permission of the publisher, except in the case of brief quotations embodied in critical reviews and certain other noncommercial uses permitted by copyright law. For permission requests, write to the author at the address below.

darbyroach12@me.com

"I went to the woods because I wished to live deliberately, to front only the essential facts of life, and see if I could not learn what it had to teach, and not, when I came to die, discover that I had not lived."

-Henry David Thoreau

Preface

It was 2012. I was sixty-two and in good health. I'd raised my three daughters, seen them through college, and given them away at their weddings. I was still close to my kids. We skied and hiked and bicycled together and never passed up a chance to talk on the phone.

Life was good. Still, for the past few years, I had felt a vague dissatisfaction with a career that had once been challenging but now seemed to be just another way of marking time. I would wake up in the dark hours of the night and ask myself the same questions: What now? What comes next? If the answer was more of the same, dull routine until dotage robbed me of my independence, then I would have to make a change.

I knew this wasn't the kind of problem that could be solved with a new convertible. No, the roots of my discontent ran too deep for that. In fact, it seemed that my possessions — my house, my car, and the other trappings that go with a middle-class life — were part of the problem. I felt like a fresh start; like I should design a new life from the ground up, focused on something I liked to do instead of something I had to do.

I had always loved to travel, and about this time I had gotten back into cycling, so I came up with the idea of combining these two passions. I would try to ride my bike around the world! Like Tolkien's Bilbo Baggins, I would wander. And like Thoreau, I would rid myself of all extraneous possessions and keep only the bare essentials. I would visit exotic lands. I would expose myself to different cultures and new ideas. I would find an answer or I wouldn't. I would see what happened.

Maybe I would write a book.

Excerpt

The man next to me nudged me with his elbow. "I've never seen them do that before."

"Do what?" I said.

"Go over an American passport the way they're going over yours." We could see the border guard examining it through the window; he would flip through the pages, look at my photo, then at me, then back at my photo. He passed it around now, and each official went through the same routine. They had found something interesting, and I was starting to worry.

I gulped, "That's not good."

The man, who looked to be an American expat, gave me a grim smile. "Well, good luck." The Cambodian border guard handed him back his passport. "You might want to give the American Embassy a call before they take your cell phone away," he added.

"Right," I said — then, "Wait, what?!" I looked around, but he had vanished into the throng of humanity streaming across the Cambodian border into Thailand.

The border guard crooked his finger at me. I leaned in the window. "Wait over there." He indicated a spot out of line next to a high chain-link fence. Several soldiers standing nearby, their rifles at the ready, looked my way.

"Uh, is there something wrong?"

The border guard pointed. "Wait over there."

I did as I was ordered and tried to appear calm, but my heart was beating in my chest like something trying to get out. There were four or five lines of people waiting to cross the border. There must have been close to a hundred people in the crowd, and they all seemed to be looking at me. I felt exposed, singled out for . . . what? What was going on? Was there something wrong with my passport? Some flaw? Or maybe they had me mixed up with someone else? Was it a case of mistaken identity? I was sweating bullets now. I glanced around; the border guards were eyeballing me, I was sure of it. I had heard stories of Westerners who had run afoul of Cambodian law and simply disappeared for reasons that no one could properly explain. I'd seen the movie *Midnight Express,* and I conjured up visions of prison and torture. They'd throw a net over me and drag me to some filthy jungle pit. My family would never know what had happened. The Thai border was right over there, not fifty yards away. Could I make a break for it?

Part One: North America
Chapter One: Washington

I had set May 6th as the date for my departure, and in the last week my friends had a going away party for me. I made a point of spending time with as many friends and family members as I could. That last week was a flurry of activity tying up loose ends and making last minute phone calls to friends I hadn't been able to hook up with personally. Finally, before I knew it, the big day arrived. My pal of forty years, Mike, had decided to ride with me for the first two weeks, and he picked me up early on the morning of the 5th. I loaded my bike in his car, took one last look around my now-empty house, climbed in Mike's Saab, and we were off.

Me 2.0

I was leaving my home near Seattle to try to ride my bicycle around the world. I had been planning the trip for several years, winding down my marketing business and selling or giving away almost everything I owned.

When I first came to Seattle in the fall of 1973, all my worldly possessions had barely filled the back seat of my brother's 1963 Oldsmobile. And now I was going around the world with even less! Everything fit into six bicycle panniers and weighed about 80 pounds. I'd agonized over every item, and I hoped I had it right, but how do you know what to pack for a trip to the ends of the Earth?

I was sixty-two and nearing retirement age, and rather than slip into dotage gracefully, I wanted to leap into this new phase of life with both feet. I had come up with the idea of trying to ride my bicycle around the world over beers with Mike, my cycling buddy. It had started out as a flight of fancy, but the more I thought about it, the more it made sense. I was looking to broaden my horizons, and what better way to do that than to travel? I'd done some bicycle touring in my twenties and knew it was a good way to get to know a place. Cycle touring is slow, but after the deadline-driven, high-stress madness of the marketing game, slow sounded pretty good to me.

It's not clear when it went from fantasy to fact, but before I knew it, I was making plans and cutting ties. Once the wheels were in motion, the project took on a life of its own. There were routes to plan, budgets to make and schedules to figure out. I gathered mountains of information and had a stack of maps. Some of my camping equipment was old and had to be replaced. I thought I'd given myself plenty of time, but when the day came to leave, there were still a dozen items on my to-do list.

Everything leading up to this day had been exciting, but now that I was really doing it, I was all doubts and regrets. As we drove down the street, my stomach was doing somersaults. What was I doing heading off into the unknown with nothing but a bicycle and camping gear? I was inexperienced, I had asthma, and I was not in very good shape. It all seemed ridiculous and irresponsible. It was a good thing Mike was driving, because if I had been at the wheel, I'd have turned around and gone straight home.

Mike and I had ridden over the Cascade Mountains countless times, so we decided to forgo that part of the ride and instead start from the town of Wenatchee, 130 miles to the east. It took several hours to reach the old family cabin, high in the mountains near the Mission Ridge ski resort, a few miles out of Wenatchee. Two of my three daughters, Brittney and Maren, and their husbands, Marty and Will, along with my ex-wife, Sue, all met that afternoon and had a small celebration. We turned in early, and I had trouble getting to sleep. Talking about and planning the trip had been fun, but it had been in the abstract. Now it was real. I'd be leaving everything and everyone I'd known for most of my life and plunging into an unknown world. I was basically homeless. The only things I now owned were on my bicycle, which sat packed and waiting on the porch for . . . what? After an hour of tossing and turning, I finally drifted off to troubled sleep.

I awoke early on the morning of May 6th and made a breakfast big enough to feed the whole party. We sat around the table and toasted the beginning of the journey with mimosas. Everyone put on a brave face, keeping the spirit light, but just beneath the surface there was a palpable sadness. No one knew how long it would be before we'd be together again. We kept joking and laughing, trying to put off the inevitable, but soon the sunlight streaking through the window told us it was time to leave.

Gathered at the end of the driveway, our small group traded hugs. I could see the tears welling up in my daughters' eyes, and it was all I could do to choke back tears myself. I knew I had to get going, but I couldn't force my legs to obey. My hands trembled and my vision blurred. *Here it comes*, I thought, *the waterworks*. Mike, sensing what was about to happen, leaned in, grabbed my bicycle, and gave it a gentle push, getting it started down the hill toward town. I looked over my shoulder at my smiling, waving family; then with a sense of firm resolve, I began turning my pedals.

On Our Way

The cyclist waved at us to pull over. "Wow," he said, "you guys are really loaded down. Where are you headed?"

I smiled, "Around the world!"

He chuckled. "No, really, where are you going?"

I shrugged. "We hope to make Waterville today . . . After that, around the world."

It took a few moments for it to sink in, then sensing that I wasn't kidding, the cyclist shook his head. "Man, I wish I was going with you." He had a far-off look. "So how many miles have you come?"

I looked down at my cycle computer, then up. "Seven."

It was a little past 10:00 a.m. and we had zoomed down the hill from the cabin, ridden through town, and were now a few miles north of Wenatchee. We pedaled alongside the broad Columbia

River, the sun shining in a cloudless sky. To our left, the water of the Columbia sparkled in an ever-shifting chiaroscuro. To the right, a sparse, dry, rocky landscape rose dramatically to the heights of the Waterville wheat country. After a fairly flat twenty-four miles, we reached Pine Canyon. Mike and I had driven our cars up the steep, winding road many times, but neither of us had ever attempted to ride a bike up it. We stood at the bottom, stared at the imposing climb, and drank greedily from our water bottles.

"Well," I said, trying to sound positive, "it's only six miles."

"Yeah," Mike replied, "and 2,700 vertical feet."

I'd weighed everything before I left, and when the heft of the bike was added in, the whole shebang weighed a little more than 130 pounds. I glanced up the hill. It was going to be a long afternoon.

It was hot now, in the high eighties, and we started out slogging along in our lowest gears. Still, even at the snail's pace of three miles an hour, we were soon sweating and huffing and puffing. "I . . . gotta . . . stop . . ." I mumbled between gasps. We found a shady spot beneath a withered pine tree and rested against the guardrail. After fifteen minutes, we started up the hill again, but didn't get very far before we took another break. That scene replayed itself countless times in those six steep miles.

After three sweaty hours, we finally rounded the last corner and emerged from the confines of Pine Canyon onto the broad, flat plain of the Waterville wheat country. From our vantage point we could see for miles. Fields of green winter wheat rolled on and on, finally merging with the sky in the far horizon. From where we were, it was a short downhill run to the small town of Waterville, and after the long hours of hot, heavy labor, we were overjoyed to let gravity do the work for a change. We had originally planned to wild camp a few miles east of town, but when we rolled into Waterville and spotted the tidy city park, we decided to camp there instead. There was a sign that said NO OVERNIGHT CAMPING and a number for the sheriff's office. "You don't think that 'no camping thing' applies to us, do you?" Mike asked.

"Why don't you give the sheriff a call, explain our situation and see if they'll make an exception?" I replied. "After all, we're semi-respectable citizens."

Mike pulled out his cell phone and dialed, paced as he spoke for a few moments, then hung up. "Talked to the deputy, he's down in East Wenatchee investigating a car prowl. He said he'd call the mayor and ask if we can camp."

"Sounds good," I said. "In the meantime, let's make dinner." As we were boiling water for pasta, a woman approached and struck up a conversation. She told us that she and her husband were staying at a hotel a few blocks away.

"Really," she said, after we'd chatted a while and filled her in on our trip, "you're really riding your bikes all that way?"

"I'm only going as far as Whitefish, Montana," Mike said.

"That's still a long way," the woman said. She looked at all our gear, and the pot boiling merrily away on my stove. "Are you camping here tonight?"

"Jury's still out," I said. "We've got a call in to the sheriff asking permission. If we don't hear soon, I think we'll just set up our tents and take our chances." We talked for a while longer, then said goodbye and turned our attention to dinner, but before we'd finished preparing our meal, a man approached. He was tall and husky, probably in his late forties, and wore an official-looking cap. Pinned to his khaki shirt was a sheriff's badge.

"You fellas got a permit?" he asked, a stern note to his voice.

Mike and I traded nervous glances. "Uh, no," I said. "We're not really camping."

"Tell it to the judge," he said. "You know, we have a vagrancy ordinance in this town. Plenty of room in the jailhouse..."

The man stood looking at us for a few beats and then burst into laughter. "I'm not really the sheriff," he confessed, "I own the hotel. One of my guests told me your story and I thought I'd come over and have a little fun with you guys. Look, I'm sorry I put you on, so to make up for it, why don't you come stay at my hotel tonight? You both look beat, so I'll give you a discount for being such good sports."

Mike

A hot bath and clean sheets sounded good, so we decided to take him up on his offer. We re-packed our gear and followed the "sheriff" to his hotel, a beautifully restored, turn-of-the-20th-century building a few blocks away. I felt guilty for spending the extra money; after all, I was on a tight budget, but that Pine Canyon had been a real stinker, and I felt I'd earned a little pampering on this, my first day on the road.

A Change of Scenery

We got up early the next morning and had a continental breakfast at the hotel, stopped at a grocery store for sun block, and then headed east out of Waterville. The country we rode through was about as different from the damp, green forests of our homes in Western Washington as it could be. A high, flat plateau, the great Eastern Washington desert rolls on from Waterville all the way to Spokane, 130 miles distant. Perhaps "desert" doesn't quite describe that expanse of land, at least not since water was diverted from the Columbia River. It's blazingly hot in the summer, but the almost-constant sunshine, combined with irrigation, provides the perfect environment for myriad crops. As we rode along beneath the scorching sun, we passed acre upon acre of alfalfa, potatoes, beans and corn. Even with all that green, there were still great stretches of parched, scrawny sagebrush, dry, brown grass, and rock.

Around noon, we reached the Grand Coulee, a canyon formed about 15,000 years ago when the ice dam holding back prehistoric Lake Missoula crumbled and released a torrent of water and ice that ripped a huge gash in the Earth's crust. The modern road that traverses the Coulee cuts steeply down through hundreds of feet of rock and back through millions of years to a mile-wide, 1,300-foot-deep gorge. We rocketed down into the Coulee, reaching speeds of thirty-five miles an hour, and stopped for lunch on the far side. As we sat among the sagebrush and ate our sandwiches, we marveled at this magnificent work of nature, once the path of a raging river, now home to coyotes and hawks.

The Coulee is scabland, and with no shade the heat bordered on unbearable. I knew it would only get hotter as the day wore on, but I tried to push my doubts out of my mind and focus on the positive. I was really on my way.

The Joker

We made about forty miles that day and camped at a park in Coulee City. The evening of the third day, we reached the little desert town of Creston and set our tents up on the lawn outside a community baseball diamond. It had turned windy, and we cooked our dinner in the nearby picnic shelter, played a few games of backgammon, and turned in. It was a pleasantly warm evening, and Highway 2 was quiet all night. The only disturbance was a freight train that rumbled through around midnight and roused me for a few minutes. But once it was past, I fell back asleep and snoozed soundly until early the next morning.

I rose at 6:00 a.m. and walked to the cafe across the street to get a cup of tea, nodding "hello" to the group of senior citizens seated at one of the four or five tables crowded into the small dining room. Our tents were visible through the cafe's big picture window, and as I sat sipping my tea, one of the old timers struck up a conversation. "What time you figure it is?" he asked after some small-talk.

I looked up at the clock on the wall. "Well, looks to be about 6:45."

"Uh huh," the old fellow said, ". . . any minute now." The whole cafe fell silent, all eyes on me.

I waited a few moments and then said, "Okay, I'll bite, what's going to happen any minute now?"

The silver-haired man blew on his coffee, added sugar and cream, and took a sip. "Them sprinklers over there, them ones right under your tents? Well, you see, they're on a timer and they'll be coming on just about five minutes from now." His statement met with a general nodding of heads and murmurs of agreement.

"What?" I shouted, jumped up, fled the cafe, ran across the street and shook Mike awake. "We gotta pack up quick," I said.

Mike sat up and looked around groggily. "Huh?" he said, "What's the rush?"

"Never mind," I said, "I'll tell you later. Just get up and get your stuff off the lawn fast!" I ran over to my tent, tripped, and fell in the door. Mike was up now and I explained about the sprinklers as I dragged clothes and equipment out of my tent and threw them willy-nilly into my panniers. We hastily dragged all our belongings to safety on the sidewalk, stumbling and dropping clothes, sleeping bags and cooking gear, tripping over each other and generally making a big mess of the whole thing. The Three Stooges couldn't have put on a better show. With our gear out of harm's way, we stood waiting for the sprinklers to come on. We waited five minutes, then ten — and then we caught on. "We've been had," I said.

We walked across the street to the cafe where we were met with raucous laughter and good-natured kidding. The old boys had been standing at the window watching us and had gotten a kick out of our antics. "Bet you never packed that fast, huh?" the old joker said, giving me a friendly slap on the back.

We laughed at having fallen for their ruse; after all, it was a pretty good joke. We sat at a table and ordered breakfast. "That's the second practical joke that's been played on us in three days," Mike whispered. "Are we really as dumb as we look?"

"No way," I replied, "we couldn't be."

We finished our breakfast and said goodbye to our new friends, who wished us well. As we mounted our bikes and started out, we could see the old guys gathered at the window waving.

We sailed out of town with the aid of a healthy tailwind that had us speeding along all day at better than twelve miles an hour. The country was flat, with only one steep hill toward the end of the day's ride. In a few short hours, we made it to our destination of Airway Heights, a town west of Spokane. We stopped at a Taco Bell and had dinner, and then I called my middle daughter, Annie. She arranged for her husband, Troy, to pick us up and drive us to their home in Chatteroy, a small community north of the city.

Annie was working the night shift, so she didn't get home until after midnight. As tired as we both were, we stayed up until the early morning talking. "Dad," she said, "I know you're going to go on this adventure, and you know you have my support, but please do one thing for me."

"Sure, Honey, anything."

"Come back home safe and sound."

One Last Goodbye

We slept in the next morning, had breakfast, and then Annie took us into Spokane to stock up on supplies. Later that evening a group of Annie's friends showed up for a barbecue. Again, as the night before, Annie and I talked until the early morning hours.

Dawn came too soon for me. I awoke and began packing my gear, but before long, I abandoned that task in favor of playing with my three-year-old granddaughter, Emi, and my five-month-old grandson, Hunter. Emi is the spitting image of Annie when she was that age, and the similarity brought back many tender memories, making the morning particularly poignant.

Annie has always been the most emotional of my three girls, and I knew saying goodbye to her would be extra hard. So I had tried to steel myself in advance. But when the moment came to part, we both had tears streaming down our cheeks. I rode out of the driveway, waved, and kept looking back until we were out of sight of the house.

The last thread had been cut. There was no turning back now.

Chapter Two: Idaho

It was a fine day for riding, sunny and warm, and at midday we crossed the border into Idaho. The roads weren't as good as they had been in Washington, though traffic was lighter. The first town we came to was Newport, on the Priest River. It was early afternoon, and the chamber of commerce offered free WiFi, so I got on line to catch up on e-mail and video-chat with my daughter Maren, back in Bellingham. "We're in Idaho!" I said.

"Wow, Dad," Maren replied, "that was quick! Where are you spending the night?"

"I don't know, Honey, we'll find someplace."

"Well, don't let the cougars get you. You know there are a lot of those man eaters up there!"

We talked for a while longer, and then it was time to get back on the road. I signed off with the same words I use each time I part from one of my girls: "I love you."

"Love you, too, Dad."

We rode out of Newport under a blue sky, reaching the town of Priest River at 6:00 p.m. We'd heard there was an Army Corps of Engineers campground a mile out of town, and when we inquired at City Hall, the woman behind the desk told us she thought it might not be open yet but that people were camping there anyway. "I have friends who spent a couple of nights there last week," she said, "and since you're on bicycles, I'm sure it won't be a problem."

But when we reached the campground turnoff, we were greeted by a sign that said, CLOSED NO CAMPING. Mike and I traded nervous looks. Neither of us said a word as we slalomed through the barricades and coasted up to the host's trailer. I knocked on the door and asked the woman who answered if we could camp. "You see," I said, pointing at Mike, who teetered on his bike nearby, "my friend and I are riding across the USA. We've come a long way today, and though I understand the park is closed, we were hoping you'd let us rest here for the night." I gave her a fine, big smile.

She shot an irritated glance at Mike, then gave me a dirty look. "Didn't you see the closed sign?" she snarled. "We're not open until tomorrow! You're not even supposed to be here. I could have you arrested for trespassing."

"Uh, well, yes, but I thought maybe . . ."

She interrupted me mid-sentence. "Come back tomorrow," she growled, and slammed the door in my face. I could see the look on Mike's face: "What do we do now?" he seemed to be saying. We had no option except to get back on the highway.

We hadn't ridden far when we spotted a dirt road leading into the woods. It looked promising, so we followed it. In a few dozen yards, we came upon a meadow that had once been the site of someone's mobile home. A forty- by twelve-foot slab of cracked concrete with some pipes sticking up and a disconnected electric panel were all that remained. We set up our tents in what had been the driveway, made dinner, and turned in, but I had trouble getting to sleep. The place had a ghostly feel to it, and as the night wore on, my imagination began to conjure up scenarios to explain what had happened to the people who had once lived at this lonely spot. Had they been the victims of some terrible crime? Killed by an axe murderer perhaps, an escapee from a nearby asylum for the criminally insane? A cunning predator who had evaded capture and still lurked in these lonesome woods, lying in wait for his next victim?

A forest sound roused me, and I quickly sat up and looked around, trying to pierce the blackness of that moonless night. "Come on," I said out loud, "quit freaking yourself out! There's nothing in these woods to be afraid of . . ." Then Maren's tease about the man-eating cougars came to mind. *Oh, crap*, I thought. *Now I'll never get to sleep.*

Chapter Three: Montana

We rose early to another spectacular day. I made breakfast, and then we retraced our route to Highway 202 and followed the Clark River east. In a few miles we passed through the small town of Clark Fork, where the landscape started to change again. The day before, we'd been riding through a flood plain, and the mountains had been far off, but now we were in the heart of the narrow Clark River Valley. Steep, wooded mountains rose on either side. In another few miles, we crossed the state line into Montana. We'd noticed that the Idaho roads had not been as well maintained as the roads in Washington, but Montana was even worse. The winters are tough in the northern part of the state, and the highways are paved with gritty material that can withstand the worst conditions. It's a strange red color and as rough as number-two grit sandpaper. I could almost feel the rubber scuffing off my tires. The shoulders weren't in good shape either, crumbling and jagged and in some places nonexistent. But the fantastic scenery made up for the bad roads.

We rode through miles of mountains and woods. Side canyons tucked up in the wrinkles of the hills cradled green pastures where livestock grazed. Off in the distance rose a fantastic backdrop of majestic, snow-covered peaks. But the roads and scenery in Montana weren't the only differences we noted. Most of the vehicles we saw were big pickup trucks, all with the requisite gun racks, driven by men wearing cowboy hats. When they got out of their trucks, we saw that a lot of them sported handlebar mustaches and wore jeans and curled-up-at-the-toe boots.

As we rode deeper into western Montana, we began to enter an even more mountainous region. We were now in among the peaks we had seen off in the distance. We'd been following Highway 202 east and now we made a left turn onto Highway 56 and headed north over the Cabinet Mountains. Highway 56 turned out to be something of an anomaly for Montana. The pavement was new and smooth, the shoulders wide and solid. But we hardly noticed; the mountains that soared all around stole our attention from such mundane matters as road conditions.

The road was lightly trafficked and wound along beside creeks and past the occasional rustic homestead. The weather was fine but hot, and we stopped often to drink from our water bottles.

We climbed for a hours; then, as dusk settled in, we started looking for a place to camp. The Cabinet Mountains are wild and rugged; steep hillsides and plunging cliffs border the winding road. It was getting late now, the sun had set behind a western ridge, and we had only a short time to find a place to sleep. As the sunlight faded, the temperature dropped, and we put on jackets. I was riding behind Mike when he suddenly braked, swerved, and made a 180-degree turn. "What's up?" I asked.

"Follow me," he said. We pedaled back down the road a few yards and Mike pulled over. Pointing to an opening in the woods, he said, "There's our campsite, made to order." We walked our bikes into the nicest, flattest mountain meadow any tired cyclist could ever want. There was a copse of birch trees, and Mike claimed a spot among them where the ground was covered with a matt of soft mulch. Because he snores so loudly, it had become my practice to pitch my tent as far away from his as I could, so I went about searching for my own distant site. Bordering the meadow was a denser forest of mature evergreens, where I leaned my bike against an old tree and began scouting. It wasn't long before I found what I judged to be the ideal spot: a flat area protected on three sides by ancient trees. The fourth side opened on a view of our meadow. A more pleasant place to spend the night I could not have imagined, and I yelled at Mike to come see.

"Pretty nice," he said, looking around with a practiced eye, "except for one thing."

"Yeah, what's that?"

He pointed to a spot not five feet from where we were standing. "That dead deer won't mind you sleeping here, but if the wind shifts you might want less pungent company." Sure enough, a rotting carcass lay almost within reach. I camped in the meadow instead.

Highway 56, Cabinet Mountains

Sometime in the predawn hours, Mike told me later, a faint rustling had awakened him. He sat up and was delighted to see that his tent was surrounded by a herd of deer. It wasn't until he reached for his camera that they noticed him and the whole herd bolted as one.

The temperature dropped below freezing that night, and the ride down into the Kootenai River Valley the next morning was bracing. But talk about the views! We wound our way through deep forests and past rushing streams, scaring up myriad wildlife as we zoomed by. Deer and coyotes bounded into the woods, and eagles took flight, startled at the last moment by our nearly-silent approach. We spent the night at a campground in Libby called the Two Bit Affair. Though it was nice to have all the modern conveniences, I missed the stellar display of our wild camp the night before, high in the Cabinet Mountains.

Cow Country

We were a day and a half east of Libby now, and mile from the small town of Rexford, where we planned to spend the night, when a pickup truck slowed and stopped. I was a few yards in front of Mike and could hear him and the driver exchanging words. "What was that about?" I asked when Mike caught up.

"That guy said if we make it to the Frontier Bar in Rexford the first round's on him!"

In a short while, we came to the turnoff for town and coasted down the hill. Rexford consists of a dry goods store, a post office, a trailer park and the Frontier Bar and Restaurant. It was a real Western bar all right, the floors, walls and ceiling made of rough lumber and the roof supported by a truss system of raw logs. One wall was filled with the stuffed heads of trophy game, testament, I suppose, to the variety of wildlife and the locals' prowess at killing them.

The patrons were cowboys and cowgirls of every age, shape and description, all appropriately attired. When Mike and I walked in dressed in our cycling gear, we were greeted with whistles, hoots and catcalls. The driver of the pickup saw us and came over. He was a bear of a man, standing six feet two inches and weighing at least 240 pounds. Our new friend put his arms around both our shoulders and proclaimed loudly, "Now listen up, you coyotes. These two tenderfeet are my pals. They're good people and I don't expect them to buy a single drink all night. So y'all show some manners and treat these fellas right or you'll have me to answer to!"

The crowd clapped and whistled in raucous approval and soon we were being slapped on the back and bombarded with questions about our "damn fool adventure." There was the typical Western good ol' boy ribbing that we happily endured the whole night long; after all, they were lining up to buy us city slickers beers.

The owner came over and we talked for a while. "Why don't you fellas camp out behind the bar tonight?" she said after we'd become acquainted. "There's a nice, grassy spot where you won't be bothered, and you can use my shower and do your laundry, too, if you want."

It was getting late now; the bar began to fill up, and the story of the two crazy tenderfeet on bicycles spread like wildfire. Evidently, our journey struck a chord with the Westerners' sense of self-reliance, because they bought us beers faster than we could drink them. As soon as we'd empty one glass, two more would appear. We drank and danced and caroused with our new friends into the wee hours, and when I finally stumbled off to bed there were still three untouched pitchers of gratis beer on our table. I staggered to my tent and after a few tries got the door open, collapsing on top of my sleeping bag. The combination of a hard day's ride and some good ol' drinking with some good ol' cowgirls and cowboys put me to sleep the minute my head hit the pillow. In other words, I passed out.

It was hard getting out of bed the next morning. I sat up and my head began spinning and my stomach was trying to turn itself inside out. I drank my water bottle dry, and then, through sheer force of will, climbed out of my tent onto the dewy lawn. "Mike," I called, "Mike, are you alive?"

A long, drawn-out groan came from his tent. "Leave me alone," he said, "I don't feel well."

I crawled over to his tent and gave it a good shake. "Come on," I said, "let's get this over with. Some exercise and fresh air is all we need."

The door to his tent came open and Mike stuck his head out. "I'm never going to drink again. I think we were over-served last night."

"Do you have to shout?" I whispered.

We made a sorry scene. We hobbled around camp like arthritic octogenarians, slowly taking down our tents and packing our panniers. With things more or less in traveling order, we pushed our bikes out to the road. We hadn't noticed the dark clouds that had been moving across the sky as we packed, and now a cold, steady drizzle fell from a leaden sky. I wiped the rain from my face. "I don't even want to think about riding in this slop," I said. "Can't we call a cab?"

"No use whining about it," Mike mumbled, zipping up his jacket. "The fat is in the fire."

I started up the hill, pausing now and then and taking deep breaths to keep from throwing up. "Fat is in the fire . . . Where did you get that one?" I said to no one; Mike was already a hundred yards up the road. My head was throbbing. I had the cold sweats and my stomach threatened to revolt with each pedal stroke. But as bad as my hangover was, the icy wind and pelting sleet were even worse. Instead of getting warmer as the morning wore on, it got colder. By the time I'd ridden an hour, I could no longer feel my fingers or toes. The sleet stung my face like hot needles. Riding through that storm would have been hard enough had we been in top form, but our hangovers made it unbearable. We finally stopped beside a graveyard and discussed what to do. Mike pulled out his map and spent a few minutes studying it.

"There's a town eight miles up ahead, Eureka. We'll stop there. Do you think you can make it that far?"

Here it comes, I thought, *I'm going to vomit.* I tried to hold it in, but the gag reflex was too strong, and I bent down and gave myself over to the big spit.

Mike watched with a look of revulsion on his face. "God," he moaned, "don't do that!" I shuddered and groaned through wave after wave of reverse-peristaltic action.

Finally my stomach was empty, and I could once again speak. "I want to quit," I squeaked, "I think there's something wrong with me."

"Quit?! Quit?!" Mike said, suddenly sounding angry, "Go ahead and quit. Just throw the damn bike over there in the bone yard. Then where are you? In the same damn place you are now. You damn fool, you can't quit out here in the middle of nowhere. You gotta go someplace to quit."

I think Mike was as surprised as I was by his sudden outburst. I guess the stress of the morning was getting to him, too. I wiped vomit from my mouth and spit out a morsel of last night's dinner. I don't know who started laughing first, but soon we were both doubled over. We laughed so hard we cried. Sometimes that's all you can do.

Whitefish

Whitefish, Montana, is a small city at the western edge of the Rockies, and Mike had arranged for us to stay with his old friends Don and Sharon, who live a few miles outside of town. Don was standing in his front yard waiting for us when we arrived. He was in his early sixties, retired from his career as an x-ray technician. He and Sharon, his wife, live on a twenty-acre horse ranch with a view of the nearby ski resort, Big Mountain. "Welcome!" he shouted, as we rolled around the last corner of his quarter-mile-long driveway. "We've been waiting for you guys!"

We settled in and spent the next two days resting and working on our bikes. Mine needed maintenance, and Mike had to disassemble his and put it in a box for the trip back to Seattle. It was nice to lie around and take it easy, but soon it was time for Mike to head home. "It's been a great trip," he said as he climbed the steps to the Pullman car. "Remember to keep the greasy side down!"

I spent that night at Don and Sharon's, and the next morning they sent me off with a big slice of banana bread that Sharon had made. Though we'd only known each other for a few days, I felt we'd formed a lasting bond. They stood in their yard waving as I rode away. It was another sad moment, but there was no time for tears. It was Monday, May 21st, 2012, and I had a mountain to climb: the great Continental Divide!

I worked my way east out of Whitefish in a steady downpour. Even though I was wearing foul-weather gear, by the time I reached West Glacier at the foot of the Rockies, I was drenched. As I climbed higher, I left the core of the storm behind, so that by late afternoon I rode in dry weather. Mike had given me the maps we'd been using, and I saw that there was a campground ahead at Stanton Creek. It was just a few miles up the road, an hour's ride, as it turned out. I walked into the small cafe and asked about camping. The man who ran the place took one look at me and said, "You came here on a bike?"

"Yup," I replied, "all the way from Seattle."

"Well then, it's free." He reached under the counter and handed me a key. "That's for the shower, you just set up anyplace you want." I thanked him and we sat and chatted while I nursed a beer. Later, in my tent, fresh from a hot shower, I settled into my sleeping bag. Soon it started raining, and then the rain turned to snow. Now the wind began to howl, and my little tent trembled in the storm.

It was early yet and I wasn't sleepy, so I watched a movie on my iPad. I had to marvel at the strangeness of it all. Here I was, high in the Rocky Mountains, in the middle of a storm, being entertained by the latest Hollywood blockbuster. What would those early pioneers who'd braved this same torturous route think if they could see me now?

There was a lull in the storm the next morning, and I broke camp in a mild drizzle. The snow from the night before hadn't stuck, but it was cold and gray. Today I would cross the Rockies, a Rubicon of sorts, and the sense of separation between my family and me increased with each spin of the wheel. The Continental Divide would represent not only a geographical turning point but a psychological one, too. Now there'd be the continent's major mountain range between us. I pedaled out of camp in a dark funk. Could I really do this? I was half hoping the Rockies would defeat me; at least I could say I'd tried. But it was only twenty-seven miles to Marias Pass, which meant that if I didn't dawdle I'd make it to the first town on the other side, East Glacier, before dark.

I climbed all morning. The weather had cleared for a while, but now the storm caught up to me and a steady rain fell. The road wound up in corkscrew fashion among jagged cliffs and past rushing torrents that fell from the heights above. As I rounded a corner, I saw a sign that pointed to an even windier road leading off into the forest. IZAAK WALTON INN ONE MILE it proclaimed. *What the heck,* I thought, *let's give it a look-see.* I took the turnoff and rode past a few cabins; then at the last curve I came to a stop and stared in amazement. There, smack in the deepest part of the deepest forest, was what appeared to be a big hotel. It was a rustic, half-timbered, four-story building with a grand drive leading up to the main portico. A few cars were parked in the lot and half a dozen camera-toting tourists wandered around the manicured grounds in rain slickers. "Well, if this doesn't beat all . . ." I muttered.

I parked my bike and went in. The petite, dark-haired young woman at the desk couldn't have been friendlier. "My gosh," she said, "you're drenched, let me get you something to dry off with." She disappeared behind a door, returned, and handed me a big, fluffy hotel towel. "Now then, "she said, "how can I help you?"

I could smell the tantalizing aroma of breakfast wafting from somewhere, and I was suddenly ravenous. Looking around the rustic lobby for the source, I saw a stone fireplace at one end big enough to burn a small shed in. Overstuffed couches and chairs formed a semi-circle in front of the flickering fire. It was the kind of place that made you want to curl up, read a Louis L'Amour novel, and take up smoking a pipe. I turned back to the young woman. "Well, I sure wouldn't mind some breakfast."

She smiled, "Just around the corner."

I settled into a booth, perused the menu, and ordered eggs over easy, hash brown potatoes, wheat toast, orange juice, pancakes, tea and a cup of hot chocolate. As I lingered over breakfast, I read a brochure about the hotel and learned that the Izaak Walton Inn was built in 1939 by the Great Northern Railroad Company as a residence for their personnel and as a gateway to Glacier National Park. Though it had never quite achieved the status of the Gateway to Glacier, over the years it had become a popular tourist destination.

I finished my breakfast and retired to the lobby, where I used the hotel's WiFi to chat with my daughters. Talking with my kids and being in such a welcoming environment raised my spirits, and I left with a renewed sense of confidence that I could make it over the Rockies after all. I was amazed at what a smile, a warm fire and a good meal had done to improve my mood.

Back on the road I continued to climb, and as I gained altitude the landscape and the weather began to take on a new character. Gone were the deep forests, replaced now by sparse evergreens and rolling emerald meadows. The twisting road gave way to long, steep, straight stretches that ran beside a raging torrent tumbling along, in a great hurry, it seemed, to reach the sea. The weather was drier, too, but the wind had picked up, and occasional biting-cold cloudbursts still fell with gale force.

It was early afternoon when I spotted the Snow Slide Inn. I let out a little whoop of joy — only six miles to the summit! The proprietor back at Stanton Creek had made me promise to stop there, so I pulled into the small dirt parking lot, went in, and ordered a cup of hot chocolate. The building was old, low-roofed and thick-walled, with deep-set windows. It looked like the kind of place that could stand up to the toughest Montana winter. Inside there were some tables and a worn Formica-topped counter. The place was so small that I could almost reach out and touch the tiny kitchen stove from the stool where I sat. It was attended by a single cook who was also the waiter. While I sat sipping my cocoa, a group of four motorcyclists came in. They asked me about my trip, and we chatted pleasantly about the joys of the open road.

"You'll be passing through Browning," one of the riders said, a serious look on his whiskered face. "Whatever you do, don't get stuck there."

"Is that right?" I said.

The motorcyclists all traded knowing looks. "Just don't, that's all," another replied. "It's a bad place."

"Yeah," said a woman dressed in black leathers, "we don't even stop for gas, we just wind the throttle back and hope for the best."

I tried to get more out of them, but they only made me promise to pass through Browning as quickly as I could. I gave them my word, finished my drink, and then said my goodbyes. Up the road several steep miles later, I realized that I had left my cycling gloves on the counter at the Snow Slide when I'd changed into warmer wool gloves. I stopped and thought about coasting back down the mountain to retrieve them, but decided it wasn't worth the effort. I'd just buy a new pair when I got to a bike store. But a few miles from the top of the pass, I heard motorcycles approaching from behind, then a beep of a horn, and looking to my left, I saw one of the motorcyclists I'd met at the Snow Slide Inn slowing down. He reached toward me, something was in his hand. It was my gloves! I grabbed them and shouted, "Thanks!" He waved and they raced off toward the summit.

The Continental Divide

Reaching the Continental Divide was a momentous occasion for me. I noted the time: 2:12 in the afternoon. On the ride up, the storm had been hitting me intermittently, but now it came on with a vengeance. The wind howled and the rain fell in horizontal sheets. I lingered at the summit only long enough to snap pictures and then began the long east-side descent, racing along with a stiff wind at my back. The road was in good shape, the shoulder was wide, the weather was clearing, and I let out a war whoop as my speedometer climbed past thirty. *This is what it's all about*, I thought, *only a dozen fast miles to East Glacier . . . It's almost a shame that it'll be over so soon* . . . Little did I know what fate had in store for me just around the corner.

But I was feeling on top of the world when I sped into East Glacier. The sky was brightening, and the wind was at my back. I was going so fast that I had to ride my brakes to keep from traveling backward in time. As I raced along, I kept my eye out for someplace flat, with a few trees, where I could camp. But eastern Montana is different from the west side of the mountains. It's drier, with less vegetation and very few trees. I spied no likely place, just barbed wire, jackrabbits, and sagebrush, so I resigned to pay for a spot in a campground in town. But when I got to the heart of the little village and stopped at a store to ask about it, the young Native American man at the counter just gave me a look. "Are you out of your mind, man, there's no campgrounds around here. That goddamn wind will turn a tent inside out."

I smiled. "Thanks," I said. I guessed I'd have to wild camp after all. But as the miles rolled by and the country became even sparser, I began to worry. Would I ever find a place? I didn't want to go much farther. I'd been on the road ten or twelve hours; my legs were heavy, and my arms ached. Soon I entered Browning, and just as I'd been warned, it was a pretty sketchy place. There were boarded-up buildings, trash blew in the wind, and a pack of wild dogs eyed me with suspicion. I wanted to be far away before I set up for the night. The problem was, I was beat. As I climbed a long hill east of town, my trembling legs almost gave out. I wobbled to a stop, hung my head, and leaned heavily on the handlebars. I was out of gas and couldn't make it much farther. I'd have to stop soon.

I made it a few miserable miles more and then saw a dirt road leading into low hills. Following it to its end near some railroad tracks, I picked a spot. It wasn't much. I wasn't out of sight of the highway and I could see battered houses across the road, which meant they could see me, too. A beat-up Chevy cruised slowly past, its young male occupants eying me with what I imagined to be nefarious intent. It wasn't a good place to camp, but I was too tired to go on. I broke out my tent and, wrestling with the wind, set it up on a rocky knoll. The ground was too hard to drive a tent peg into, so I weighted down the guy lines with piles of rocks. The wind was really rocking and rolling now. I crawled inside and wiggled into my sleeping bag; then suddenly, a strong gust laid my tent flat. I lay on my back with the walls and ceiling pressed tightly against my body. Soon my tent would be destroyed by that terrible wind. I knew I'd made a mistake to try to camp in it. I glanced at my watch; it was 6:30. I had a few hours of sun left, but not nearly enough time to make it to the next town, Cut Bank, thirty-one miles farther east. *Well, I've got to do something*, I thought, *I can't stay here!* So I packed up camp and got back on the road.

Then something just short of miraculous happened. The same wind that had defeated my attempt to camp now pushed me along at twenty miles an hour! "I just might pull this off," I said. I'd been talking to myself for the past few hours — not a good sign. The wind kept up, the road was flat or slightly downhill, and I rolled along at breakneck speed. Soon, I was twenty miles from Cut Bank, then ten miles, then five. Now I could see the little town off in the distance. I was going to make it! It was a good thing, too; I had been on the road for more than fourteen hours, and I was beyond exhaustion.

I was almost there when I hit a bump and felt that heart-sickening crunch that can only mean a flat tire. I rolled to a stop. Sure enough, my front tire had blown. A hill led up to the town, and though it was only a few hundred yards long, in my exhausted state it looked like Mount Everest. Instead of making a roadside repair, I pushed my bike the final distance. As I struggled up the grade, I could see the brightly-lit Super 8 Motel sign, and I set my sights on it.

Night had fallen by the time I reached the hotel. I stumbled in and staggered up to the front desk. "Do you have a room?" I asked the clerk.

The clerk looked me up and down. I was sunburned and wind whipped. My lips were chapped and my eyes were bloodshot. My hair was a tangled mess, and my sweat-soaked clothes were caked with grime. I smelled like a bum. "Man," he said, "you look like you've been rode hard and put away wet."

Indeed. I had climbed 5,000-foot Marias Pass in a howling storm, ridden eighty-six grueling miles, and had a high-speed flat tire, but I'd made it to Cut Bank. And now all I wanted was a place to lie low and lick my wounds. "You don't want to know," I mumbled. "Now what about that room?"

I soaked my battered body in a warm bath, dozed in the tub for an hour, went to bed and slept the sleep of the pure at heart. It had been quite a day, my longest and most challenging so far.

Cold Feet

The ride over the Rockies had been an ordeal, but what I was about to face made that challenge seem like a walk in the park. I was several days east of Cut Bank when things turned deadly. I had camped in the little town of Hingham the night before and a howling windstorm kept me awake most of the night. As soon as it got light, I'd poked my head out. Dark clouds roiled a gray sky. The wind carried the scent of rain. It was marginal cycling weather, but I couldn't bear the thought of spending all day and another night in my tent, so I made a hurried breakfast, packed up, and pedaled out to the highway. A mile farther, I passed a roadhouse just opening and stopped to pick up food for the trip ahead. The owner, a hippie-looking fellow a few years younger than I, had shaken his head. "You might want to go back and sit this one out," he said. "Looks like it's gonna get ugly."

"Yeah, I was thinking the same thing," I replied, "but Havre's not far is it? A little over forty miles?"

"About that," he said, "but it could be a long forty miles."

I'd gone back out and read the sky. A new bank of mean-looking clouds had bunched up and were crowded in low. A stiff wind blew out of the east, but though it was ugly, I'd been riding in similar weather for the past few days and it hadn't been anything I couldn't handle. I'd figured today wouldn't be much different, so I decided to make a run for it. It was a calculated gamble, but I got on my bike and headed into the wild anyway.

Montana Highway

That had been twenty miles back. Now the day grew suddenly dark as dusk, and off in the distance I could see an approaching storm. It looked like a big one, moving fast. In half an hour, it was upon me, hitting suddenly in full force. An icy rain stung my skin, the wind blew me from one side of the road to the other. The storm seemed to be coming from all directions at once, and a gust hit me with such force that I was knocked to the ground. There was no sense in getting back on the bike now, the wind was just too strong. So with a rising sense of dread, I started pushing it up the road. I stumbled along through the deluge, staggering to a stop and bracing against each freezing onslaught. A long, sustained squall hit, and it took all my strength to keep from being blown away. I leaned into the gale, but it was no use. I stumbled, giving up ground and struggling to keep my footing; then I fell backward and tumbled into a ragged tangle of ditch weed. I lay there for a few minutes. *That's it*, I thought, *I know when I'm beat. It's time to give up*. That's when Mike's words came back to me: "You can't give up here, you gotta go someplace to give up!"

I picked myself up and put my thumb out as off in the distance a lone red pickup approached, slowed, then sped past. As I watched the truck disappear into the haze of that stormy eastern Montana highway, I felt the queasy beginnings of The Fear stirring deep inside.

There wasn't much traffic on the road that morning. The locals knew enough to stay home when the weather got this bad. I tried to see back west through the heavy wind-driven rain, hoping another ride would come along, but no, the road was empty.

There are few trees in that part of the American West. Rolling hills and rocky escarpments dominate the landscape. In the absence of natural barriers, the storms come on with a vengeance. When it gets really ugly, staying out in the weather isn't an option; shelter becomes the only hope. And I knew that if I didn't find some soon, well, I wouldn't be the first tenderfoot to be gobbled up by this rugged land. Up ahead I could make out a line of tall trees, and I struggled toward it. It had been planted ages ago as a windbreak to shelter a long-gone home. A broken foundation was all that remained. I hoped that if I could huddle among those trees, I might last out the storm. Now my thoughts came slowly and my body responded sluggishly. I realized that I was in a bad way. *If I can just make it to those trees*.

I was having trouble pushing my bike. My hands were numb and my legs felt like logs. I couldn't feel my feet. It seemed to take an eternity, but eventually I reached the trees. Setting up my tent was out of the question. I stood there staring stupidly at my bike and my gear, all of it useless in this horrible wind and rain. I couldn't seem to concentrate; *if only the wind would die down for a few minutes and give me a chance to think* . . . Then, out of the storm, a black pickup appeared, slowed, came to a stop, and the window rolled down. I stumbled over and looked in. The driver said, "You okay or do you need a ride?"

I giggled hysterically, "Oh, man," I said, through chattering teeth, "I n-n-need a r-r-r-ride!"

Saturday Night in Havre

We rode along in silence. The soft purring of the truck's heater was the only sound. I stared out the windshield, letting myself be mesmerized by the rhythmic back-and-forth motion of the wipers. Still amazed that I had escaped, I didn't want to break the spell. For all I knew, this nice warm truck was simply part of an elaborate hallucination cooked up by my hypothermic brain to ease the slide into eternity. What if I were really lying back among those trees breathing my last few breaths? The thought, as improbable as it may seem now, sent shivers down my spine. I had read *An Occurrence at Owl Creek Bridge* in high school . . .

Finally the driver spoke. "The reason I happened along," he said, "my father-in-law saw you earlier, said you might be in trouble, so I thought I'd check on you." He smiled. "Name's Chad. My dad, my brother and I grow wheat. Got 140,000 acres under cultivation."

A small manic laugh escaped my numb lips. "I was a goner back there," I said, the words tumbling out. "Man, I don't know what I'd have done if you hadn't come along . . . really cold and that storm . . . it came on so fast . . . knocked down a couple of times . . ."

"Whoa," Chad said, "slow down! What are you doing out here in this weather anyway? Even the jackrabbits find a hole when it's this bad."

"I started out from Hingham this morning . . . thought I could make it to Havre before it got too hairy. Thought I could handle it."

He nodded. "Not from around here, huh?"

"Seattle, I'm attempting to ride around the world."

Chad grinned. "Really?! Around the world?!"

"Yup."

"I've always wanted to travel," he said, "but what with the farm and the family, I don't get to go too many places. For me, a trip to Denver is a big deal."

As my mind thawed, I began to take notice of my surroundings. The truck was new; it still had that smell. It was first class all the way, double cab, leather interior, custom built-in wheelchair . . . It was then that I noticed Chad was using hand controls to operate the throttle and brake. He looked to be in his early forties and had mentioned that he was married with two kids. There was an easy-going air about him; I'd have liked him even if he hadn't saved my life. "Back before I broke my neck," he said matter-of-factly, "I used to love to go camping, backpacking, all that stuff." He gave me a look, "Around the world," he said wistfully, "sure wish I was going with you."

We chatted for the rest of the eighteen miles to Havre. Chad wanted to know all about my trip, where I was going and how long it would take. By the time we reached a motel, snow had begun to fall. As we parted, I thanked him profusely. "Look, Chad, I won't insult you by offering you money, but how about if you e-mail me your address and I'll send you a post card from someplace exotic?"

A big grin broke out on his face. "That sounds just fine," he said, "just fine."

I spent the next two nights waiting out the storm in a Havre motel. A lot of people had the same idea. Families in SUV's, state road crews, even the eighteen-wheel jockeys were getting off the road. I got a room on the second floor where I had a good view of the storm as it raged outside.

I hadn't eaten much and was ravenous, and I nearly cleaned out the motel vending machines. I ordered a pizza, which miraculously appeared at my door within the promised thirty minutes!

This was the first rest day I had since Whitefish, and with little to do except sleep and eat, I now had time to reflect on the journey so far. Before this trip, I'd done some weekend and week-long rides, and I knew going in that cycle touring wasn't all smooth roads and sunny weather. But there was a psychological component associated with long-distance riding that I'd had no way to prepare for. I had tried to keep things light, but it seemed that I was homesick half the time. I understood that there would be a period of adjustment, but I never imagined it would be this hard.

I was discovering that I wasn't very good at cycle touring either, which shouldn't have come as a surprise. I've never been good at athletics. My friends describe my skiing style as "a series of linked recoveries." And now I felt like I was lurching from one crisis to another, and this last one had nearly cost me my life. I was sure it would only be a matter of time before I fell prey to a disaster of my own making. I knew my family was worried about me, too. If things went really wrong, it would be up to them to pick up the pieces. I felt guilty for having put such an onerous responsibility upon their shoulders, and I fell into a dark funk. I paced around the room. I went to the window and watched cars splash through the frozen slush. A piece of half-eaten pizza was left in the box, and I sat on the edge of the bed and nibbled on the stale crust and drank the dregs of a flat Coke.

I stretched out and tried to sleep. *Things are bound to look better in the morning*, I thought.

Like I'm in a David Lynch Movie

The only people who know where The Edge is are the ones who have gone over it. Hunter Thompson said that, and I was beginning to think I understood what he meant. The storm that had taken me so close to disaster was still vivid in my mind, and the lesson it taught me had stuck. Though it was frightening in its fury, there'd also been a kind of bent appeal to the experience. You didn't seek out The Edge unless you had a death wish or were crazy or drunk. It was the kind of place you stumbled on only by accident or stupidity, and if you'd been there and you were lucky enough to return, you'd never be the same. At The Edge, all pretensions fall away. Longing, confusion, and even fear give way to a kind of stark clarity and an appreciation for the temporary nature of life, and that, I think, is a kind of wisdom in itself.

From Havre, it took me three days to cover the 209 miles to Wolf Point, where I spent the night shivering through a thunderstorm at a public park near the edge of town. At Wolf Point, I left Highway 2, crossed the Missouri River, and headed south on Highway 13. There are more than sixty hills between Wolf Point and Circle. I know this for a fact. When I reached the top of one hill, I could see the next hill, and the next one, and the one after that. Every once in a while, I'd see off in the distance a clump of trees, a barn, a house, and grain silos.

The day had started out cool, but by afternoon the temperature was hovering around ninety degrees. I was riding south, so I had the sun in my face all day, making it feel even hotter. As I neared the town of Circle, the road took a bend to the west and I was now battling a strong headwind. Coming at the end of a long day of climbing hills, this last-minute challenge put me in a foul mood.

"I ride up these goddamn hills for five hours, then they throw in a damn headwind just to piss me off," I muttered. I wasn't sure who "they" were, but as my trip progressed and I faced new obstacles each day, there had begun to form in my mind the existence of an all-powerful force tasked solely with making my life miserable. If I rounded a corner and faced a long hot climb, I'd curse and growl, "Well, sure, there's another damn hill, they just couldn't leave well enough alone!" Of course I didn't really believe there existed a cabal of supernatural beings magically manipulating terrain and weather just to cause me suffering. It was simply weariness and my own inability to cope with hardship bubbling to the surface.

I'd been travelling for twenty-eight days, and in that time I had to face many hard truths about myself. The road had exposed my every weakness in such a way that it was impossible to ignore or rationalize. Alone out here, try as I might, I couldn't find anyone else to blame for my problems.

But if the road was merciless in exposing my shortcomings, it was also generous in giving me the opportunity to build on my strengths. I hadn't weighed myself, but I knew I was losing fat and getting stronger. I was making more miles each day, too. In the beginning, forty miles was a day's work. Now I was knocking off sixty or more. I was comfortable sleeping in my tent, and I felt almost claustrophobic when I bunked indoors.

Tonight would be spent under the stars, and I was looking forward to a good night's rest in the fresh Montana air. I finally came to the outskirts of Circle, rode into town, and stopped at the first place I saw that had cold drinks, a small Sinclair service station. It was a low, flat-roofed building, painted white with a red stripe halfway up. It sat on a corner lot by itself; the nearest other building was a motel a quarter mile to the east. The area in front was gravel, with a concrete apron where two gas pumps sat. Weeds grew through cracks in the cement. Directly behind the pumps was the door. Next to that, and taking up two-thirds of the building, was a repair bay, and idling in it was a perfectly restored 1968 Dodge Charger in metallic blue with a black vinyl top and blinding-white interior.

As I walked through the door, I noticed two teenaged girls. That they were sisters was unmistakable. They shared the same high cheekbones and wide eyes. Their skin was deeply tanned, and they wore their dark hair pulled back and secured by rubber bands. Both were tall and dressed in shapeless boy's clothes: checkered long-sleeved shirts, faded jeans, and work boots. One looked to be sixteen or seventeen, the other a year or two younger. The elder sister stood in the doorway, listless, staring out of heavy-lidded eyes at the vacant lot across the road. The younger sister leaned against the wall; she seemed to be looking at nothing at all. Neither acknowledged my presence. Instead, they maintained the same distant expressions.

The clerk, who doubled as the mechanic, had finished working on the Charger. He stood behind the counter next to an ancient cash register, writing up a bill. An older, white-haired, heavyset man came in from the service bay, wearing a tan cowboy hat and silver-tipped cowboy boots that made a heavy clunking sound as he walked across the wooden floor. He had a round, puffy face and small, close-set eyes. His nose was heavily-veined; he looked like a heavy drinker. Around his neck was a bolo tie bound with a white-veined agate in a silver setting. "You put the good stuff in?" he asked.

The mechanic looked up. "You bet," he said, "she oughta run like a dream now." He pulled a shop rag from his back pocket and wiped his brow, then his hands. He looked to be in his mid-forties, had a pinched face, and his brown, disheveled hair sported a scattering of gray flecks.

"Good," said the white-haired man, "where's the rest of it?"

"I put it in the trunk."

The white-haired man nodded, examined the bill, nodded again, paid, then went out, got in the Charger, and backed it out so that now it sat in front of the open door. As if by a signal inaudible to everyone but them, the girls walked out and got in the back seat. I saw the white-haired man turn and say something to the girls.

The mechanic and I watched the Charger accelerate out of the lot, spew gravel, then burn rubber when it hit the pavement. We could hear the roar of the engine long after the car had disappeared over a rise. I looked at the mechanic and for just an instant our eyes met. He shrugged, "What are you gonna do?" he said.

Plate Tectonics

I'd been fighting against this burning, soul-scorching headwind all morning, struggling toward a small town where my map promised there'd be a grocery store. I checked my computer: another eleven miles and I'd be there. I fantasized about the store. It would be air-conditioned, and there would be cold drinks. I'd go in out of this terrible wind and buy a Coca Cola. There'd be a deli and they'd have my favorite sandwich, tuna salad. As I rode on and the wind became even worse, I added a campground with hot showers; then the campground became a motel with air conditioning, big beds and clean, cool sheets.

It was midmorning. I'd camped at Circle in a vacant field across from the Sinclair station the night before, and had been on the road for a couple of hours now. I was averaging four miles an hour and moving slower than continental drift. At this rate, Mt. Rainier would reach the East Coast before I did. It would be another two hours before I got to the store, and many more before I arrived in Glendive, where I planned to spend the night. I blocked everything out of my mind. *I'll just make it to the store,* I thought, *nothing exists beyond that. There is no wind.*

From a mile out, I could see the cluster of buildings and the grove of trees that marked every small town in that part of the state, and I pedaled even harder. My heart was bursting with joy when I saw the sign. I was too far away to read it, but I knew it had to mark the store. I put my head down and raced the last quarter mile, then coasted into the parking lot of the boarded-up building. *I must be seeing things* I thought, *this can't be.* I rode around to the side and back, hoping against hope that I'd find what I had been praying for, but no, there would be no sympathy for the devil this day. The place was out of business. I was ready to weep; my heart was in my throat. Then my cell phone rang.

"Hello," I croaked.

"Dad?" It was my middle daughter, Annie. "Dad, are you okay? You sound terrible."

"Oh, hi, Honey," I said. "Yeah, I'm fine, I think we have a bad connection." I didn't want to worry Annie, so I assumed a light-hearted tone to disguise my dark mood.

"Well, that's good," she said. "You had me scared. Where are you?"

"I'm a few miles out of Glendive, Montana," I said. "How are you?"

"I'm fine. What's the weather like?"

I looked down the road, holding my hand up to block the wind, "It's nice," I said, "warm and sunny, not a cloud in the sky."

"What's that loud noise?"

I guess the phone was picking up the howl of the wind. "There's a train passing by," I lied. We chatted a bit more, but after a few minutes, it was clear that I'd have to invent one very long train to explain the never-ending roar of the wind. "Well, Honey, it's been good talking to you, but I'm going to get going now; I've got a ways to go."

"Okay, Dad," Annie said. "I just called to make sure you're okay. Be careful! I love you."

"I love you, too," I said, and broke the connection.

As I was getting ready to start, a police cruiser drove by, slowed, turned around, and pulled up next to me. "Are you all right?" the cop asked.

"Yeah," I said, "just taking a break."

"This stretch of road is my beat," he said. "I saw you earlier and you looked like you were having a tough time. I'll be patrolling all day, so if you need help, flag me down."

I was filled with a sense of gratitude for the sudden expressions of concern — first from my daughter, and now from this complete stranger. "Wow, that's really nice of you," I said, "but I think I'm gonna be okay."

The wind continued to blow hard all day, and the next twenty-five miles were a horror show. As I neared the outskirts of town that evening, I saw the officer drive past again. He waved and I gave him a shaky thumbs-up. It had taken me ten hours to cover those awful fifty miles. I pushed on to the first supermarket I saw, stumbled in, and finally got that nice cold Coke I'd been dreaming of. I sat outside next to my bike and drank my soda and ate a banana and rested. The bag boy stopped and asked how I was doing. "Fine," I said, "just rode in from Circle. Man, that wind is something."

"Yeah, well, that sounds like quite a trip. You take care, now," he said, and walked back toward the store.

"Hey," I called after him, "where's a motel?"

He turned and pointed. "Ride across the bridge, take a left at Main, go over the overpass. There's a bunch of them."

Glendive is a community of around 5,000, and the old part of town lies just east of the Yellowstone River. West of the river, supermarkets, fast food joints and big-box stores have sprung up. I crossed the bridge into old Glendive and rode north toward Interstate 94, past nondescript brick storefronts, new convenience stores, and the massive Burlington Northern Freight Depot. In a mile, I crossed the Interstate 94 overpass and pulled into the Comfort Inn Motel. A fifty-something woman leaned on the railing outside the front door, looking like she needed sleep about as badly as I did. She was smoking a non-filtered Camel, and as I passed, she smiled. "I'll be right in," she said, "just let me finish my butt."

I nodded. "Sure, you bet, no hurry."

She looked at my bike. "You come a long way?"

"Yeah," I said, "I guess." I didn't want to tell her about my day or that I'd ridden from the West Coast. Talking seemed like too much work. I just wanted to lie down. I checked in, took a shower, turned the air conditioner on high, and plopped down on the bed. My stomach was growling; I knew I should eat, but first I needed to rest my eyes for a minute.

I'll Have the Tuna Melt and Fries

I woke up shivering. The room was freezing; the air conditioner rattled and groaned and blew cold air. I got up and turned it off, checked my watch, and saw that it was after 10:00 p.m. I'd slept almost five hours! Now I was ravenous, and I needed more than the candy bars and Cokes in the vending machines, so I ventured out. I spotted a twenty-four-hour restaurant a block away, and bending into the wind, I made my way toward it.

A haggard-looking family of four sat at one of the booths. At the counter, truck drivers hunched over plates of stale-looking food. A flickering neon light pulsed overhead, emitting a loud buzz as it cycled on and off. On the walls were reproductions of Western-themed oil paintings: a cowboy riding a bucking bronco, an Indian astride his palomino, a still life titled Boots 'N Saddle. In the center was a salad bar offering wilted lettuce and suspect tomatoes. I sat down at a booth and perused the menu. Chicken fried steak, cheeseburgers, meatloaf—all standard fare for this kind of place, but I saw nothing I could eat. Being a vegetarian can sometimes be inconvenient, and it was starting to look like I might have to settle for a vending-machine dinner after all.

The waitress came over to my table. "What can I get ya, Hon?" she said. She was in her late twenties, with streaked blond hair bunched up on top of her head. She wore a pink-and-white-striped uniform. Her name tag read Cindy. She had a cheery air that seemed out of place in this drab establishment.

"Could you fix me a grilled cheese?"

"Why sure, how about a tuna melt?"

"Yeah," I said, "that would be great." I looked around the sad restaurant. "Can you make it to go?" The place was bringing me down, and I didn't think I could stay there much longer. I took my dinner back to my room, and it was about as I expected: soggy fries and stale bread. But I was so hungry that I wolfed it down anyway, enjoying every bite.

The wind was still howling the next morning, and after the grueling trip from Circle the day before, I was in no mood for a repeat performance. I'd decided to take a rest day, so I went to the front desk and asked about keeping the room for another night, but it was booked. I got the same story at the two or three other places, so I resigned to camp. The night before, I'd spotted a campground icon on my map, and I had a rough idea where it ought to be. I got on my bike and made a swift trip back to Glendive.

The campground bordered the Great Northern Line on one side, and to the west was the Yellowstone River. I paid the ten-dollar camping fee and set my tent up on a grassy spot next to the railroad tracks. Stowing my gear, I rolled out my sleeping bag and took a nap. When I awoke an hour later, the wind had died down, the sun was high in the sky, and the inside of my tent was stifling. I'd been off the road for nearly twenty hours now and wasn't used to sitting still for so long. Though I wasn't fully rested from the ordeal of the day before, I was filled with nervous energy, and I needed something to do, so I rode into town. I stopped at a taco shack and had lunch, then rambled around the residential neighborhoods looking at the neat houses with their meticulously-manicured yards.

And Now, For My Next Trick

I was puzzled by how nicely kept every lawn was. Even houses that were run down had recently-mown yards. The answer to the mystery, I discovered, was that wood ticks are a hazard in that part of the country and they need tall grass to thrive. Some communities had passed ordinances requiring certain standards about yard care. If the homeowner was negligent, the city work crew would do the cutting themselves. I know this because I read it on the bulletin board at the Glendive Public Library, where I'd gone to plug into the Net and Web-chat with my kids, catch up on e-mail, and read the latest news on The Huffington Post. I checked the weather, balanced my checkbook, and read the local paper.

Now it was 12:30 and I noticed that the place was beginning to fill up with small children accompanied by parents or older siblings. *Well, why not?* I thought, it is a library. Then more children showed up, then still more, until there was standing room only. I'd seen a kiosk advertising a magic show, and though I hadn't noticed the date, I hoped it would be today. "Is there really going to be a magician?" I asked the librarian, maybe a little too eagerly.

She looked at me over the top of her glasses. "How long have you been on the road?" she asked.

"This is my fifth week," I muttered. "What about the magician? Will there be a clown, too? What about balloon animals?"

"Well, you'd better find a chair," she said, indicating an area. "You can sit over there . . . with the rest of the kids."

I laughed and clapped with the other preschoolers as the magician pulled a rabbit out of his hat, made an egg disappear, and miraculously restored a rope he'd cut in half just seconds before. It was a great show, and afterwards we got to enter a drawing for a new bicycle. Second prize was a Slip 'N Slide.

Chapter Four: North Dakota

The song says, When you walk through the storm hold your head up high. That might make a good bumper sticker, but when you're riding a bicycle through a North Dakota gully washer it's better to keep your head down. It was raining so hard that I could barely see. To keep from straying into the freeway traffic on my left, I focused on the fog line and kept my front wheel a foot or two to the right. Occasionally, I'd peek up to see the road ahead, then duck down again when a car or truck passed and kicked up a wall of water that would otherwise hit me in the face.

The day hadn't started out stormy. In fact, it had been clear and warm and windless when I left the campground in Medora, fifty miles east of Glendive. I had been in high spirits, certain that the bad weather was finally behind me. But by midmorning, the sky to the northeast had darkened. Black clouds bunched up and rolled across the horizon. Far off I could see the slanted drapery of rain falling on the distant plains. By the time I reached the Highway 85 interchange, the leading edge of the storm had reached me and rain had begun to fall. I rolled up the off-ramp and took shelter under a Chevron canopy, one of a complex of gas stations, convenience stores and fast food joints clustered around the cloverleaf. It was my second day riding on the freeway, and to my surprise, I'd found it enjoyable — that is, until this storm hit.

I leaned my bike against the window of a small market and went in. The man and woman who ran the store offered to let me sit at their table in back until the rain stopped. I ate donuts and drank tea; then, after half an hour, there was a pause in the storm. I figured I might be able to make it to the campground in Dickinson before the heavy stuff hit, so I thanked the store owners, went out, and got back on the freeway.

I'd picked up Interstate 94 at Glendive and crossed the Montana border into North Dakota just west of Medora. I had been glad to put the brutal Montana weather behind me, and had great hopes for North Dakota, but now, as I wiped road slush from my face, I was beginning to wonder. It was looking like one of those out-of-the-frying-pan-and-into-the-fire kind of deals. I took the first exit for Dickinson and found myself riding through an industrial area. The storm was just too much, and I knew I'd have to get off the road soon. But short of knocking on the door of one of the factories, there was nowhere for me to go. Then, in several miles, the surroundings started to take on a more urban feel; strip malls replaced recycling plants, and I began to look for a place where I could get in out of the weather. I came to a stretch of road under construction where traffic was being routed around torn-up pavement. I rolled to the front of the line of cars to where the flagman, a Hispanic man in his 20's, stood. He looked at me and smiled. I smiled back, and we both shrugged in understanding, brothers in our soggy misery. In another two miles, I spotted a Hardies burger joint and dashed inside, sat at a table, and peeled off my drenched rain gear. People turned to watch, and they spoke to me as I settled in.

"Wet enough for you?"

"You're not riding in that slop are you?"

"I saw you on your bike, you must be freezing."

I smiled and shook my head. "It's pretty hairy out there, all right."

They were the locals: oil-rig roughnecks, teenagers, housewives, and a work crew that had been pumping out a flooded intersection across the street. We were all gathered in the same place for the same reason. I guess there's something about violent weather that brings people together. We watched cars splash through the flooded intersection, making wisecracks, astute observations, and predictions about how long the storm would last. In that half hour, we became a sort of community. We talked and joked, swapped advice, and traded life stories until the rain stopped and the sun broke through. Then the gang parted and we went our separate ways.

Le Plat Du Jour

I had learned that the best time for riding was early morning, so most days I would rush around and get going by 7:00 or 8:00. Because it was quicker than cooking, I'd fallen into the bad habit of stopping at convenience stores for breakfast. Back home, I rarely ate the pre-packaged swill that had lately become my morning staple. Each time I'd have a Hostess Fruit Pie in the parking lot of a 7-11 I'd feel guilty and then sick to my stomach, and I'd vow to purchase better food at the next supermarket. But when the next morning rolled around, I'd again be wandering the aisles of the nearest Quickie Mart.

Though I wasn't doing much for my body when it came to breakfast, I ate pretty well for the other meals. Lunches were usually whole wheat bread with peanut butter and sometimes jelly. I had experimented with cheese, but that turned rancid in the heat. I'd snack as I rode. I always had a package of cookies or crackers within easy reach. Dinner was the big meal of the day. I'd cook pasta, rice or couscous with pesto, masala or tomato sauce and fresh or canned vegetables. I guess eating relatively healthfully the other two meals helped me justify my junk-food breakfast habit. That morning in Dickinson I had a breakfast of Doritos, Ho Ho's and a stale maple bar in the parking lot of a Cenex gas station just north of the freeway interchange. I headed out on Old Highway 10, which, I was told, had been the major east-west route before I-94 went in. Also known as Old Red 10, the road meanders along past fields and farms and through the small towns of Taylor, Richardton, and Hebron.

The morning had started out foggy but bright, and the sun lit the air so that it glowed. It was as though I were inside a cloud. As I pedaled along, mist swirled around and spread out behind like the wake of a ship. The atmosphere was charged with a kind of living, fluid electricity; I could sense the energy all around. The road twisted and turned and climbed and descended over rolling hills, and I drifted through this dreamscape in a kind of blissful trance. It all seemed so right and good and beautiful that it made me a little sad to know this moment would soon pass and never come again.

I spent that night at a campground in Glen Ulin, and camped near Bismarck the next day. From there, I rode south along the Red River to Hazelton.

Ruthie and Jay

I rose early, broke camp, and rode out of Hazelton heading for my next campsite in the small town of Gackle. I'd had two good days of tailwinds since Dickinson, and out on highway 34 the wind blew at a steady fifteen miles an hour. The sky was clear, the air was warm, and I anticipated a grand sixty-three-mile lark. For the first fifty-five miles I barely turned a pedal. The road cut through miles of green fields, and every once in a while I'd pass a small lake. The two-lane back road was flat and straight, with only a slight jog to the north about fifty-eight miles into the ride, and that's where the trouble began: The wind that had made my ride nearly effortless now turned against me. I had only five miles to go, but riding in that tempest turned out to be a lot more work than I had bargained for. It was the worst windstorm I'd been in since that day outside Havre, and it was getting to me. The wind would send me toward the edge of the road, and I'd overcorrect so that I wound up swerving from the shoulder to the center line and back to the shoulder again, weaving like a drunken sailor. It was early evening now, and I could see Gackle in the distance; a few lights were just coming on when a blue minivan pulled up alongside. I could hear a woman's voice over the roar of the wind.

"Hi," she said, "where are you going?"

"Gackle," I replied.

"Where are you staying tonight?" she asked.

"The campground."

"Can you make it that far? This wind is pretty bad."

I leaned in the window, keeping a firm grip on my handlebars. "How far is it?"

"About a mile. Can you make it?"

"Yeah, I can make it."

"Well, I think you should stay with me tonight. My place is up ahead on Main Street; it's the double-wide mobile home on the right. I'm going to go ahead and I'll meet you there. Remember, the white trailer on the right, the only mobile home in town, you can't miss it. I'll leave my van out in front."

I nodded. "Okay, I'll see you in a few minutes."

Soon, I reached town. As I pedaled slowly past the first few houses, I could see up ahead a young man and woman and two small children.

As I neared, the young man called out to me from the sidewalk. "Hi," he said, "welcome to Gackle!" I smiled and waved and wobbled on. The young man came out into the street and walked along beside me. "So, where are you coming from?"

"Seattle," I said.

"Wow, long way!"

I stopped and stood astraddle the top bar. "Yeah, it's a long way." The wind was not as strong in town; the few buildings that lined Main Street blocked the worst of it, and it was a real treat to be able to stand still without having to brace myself.

The young man looked to be in his twenties, trim and fit. He waved to the woman who stood on the sidewalk. "Honey, come over here, I want you to meet someone. This is my wife," he said, "and I'm Jason."

"Glad to meet you," she said.

"Hey," Jason said, "wait here a minute, I've got something for you." He dashed across the street and into a nearby house. In a few minutes, he returned and handed me a fistfull of small packages. "Those are Honey Stingers. They're an energy supplement that my company makes."

I took the packages and slid them into my handlebar bag.

"Thanks a bunch," I said, "I could use some energy."

Just then I saw the woman from the van coming down the street, with a man at her side. "There you are!" she said. "Come on, we've got to get you inside. By the way, I'm Ruthie, and this is Jay, my neighbor."

"I'm Darby," I said, and we shook hands. I thanked Jason and his wife and went with Ruthie and Jay up the street. We rolled my bike into the garage and leaned it against a workbench. Ruthie took me by my arm and led me into the trailer. "Now you sit down and rest," she said. "Later, I want to hear all about your trip."

Both Ruthie and Jay were drinking whiskey, and Ruthie asked if I wanted one.

"Sure," I said, though it was the ice that enticed me more than the whiskey.

Ruthie was slim and tall, with an infectious laugh. "How old are you?" she asked as she rattled ice cubes into a glass. "I'm sixty-one. Jay here is the same age." Ruthie went to the cupboard and pulled out a bottle of Johnny Walker Black Label. "My husband is in Minnesota, he's a rep for a medical supply company. We've known Jay forever; he and Bob, that's my husband, have been friends since the first grade!"

"Can you put some water in my drink?" I said.

Ruthie splashed three fingers of Black Label in my glass, came around the kitchen counter, and handed it to me. "Oh, don't worry, the ice will cut it down, just let it melt a while." She sat in a lounge chair and leaned in, her elbows braced on her knees, her hands cradling her face. "Now, what are you doing out in this kind of weather?" She sat listening with rapt attention as I told my story. "Well, that's just about the coolest thing I ever heard," she said when I'd finished. "But it's crazy, too, you know that, don't you?"

"I guess," I said.

"Well, some people think I'm crazy too, so I suppose we'll get along just fine. Now, while I make dinner why don't you and Jay go out to the farm?"

"Farm?" I said, "there's a farm?"

Climate change

Jay, who hadn't said much, stood up and walked to the door, motioning for me to follow. "Come on," he said, "and bring your drink." We got in Ruthie's van and drove out of town, then turned onto a dirt road. We drove a few miles farther through fields of native grass dotted with small lakes, and finally arrived at an old white farmhouse. A big red barn sat on a rise overlooking a pond. "These lakes weren't here ten years ago," Jay told me, "they were just low spots in the hay fields. The water table has risen so much they filled in." He shrugged. "Climate change I guess." Jay brought the van to a stop and we got out. He was, I found out, a Vietnam veteran. He'd been a Navy SEAL and had seen a lot of action.

"I guess I better not get you mad at me," I joked.

Jay smiled, "I've changed a lot since those days. Now I just take things easy." He was the polar opposite of Ruthie, quiet and contemplative, speaking in a soft voice. He had a broad, friendly face with an easy smile that came on slowly and spread across his face in a wide grin.

As we walked around the farm, Jay showed me an old well with a hand pump that still worked. We explored the barn, and then Jay looked at his watch. "Hey, we better get going, Ruthie will have dinner ready by now." We got in the van and drove back to Ruthie's trailer and ate, after which I took a shower and bedded down in a spare room. The next morning, Ruthie fixed breakfast for Jay and me and we talked about my destination for the day. I pulled out my map and pointed to a campground sixty miles away on the Sheyenne River.

"You can't go that way," Ruthie said, "the bridge is washed out and the road is closed. You have to detour forty miles."

My heart sank. "Damn," I said, "forty miles? That'll take me almost a day!"

Ruthie thought a moment, went over and picked up the phone, dialed, then spoke for a few minutes. "It's all taken care of," she said, "I called someone I know at the highway department, told them you'd be coming through on your bike, and they said they'd let you pass. There's an old bridge, and you have permission to use it. You can camp at your campground after all."

As I was packing my panniers, I discovered that Ruthie had done my laundry. My clothes were neatly stacked on the bed. Later, Ruthie, Jay and I stood in front of her trailer taking extra long to say goodbye. We took photos and hugged, and then I got on my bike and rode away.

I'll never forget Ruthie and Jay. They'll always hold a special place in my heart.

Chapter Five: Minnesota

It had rained every day since I'd crossed the border from North Dakota to Minnesota three days before. I'd picked up the Lake Wobegone Trail in St. Joseph and had ridden to its end just west of St. Cloud. It had rained hard all day, and I stopped and huddled in a picnic shelter with a dozen or so other cyclists. It had been enjoyable talking with them, but it was late afternoon now, time to go.

There was a campground east of town, and by the time I arrived, the storm had paused, though black clouds still roiled and tumbled across the sky. I knew it wouldn't be long before another downpour hit. I set my tent next to a fifth-wheel camper and struck up a conversation with the man who occupied it. He was in his mid-thirties, nicely dressed in upscale, casual clothes and carrying a slight potbelly. "I freelance for insurance companies," he told me. "There's been a lot of bad weather and flooding this year, and I do damage inspections and repair estimates. I work for a number of different companies, and I'm busier than I've ever been."

"There have been a lot of storms?" I asked.

"Worst year on record. Climate change is really taking a toll on the insurance companies." He looked up at the darkening sky. "Tonight's gonna be a killer . . . Are you sure you'll be okay in that tent?" He pointed to my yellow REI Half Dome.

My tent was now quaking in the wind. "I think I'll be okay," I said.

"Well, if it gets too bad, come over to my place. I'll leave the door unlocked. There's an extra bed, and you're welcome to it."

As I lay in my sleeping bag, I realized that it was June 17th, Father's Day. Feeling a twinge of loneliness, I hooked up to the Internet and connected with my middle daughter, Annie.

"Hi Dad," she smiled, "where are you?"

"I'm in St. Cloud, Minnesota," I said. It was dark now, and the only illumination came from the glow of the iPad screen, giving my face a ghostly appearance.

"It's night, where you are?"

"I'm a few of hours ahead of you, plus there's a storm coming." At that moment, a lightning bolt lit up the tent like a high-powered strobe, followed by booming thunder. As if on cue, the video scrambled.

When the screen came back on, Annie was wide-eyed. "Holy cow," she said, "what the heck was that?!"

"Oh, just a little thunder and lightning, nothing to worry about." A strong gust of wind hit the tent, making it rattle and groan and flap with a noise that rivaled the crash of thunder.

"Dad!?" Annie said. "You'd better get to shelter, it looks like you're about to be blown away!"

"It's not as bad as it looks, Honey," I said, "I've been in worse." There were two or three lightning flashes that I'm sure would have looked to anyone watching like the coming of Armageddon, and again the screen went blank for a moment, then flickered back on. "Really" I said, "it's just a little storm."

"Well, it sure doesn't look little," Annie said. "I'd feel better if you could get inside. Is there someplace safe where you can spend the night?"

"I tell you what . . ." A series of lightning strikes and a roll of thunder interrupted me ". . . if it gets too bad, the guy in the RV next door said I could bunk with him. If it looks like I'm in danger, I'll go over, he's not ten feet away."

"Well, happy Father's Day anyway. Let me know if you're still alive in the morning."

"That's the spirit."

"Okay, Dad, I can't take much more of this. You be sure to e-mail me tomorrow, promise?"

"I promise. Good night, Honey. I love you."

"I love you too, Dad," Annie said. "Be safe."

We broke the connection. I scrunched down in my sleeping bag and soon drifted off to sleep as the storm passed through on its way south toward Minneapolis, my next destination, too.

Craig's House

I was anxious to reach Minneapolis because I was going to get to see my friend Craig. He and I had been studio mates at The Rhode Island School of Design many years before, and I was looking forward to reconnecting. I wanted to take the shortest route possible, which, it turned out, was Highway 10, a sixty-five-mile straight shot southeast. I got up early to a clear day and, map stuffed in the back pocket of my cycling jersey, started out from St. Cloud.

Highway 10 had four divided lanes, debris-strewn shoulders, and heavy traffic. It was a freeway in everything but name. I had thought about cobbling together a tangle of back roads, farm roads and dirt roads, but I had a long way to go, so I opted for the more direct but more hazardous route. The first eight miles weren't too bad; then I hit a stretch of highway construction that closed the northbound lane, funneling traffic for both directions into the two southbound lanes. That meant that the traffic volume normally carried by four lanes was now crammed into just two, and the result was motorized anarchy.

The cars were fine, but the eighteen-wheelers hung over the fog line, and I had to ride on the edge of the pavement to keep from getting hit. A few miles into the work zone I was riding along, breathing diesel fumes and getting pelted with flying road junk, when a big rig whizzed past on my left. He was so close that I could have reached out and touched one of the spinning tires. I tensed up and steered a line for the gravel at the edge of the road. There wasn't much room; a miscalculation of a few inches would land me in the ditch. Then it happened. From behind, I heard a terrible roar, a jangling of metal, and a horn blast that made my ears ring. It seemed that a big, fire-breathing road behemoth was bearing down on me. If I didn't act quickly, I'd be crushed.

I couldn't go to my left, and if I stayed on my present course, whatever it was that was behind me would gobble me up for sure. My only hope was to execute a crash landing by steering into the grass at the side of the road. Just as I was about to ditch, I noticed something out of the corner of my eye. A freight train was passing on the right, and as it did, the engineer blew the horn again. It was the same horn that had just scared the bejesus out of me. I had mistaken Casey Jones for the Grim Reaper! I swerved, straightened, slowed to a stop, and shook my fist at no one in particular. Getting off my bike, I walked down into the grass median between the highway and the tracks. My hands shook and my knees went weak, and it took a while to gather my wits enough to get back on the bike. I vowed to get off that Highway to Hell and finish the trip on back roads; it would take me longer to reach Minneapolis, but at least I'd get there.

My friend Craig is a diehard cyclist who had planned to ride with me for a while, but during one of our phone conversations he told me that he'd had an accident and hurt his shoulder, and wouldn't be able to join me after all. "But look," he'd said, "when you get close to Minneapolis, give me a call and I'll come pick you up."

I'd told him that wouldn't be necessary, but as the day wore on and the temperature and humidity rose, I began to think about taking him up on his offer. After abandoning Highway 10, I had been zigging and zagging back and forth across the Mississippi River, riding through the little towns of Monticello, Olsego, Elk River and Dayton. I'd been covering a lot of miles east and west but making slow progress south. By late afternoon, when I rolled into Coon Rapids, I had ridden more than eighty miles but hadn't yet reached the outskirts of Minneapolis. Finally, as I struggled along in the muggy heat, I decided to call Craig.

"Sure," Craig said, "I'll be glad to come get you. I'll meet you in the parking lot."

There's a park at Coon Rapids through which the Mississippi

River runs, and I was sitting beneath a tree there when my phone rang. "Hey," Craig said, "I'm stuck in traffic, it's probably gonna be another hour before I can get to you."

"That's okay," I said, "take your time."

"I'm sitting in bumper to bumper traffic, there must've been a crash or something. I haven't moved in five minutes."

"Well, don't worry about it. I'm in the shade and everything is . . ." Just then, I felt a tap on my shoulder and I turned around. It was Craig. He had parked his car and snuck up behind me. He put his cell phone away and handed me an ice-cold beer. "Thought you might be thirsty," he smiled.

"Oh, you magnificent bastard!" I laughed, and took the beer.

We loaded my bike into Craig's car and drove an hour south to his early-20th-century, two-story home in the tree-lined Hiawatha neighborhood of Minneapolis. His wife, Jeenee, and daughter, Seeley, were out of town, so it was just the two of us. We sat around drinking cold brews and reminiscing; then I took a quick shower and we headed into the city.

Craig took me to one of his favorite restaurants, the Birchwood Cafe, where I had a vegan sandwich made with pumpkin, sunflower seeds, radishes, and a whole bevy of other greens. After the basic foods I'd been eating on the road, that sandwich was a treat. Later, we walked around the Seward neighborhood and talked about old times. Craig has a great sense of humor and had me laughing so hard I could barely walk, and I finally had to beg him to stop. We were back at his place well before midnight, and I collapsed on the couch and was asleep in a few short minutes.

My daughter Maren had mailed a box to me, care of Craig, with a supply of my asthma medicine and two spare tires. The next morning, I opened the box and was delighted to find, in addition to the expected items, some surprises: protein bars and my favorite chocolates, a new pair of cycling gloves, and a camp towel to replace the one I'd lost in Montana. Since I'd lost my towel, showering at campgrounds had become something of an art. If the bathroom had paper towels, I could dry off with them, but sometimes I'd have to use one of those electric wall-mounted blow driers. At one campground neither paper nor hot air was available, and I dried off as well as I could with a plastic shower curtain.

My stove had malfunctioned in North Dakota, so I needed to visit the Minneapolis REI to get a rebuild kit. I'd also broken my watch and was in the market for a replacement for that, too. Craig fixed breakfast, and then we headed into town to run my errands. By early afternoon, I'd gotten everything I needed, and it was time to pick up Jeenee and Seeley at the airport.

Craig is a book designer and a gifted painter. Jeenee is a graphic designer, too, but also sings professionally. Seeley, their fifteen-year-old daughter, is smart as a whip and traded quips with me blow for blow as we drove home from the airport. After Jeenee and Seeley stowed their baggage, we went into St. Paul, where they treated me to dinner at a Japanese restaurant, Tanpopo, in the Lowertown neighborhood. Back at the house, Jeenee got their dog, Chaz, to chase his tail. It had me rolling on the floor. I sat on the old couch and basked in the warm glow of family and good fellowship. It was a pleasant feeling, but I guess it made me miss my own family a little, too.

The enormity of riding across the North American Continent was too much to grasp, so I had gotten in the habit of setting mid-range goals of 200 to 500 miles to break the trip up into manageable chunks. My next goal was the port city of Manitowoc on the shore of Lake Michigan in Wisconsin, 400 miles east. From there, I'd cross the lake on the S.S. Badger, the last coal-fired steamer on Lake Michigan, to the town of Ludington, in Michigan.

Craig offered to drive me to the edge of town, so we lingered over breakfast and then drove twenty miles south of the city. It felt a little like cheating, but it was late morning, and hitching a ride saved me the frustration of the difficult route-finding always associated with getting out of any big, unfamiliar city on a bicycle.

We crossed the Mississippi River into Wisconsin at Hastings, and Craig dropped me off in a supermarket parking lot. It was hard saying goodbye. I loaded my bike as quickly as I could; then, with a handshake and a hug, I was off.

Chapter Six: Wisconsin

On my own again with the flatlands of Minnesota behind me, I was now in the rolling hills of Wisconsin. I rode on Highway 35, also known as the Great River Road, which runs along the banks of the Mississippi River, climbing and descending through lush forests and past rocky cliffs. My plan was to make a short day of it, riding only fifty miles to the little Mississippi River town of Pepin, where my map promised I would find a campground.

I was within a few miles of Pepin when the clouds opened up and it began to rain. It came down so hard that the rain splashed back up several feet, creating an opaque wall of water and road grit. Cars would suddenly materialize out of the storm, whiz past, and disappear just as quickly. It was a disaster waiting to happen. I was creeping down a shoulderless section, praying for a place to get off the road, when I spied a rest area. Pulling in, I rolled my bike under the small six-by-six-foot shelter, stripped out of my wet duds, dried off with my new towel, and donned dry, warm clothes. *I'll give it an hour and a half*, I thought; *if it doesn't let up by then, I'm camping right here!* I tried not to notice the NO OVERNIGHT CAMPING sign.

The overlook where I huddled was a hundred feet above a wide section of the river called Lake Pepin. I whiled away the time watching lightning strike after lightning strike light up the rain-darkened sky. Thunder rolled through the fog-shrouded hills; *apparently*, I thought, *the gods are angry tonight*. Darkness fell, and the storm got worse. It was too late to get back on the road now; I would have to spend the night where I was. There was a concrete-block bathroom nearby, and I toyed with the idea of sleeping in it. As I mulled it over, the rain let up. I quickly set up my tent and climbed in just as the storm started again.

I had picked a spot that was partially hidden by bushes next to a stand of trees. As it turned out, it was a poor choice. I was between the highway and the Great Northern railroad tracks, and all night long, lights from passing cars would illuminate the inside of my tent as they rounded a corner. Worse than that, long freight trains rumbled by every few minutes. I hadn't known it when I pitched my tent, but it was a mere ten or fifteen feet through the woods to the tracks. Each time a train roared past, I'd be jolted from my half-sleep. The noise was so loud, and the trains seemed so close, that for a drowsy instant I would think I was about to be run over. I slept little, and as soon as it was light enough to travel, I got back on the road.

Mississippi backwater

The day dawned clear and bright. A wispy fog clung to the ground and I sailed down out of the mountains through an ethereal landscape of steaming earth and weeping forests. Despite being tired, I enjoyed my ride through that weirdly beautiful place. In eleven miles, I came to the small town of Pepin, where I had originally planned to camp. Stopping at a small store just opening up, I bought my now-usual junk food breakfast.

I rolled on through the small towns dotting that section of the Wisconsin Mississippi: Nelson, Alma, and Cochrane, each village conjuring up images of what had once been thriving riverfront commercial hubs, now mostly on the decline.

It was early afternoon and hot when I reached the little community of Fountain City. I spotted a Coke machine on the porch of what looked like an Elks Club and pulled in. I put my money in the slot but nothing happened. Then I realized that the building was boarded up and the vending machine was dead. I gave the Coke machine a good kick, and when I turned around, I saw a police car pull up. *Oh crap!* I thought. I was unshaven and my clothes were stained with sweat and road grime. I smelled pretty funky, and I'm sure I gave off a hobo vibe. Was I going to be busted for vagrancy? The cop, a young guy in his late twenties or early thirties, stuck his head out of the cruiser window. "How you doing?" he asked.

I smiled back. "Pretty good. I just stopped to get a Coke. I guess the machine is kaput."

He glanced at the machine, then back at me. "Yeah, that thing hasn't worked in years." He paused and seemed to give me the once over. "Where are you headed?"

There's a town every few miles along this section of the river, and I had to think . . . "Uh, Onalaska. I'm heading east from there to go to Manitowoc. Going to catch the ferry across the lake."

"Are you coming from Minneapolis?"

"I rode out from Seattle."

He thought for a moment. Was he going to arrest me? I had, after all, damaged private property when I'd kicked the Coke machine; we both could see the big dent. "There's a good trail up ahead, why don't you take that. You can get off the highway for a while."

"There's a trail?" I said, happy to draw attention away from the Coke machine.

"Yeah, it's hard-packed dirt, but you should have no trouble." He looked at my tires. "What are those, 35's?"

"Yup," I said, "I've ridden on dirt, and they work fine."

"I ride that trail all the time on my mountain bike" he said. "There's a three-dollar fee, but if the ranger stops you, just tell them your story, and I don't think they'll make a big deal out of it." It turned out the cop was an avid bicyclist too, and when he'd seen me cruise through town, he decided to see if he could help out. "I know what a hassle traffic can be on a bike," he said. "Let me lay out a route for you."

I followed his directions, found the trail, and in fifteen miles rolled into the riverfront town of Trempealeau. It was midafternoon and sweltering, so when I saw a Stella Artois sign in the window of the Trempealeau Hotel Bar, I couldn't resist. Stella is my favorite brand, and a long-shot between Manhattan and Seattle. To find it here in the Heartland seemed like an omen, so I parked my bike and went in. The place was all parquet and ferns, with a long, polished bar and a brass foot rail. I pulled up a stool and ordered. As I sipped my cold Stella, I chatted with the bartender, a young woman with short blond hair and a tattoo of an American eagle on one forearm. "Is there a place to camp around here?" I asked. "I saw a state park on my map."

The bartender nodded. "Yeah, that would be Perot State Park. It's just a few miles north." She absently wiped the bar with a cloth. "You're not from around here are you?"

"Seattle," I said.

"I figured West Coast."

"Really?"

"Yeah, you have that accent."

I laughed. "You're the one with the accent."

She smiled. "I guess it depends on where you're at."

"No matter where you go, there you are."

"Hey," she said, "that's a good one. Can I use it?"

"Well, it's not mine, it's from a movie, but sure, be my guest."

I finished my beer and rode to the state park, where I paid fourteen dollars for a grassy spot in a small clearing. Later, around 3:00 a.m., I was sleeping soundly when I became aware of a presence. Someone — or something — was in the tent with me! I sat up and peered into the darkness. I heard a low, menacing growl and saw a pair of mischievous eyes; whatever it was, it wasn't afraid of me. Now it began to move. I could hear the rustle of nylon and felt a tug on my sleeping bag. Drawing my legs up to my chest, I let out a yell, grabbed my flashlight, and promptly dropped it. I fumbled around, found it, and shined it at the intruder. The raccoon blinked in the glare of the light, snarled, then pulled my two-pound bag of granola through the hole he'd made in my tent. My pepper spray was around there someplace, but by the time I'd located it, Rocky was waddling into the forest with my week's supply of breakfast. I could see him sauntering off, and before he melted into the darkness, he turned and gave me a dismissive sneer — the raccoon version of the finger, I suppose.

The next day I examined the rip the raccoon had made in my tent. It was about five inches high and looked like it had been cut with a scalpel. Equipped with such sharp claws, that raccoon would have been more than a match for me. I was glad I hadn't started a fight with him after all.

The Tea Thief

I reached Manitowoc around 6:00 in the evening of the third day out of Trempealeau. Still, I had seven hours to kill until the S.S. Badger departed for the crossing of Lake Michigan at 1:00 a.m. I bought my ticket and then lounged around the lobby. I called my daughter Brittney, and we caught up on events back home; after that, I went inside and read every magazine and rack brochure in the place. On a table in the corner was one of those free self-serve coffee machines with three spigots, one labeled COFFEE, another DECAF, and the last HOT WATER. There were sweeteners, half a dozen flavors of creamers, a stack of cups, stirrers, and a box of tea bags. I decided I'd like a cup of tea, so I got in line behind an elderly gentleman who was making himself a cup of tea, too. While he was busy adding sugar, stirring it, then tasting it and adding more sugar, getting it just the way he liked it, I reached around, grabbed a cup and a tea bag from the box, and stuck some tea bags in my pocket; they were free, after all.

The old guy gave me a look that if looks could kill . . . I guess I might have been invading his space a little, but I was puzzled why my small intrusion would cause such intense resentment. *Well*, I thought, *he's old; you gotta cut him some slack.* I shrugged and smiled. "For later," I said, leaned in, and took a few more tea bags. Now I could tell the old boy was really fuming. He grabbed the box, gave me another dirty look, and stormed out of the waiting room.

I stood there with my mouth open. The old dude had swiped the whole stash! Later, I asked one of the women working the desk if she would mind putting out another box of tea bags; a cranky, old man had stolen the last one. I smiled and rolled my eyes as if to say, "Can you believe the gall?"

She gave me a funny look. "Tea bags?" she said, clearly bewildered. "We don't have tea; you have to bring your own."

Chapter Seven: Michigan

After twenty miles of pedaling, I was right back where I'd started. The S.S. Badger sat belching black smoke at her berth just the way I'd left her two hours earlier. The four-hour crossing of Lake Michigan from Manitowoc to Ludington had been uneventful. My fellow passengers had disappeared once we left the dock. I suppose they'd all had staterooms; after all, it was past 1:00 a.m. by the time we'd gotten underway. The Badger is the last of the coal-fired steamships on the Great Lakes, and she's showing her age. Her linoleum is cracking and her paint is chipped. I'm sure the S.S. Badger is perfectly seaworthy, but there's something sad, and a little creepy, about being the only waking passenger on an old ship's night crossing.

After roaming the eerily empty vessel for an hour, wandering up and down vacant stairways and deserted passageways, I'd settled into the TV lounge to watch reruns of Breaking Bad. I dozed, but got no real rest, so that when we pulled into port in Ludington, Michigan, I was stumblebum tired. My original plan had been to ride forty-five miles to a campground I'd marked on my map, but while on the ship, I'd read a brochure advertising a state campground just a few miles out of Ludington. We pulled into port at 6:00 a.m. "I'll see how I feel," I mumbled as I changed out of my street clothes and into cycling gear.

Once on the bike, I realized how tired I was, so I opted for the nearby state park. But when I got there and asked about a space, the host, a heavy man in his sixties, told me I'd have to "Go check in at the registration building."

"Where's that?" I asked.

"Oh, you passed it about five miles back." He glanced at his watch. "They ought to be open in an hour."

I smiled dopily, turned my bike around, and started back the way I'd come. Normally, that kind of setback would put me in a foul mood. But it was a grand morning, the scenery was spectacular, and I was in high spirits. Dunes lined the quiet two-lane road, and I entertained myself by cutting through the many small sand drifts that had blown onto the pavement. I'd line up on one and hit it at full speed, sand spraying from my tires almost the way snow does from skis on the first run of a good powder day. That kept me entertained until I reached the registration building, where I settled in at one of the picnic tables and made a breakfast of raisin bran and powdered milk. Halfway through my second cup, the ranger showed up and rented me a spot.

Hot diggity, I thought, I could almost feel the pillow beneath my head. But when I reached my assigned campsite, I was dismayed to find it was occupied. When I returned to the registration booth and told the park ranger, she shrugged. "Checkout time is 1:00 p.m.; I guess you'll just have to wait." I couldn't stay awake that long, so I got a refund, thanked the ranger, and headed back to Ludington.

Now more tired than ever, I stood where I'd started, staring groggily at the S.S. Badger. I couldn't afford a motel, so I had no choice but to get back on the road.

By now I had a pretty good feel for my bike. I had it dialed in just right, like it was a part of me. I could sense the texture of the pavement through the frame vibrations, and I merely had to think and the bike responded. I'd spent so much time riding the thing that I could almost do it in my sleep. It was late morning now, and the temperature hovered in the low seventies. It was a beautiful day for cycling, and I rode along in a happy daze. I was so tired and sleepy that I could barely keep my eyes open, and I blinked out for a few seconds. As my bike strayed into the gravel on the outer edge of the pavement, I came to with a start, corrected my course, got back on the road, and continued. But it wasn't long before I dozed off again. This time I drifted into the middle of the road. Luckily, there was no traffic at that moment, and I steered back toward the fog line. I don't know how I managed to ride while I was out for those brief seconds, but I suppose some basic motor functions remained active even as my conscious brain took a break.

The third time I dozed off, I awoke just as I was about to run into a foot-high curb in the small town of Scottville. I swerved and pulled hard on the brakes, barely avoiding a collision with a parked car, then teetered to a stop in the middle of the street, causing a minor traffic jam. *That's enough of that,* I thought. I would find a park bench to sleep on if I had to. Then I saw a sign advertising the Scottville Riverside Park. I turned off, followed the signs, and in a few miles crossed the Pere Marquette River and pulled into the campground.

The young woman who registered me had two small children bouncing around the office. They ran and clung to their mother's leg when I walked in, shy, I guess, in the presence of a stranger. One was a boy about seven years old, the other a younger girl, four or five. I paid the twenty-five-dollar fee and talked with the woman for a few minutes; then the little girl followed me out and stood at the door. "Hey, mister," she said, "how come you have a little girl's helmet?"

I had bought my cycling helmet at an REI sale, and the only color available was white and pink, so yes, it did look somewhat "little girlish," though I liked to think of it more as an expression of confidence in my masculinity.

"Why do you have a little girl's helmet?" I asked, feigning indignation.

She looked puzzled for a moment; then, "Because I'm a little girl!"

"I know you are, but what am I?"

Now she caught onto the game. "I know you are, but what am I times a hunnert!" She grinned.

"You're rubber and I'm glue . . ." I prompted.

". . . Everything you say bounces off'a me an' sticks to you!" she said, clapping her hands gleefully.

I could tell the little girl would have liked to continue the game, but I was badly in need of sleep so I said goodbye and pushed my bike to a spot near the slow-moving, clay-colored river and set up camp in the shade of a big oak tree. Within a few minutes, I was sound asleep.

Sometime in the afternoon, I woke up to a stifling-hot tent. It felt like a sauna, and I was pouring sweat. I dragged the tent to the shade of a tree, then fell back asleep and didn't wake up until after the sun had set. I broke out my stove and cooked a dinner of pasta with pesto and tomatoes. It was a gorgeous evening, and I took my meal to the bank of the river, where I sat and watched the fireflies put on a psychedelic light show.

The next day was hotter than a two-dollar pistol, but the road was flat, and I made good time. I camped near a lake just west of Clare that night, and the day after that, I picked up the Pere Marquette Rail-Trail, which led me southwest toward Lake St. Claire and Canada.

I had been having trouble with my kickstand for several weeks now; it kept working loose. I would have to tighten the bolt almost every day, but it just wouldn't stay secure. I finally pulled into a bike shop in the little town of Clare and asked the mechanic to have a look. "The kickstand dented the frame," he told me, "that's why it won't stay tight. You'd better take it off before it does serious damage."

I was horrified. "My frame is bent?" I said. "What does that mean?"

The mechanic smiled. "Don't worry, it's just a small dent, and I don't think it will affect anything. Just lose the kickstand and you'll be fine."

"Okay," I said, "let's take it off, you can keep it or give it to some other biker."

As the mechanic worked on my bike, he looked around at all my panniers, dry bags, and assorted other baggage. "Man," he said, "I'll bet this rig is really heavy when it's loaded up. Must be a lot of work to move it down the road."

"Tell me about it," I said.

Things That Go Bump in the Night

The forests in Michigan are well suited for camping. The ground where I had pitched my tent was covered with a spongy mat of dried leaves and mulch, making for a nice, soft bed. *Everything a wild camper could want,* I thought. I could see the road through the trees, but I didn't think drivers could see my tent unless they were looking for it, so I started out feeling secure in my stealth camp in these remote Michigan woods. But in the back of my mind I had the nagging feeling that something wasn't quite right.

I had followed the Pere Marquette Rail-Trail all the way from Clare to Midland, where I got back on surface streets. I'd made good time and was now a few miles south of Saginaw. If everything went right, I'd be entering Ontario, Canada, the day after tomorrow. I'd picked up the pace lately and set a new personal record of almost a hundred miles that day, and I was dog tired. I'd been looking for somewhere to set up my tent since late afternoon but hadn't found a suitable spot until some hours later, when I spotted a dirt road leading off into the forest. I'd followed it, found this small clearing, and pitched my tent, skipped dinner, crawled into my sleeping bag, and settled in for a well-deserved rest. In a few minutes, I was dozing. Then I jerked awake. *What was that?* I thought. Then I heard it again. Something was moving out there in the dark; I could hear the leaves and branches crunching and crackling. I dared not shine my light for fear of drawing attention to myself.

I'd done a lot of camping in the wilderness of my home state of Washington, much of it alone. I'd never felt the slightest bit uncomfortable or frightened sleeping in the most remote regions of the Cascade Mountains, but here it was different. There were people around, and they can be more dangerous than even the most ferocious wild animal. As the night wore on and the sounds of voices from nearby residences echoed eerily through the woods,

I became more and more paranoid. A time or two, I thought I heard banjo music. As tired as I was, I just couldn't stay asleep. Some atavistic sense of self-preservation kept me half awake. It was a moonless night and dark as coal; tree branches tangled in close overhead like tentacles, blacking out the stars, and for some reason I felt exposed and vulnerable. The woods are alive at night with nocturnal creatures and I could hear them scurrying about in the inky blackness. The hairs stood up on the back of my neck. It was like I was in one of those Stephen King novels where the protagonist discovers he's unwittingly set up housekeeping on top of an ancient Indian burial mound.

At each night sound, I would snap out of my stupor and peer nervously into the darkness. After a while, I would drift back into semi-slumber until another sound jerked me awake and I'd sit wide-eyed with my pepper spray at the ready. This happened again and again until the sky lightened enough for me to bug out. I couldn't wait to leave that place.

My wild camping experience had been a bust, so I decided to stay the next night in the exact opposite, a KOA. Kampgrounds of America is a chain of highly-developed facilities with so many luxuries that they border on resorts. The one I stayed at that night near Waterford Township had a man-made lake, a restaurant, an outdoor disco complete with DJ, a miniature golf course, a small market, and myriad other family-oriented activities and amenities. After sleeping in the woods the night before, the place looked like a little slice of heaven. I rolled in and pitched my tent in the "primitive" area.

Primitive in a KOA means there are only two bars of WiFi and you have to light your own campfire. It wasn't much of a wilderness experience, and it had a shuck and jive feel to it, but I enjoyed every decadent moment. I felt warmed by the presence of other campers and safe in the knowledge that the sturdy KOA security patrol would keep me safe while I slept.

Chapter Eight: Ontario

I started out the next day rested and feeling strong. Around midday, I crossed the St. Clair River at Marine City. The ferry ride into Canada took ten minutes and cost one dollar. When I got to Canadian customs, the border guard asked for my passport; then, "What is your purpose in visiting Canada?"

"Just passing through to New York," I replied. "I'm going to ride the Erie Canal."

He gave my bike and me the once-over. "How long do you plan to stay in Canada?"

"Oh, four or five days, I guess."

"What do you do for a living?"

That was a hard question to answer. Back home, I was a graphic designer, but now I wasn't sure what I was. Was I a seeker or just a bum on a bike? "Well, I'm an artist, but I'm taking some time off," I replied.

"Oh?"

"Yeah, I'm riding around the world."

"How long will that take?"

"Not sure. A year, maybe more."

"Must have a nice boss to let you off for so long."

"I don't have a boss, I have my own company, or rather I did."

"Okay, wait here." He walked off with my passport and came back ten minutes later. "Do you have any weapons?" he asked.

I had two Swiss Army knives and a small can of pepper spray. The knives were buried deep in my panniers, but the pepper spray was sticking out of my handlebar bag in clear sight. "No," I said. "I do have this." I pulled out the little red spray can. "For dogs."

He held his hand out. "That's illegal in Canada," he said. "I'll have to confiscate it."

I handed it over. "I didn't know, in the US . . ."

"You're in Canada now," he said, waving me through the gate. "Have a nice day."

I pedaled out of the customs complex and onto Canadian Highway 33. The road followed the St. Clair River south past modest but well-kept homes on the landward side, and private docks next to the water. I must have seen twenty docks in five miles. They ranged from simple wooden structures with a few lawn chairs and a cooler to elaborate, two-story affairs with slips for ski boats, diving boards, and what looked like wet bars. It was a warm, sunny afternoon and the humidity wasn't too bad — a perfect summer day, and at each dock, whether humble or extravagant, young bathing-suit-clad Canadians frolicked in the sparkling waters of the St. Clair River.

As I trundled past, I fantasized that someone would call out to me, "Hey, come on over and join in the fun!" But it was not to be. I tried initiating contact by waving at the merrymakers, but got no response. I suppose they were on to that trick. Almost every dock had a PRIVATE PROPERTY NO TRESPASSING sign.

Soon, the road curved away from the river and headed east again. My plan was to camp at the Rondeau Provincial Park, which sits on a spit that juts into Lake Erie ninety miles farther on. It would be a long day, but I had gotten an early start and there would be many hours of sunlight. Still, I'd be sticking my neck out. There would be no place to camp after I passed the small town of Dresden, thirty miles short of the campground. If I had two hours of sunlight left when I reached Dresden, I'd continue; otherwise, I'd stop there for the night. I rode hard and fast all day, keeping a close eye on my watch and my odometer.

If You're Gonna be Stupid, You'd Better be Tough

I rolled into Dresden with a little less than two hours of daylight left. At a grocery store, I stopped and gulped down a pint of chocolate milk, ate a protein bar and a banana, and then, without giving it much thought, started out. After an hour, I came to an intersection and took what I *thought* was the right road. It had been a long day. I'd already clocked more than eighty miles and had thirty to go, but I felt strong, and I was confident that I'd be snug in my sleeping bag before dark. I rode happily along past endless cornfields, enjoying the warm evening breeze. But when I glanced at the small compass I kept pinned to my handlebar bag, I was surprised to see that I was heading south. *Hmmm, that's weird*, I thought, *shouldn't I be going east?* I knew that roads have a way of twisting and turning, and I wasn't worried yet; I figured it would take me in the right direction soon. I rode on into the dusk, and still my compass pointed south. After another half hour, I stopped and checked my map and discovered that I'd made a wrong turn ten miles back.

I was in good enough shape now to push hard for long stretches. In fact, I found that I enjoyed the feeling I got from exertion. Earlier in the day, I'd ridden up some low hills, and instead of shifting into an easier gear, I'd stayed in high gear and pedaled as hard as I could. The feeling bordered on euphoria. It was a kind of floating sensation that is hard to describe. It was almost as if I were disconnected from my corporeal self and hovering in some non-space. My breathing was deep and fast but regular, and my legs turned the pedals almost on their own. It seemed that I could keep it up indefinitely. I know it sounds odd, but the best way I can describe the feeling is that the effort was so great that it was nearly effortless. And now I would call on my new-found strength to get me out of this jam.

The sun had set. I'd have to make up for lost time, so I turned around and pedaled like mad, racing against the darkness and reaching the intersection where I'd made the wrong turn just as night fell. I checked my map and compass to make sure I was now on the right road.

My headlight put out enough light for oncoming cars to see me, but not enough for me to see the road well. The shoulder started out good and solid but soon deteriorated into a soft, gravelly moat. It was bordered on one side by steep drop-offs into the ever-present cornfields, and on the road side by a sharp, six-inch asphalt ledge. The shoulder was in such bad shape that I had to ride on the pavement and was nearly sideswiped by passing trucks. One white Ford F150 came so close that I had to swerve into the moat. As I bumped along, I careened over the carcass of a dead raccoon and almost wrecked. After that near-disaster, I decided to get off the road and sleep wherever providence put me.

Then up ahead I saw the lights of what looked like a small town. I prayed there would be a place to camp, and I pinned my hopes on those distant twinkling lights. But when I reached the small crossroads village of Kent Bridge, I was disappointed to find that it was just a rural intersection with a closed-down store and a few houses buttoned up for the evening. Checking my watch, I saw that it was after 10:45 p.m. I headed back toward a swath of green I'd passed coming into town; I'd sleep there tonight.

It was July 1st, Canada Day, and behind the houses across the street from where I'd laid my sleeping bag, someone was setting off fireworks. I scrunched down and tried to block out the booming and flashing of the pyrotechnics. I'd set up camp in a swale of grass near a railroad siding where trains came and went all night long, their loud clanking and clunking adding to the general cacophony of the Canada Day celebration. But even with all that ruckus, I drifted off to deep sleep.

First, Be a Good Animal

It was 5:30 a.m., and off to the east the sky was brightening. I packed up and got on the road. There's something about starting the day on a bike. There's a feeling of optimism and adventure and the sense that anything's possible and nothing's for sure. It's quiet, and the air is pure like scentless perfume. The dust hasn't kicked up yet, and it's so clear that you can see forever. Whizzing past in a car, you get a rough idea of what it's like, but you're separated from the world by so many layers that you never get a real feel for the landscape. Cycling lets you tap into the true nature of a place and experience it with your soul. The sun on your face, the beckoning horizon, and the rhythm of your breathing all conspire to fill you with the simple joy of being alive and on the road.

The road I was on that morning, bordered on either side by cornfields, was straight, flat and empty, except for a four-legged creature standing in the center of the pavement a hundred yards ahead. From far off it looked like a dog, but as I got closer I discovered that it was a small red fox, the white tip of her tail flashing in the glow of the sun just breaking. I expected her to dash for cover, but she remained motionless even as I coasted to within a few feet.

She was intently watching something at the side of the road, breakfast perhaps, and didn't notice me until I was nearly upon her. She glanced my way; there was a spark of recognition, and with an almost human expression of indignation, she turned and darted into the cornfield. Our eyes met for just an instant, and that glimpse into the wild sent shivers down my spine.

That, I thought, *is why I'm on this trip*. My encounter with the fox was one of those moments that only come about by chance. I would have missed it if I hadn't made a wrong turn, and suddenly all the fatigue, stress and discomfort of the night before made sense. My fox moment set the tone for the rest of the day, and though I was sleepy and tired, I rode along in a dopey, happy mood, singing snatches of songs and waving at motorists.

Chapter Nine: New York

I skirted the north shore of Lake Erie, camping at the little beach towns along the way: Port Stanley, Port Rowan and Evans Point. I ran into some rain squalls, but the weather was mostly fine, and the roads were good. I reached the Peace Bridge, which spans the Niagara River, five days after crossing into Canada. Riding past a two-mile-long line of cars waiting for customs, I stopped at the arc of the bridge high above Lake Erie. As I took a photo, a station wagon with two teenage girls in it inched up beside me. One girl stuck her head out and yelled something that was lost in the wind, but her smile and thumbs up conveyed her support. I waved back, then pushed off and coasted into the USA.

Erie Canal

I made it through Buffalo pretty well, but soon got lost and had to spend the night in a motel. The next morning, I found my way to the start of the Erie Canal at the town of Towanda. I thought the State of New York would make a big deal out of the Canalway Trail, but it doesn't. I wandered around for half an hour until a pedestrian pointed it out to me. "Are you lost?" he asked. He was in his late forties or early fifties and wore shorts and a blue t-shirt that bulged around his stomach, showing a thin sliver of pale flesh. The small shorthaired terrier he was walking sniffed at my shoes.

"Yeah," I said, and pointed at the nearby waterway. "Is that the Erie Canal?" It didn't look like much.

"Uh-huh, that's it. The trail is kind of confusing, but I've got a good map back on my boat. If you want, I can give it to you," he said.

We walked along the promenade past crowded restaurants, bars and ice cream parlors to his sailboat. I leaned my bike against a post and climbed into the cockpit. We chatted a while, and he told me that he had been living in California when he and his wife decided to chuck it all and take a trip around the world by sailboat. His name was Frank; he said they had purchased their boat and started out in Green Bay and were now headed out the Erie Canal to the Atlantic.

"We're going to sail to the Panama Canal, then maybe New Zealand," he said as he rummaged around in the cooler and handed me a cold can of iced tea. "I've never ridden the whole Canal, but the parts I've done were pretty good. You should have a fine time." We wished each other luck on our respective adventures; then, with Frank's map in my jersey pocket, I headed east along the Erie Canal.

Sections of the trail are paved, but most of the surface is what the brochures called stone dust, which is a fine layer of light-colored, sand-like topcoat over a hard-packed subsurface. My tires kicked up the dust and coated everything with a thin veneer of gray. By the time I stopped for lunch at a trail-side park, my bike and I were covered with the stuff; I looked like a zombie. I had taken off my jersey because I was sweating so much and the stone dust stuck to my bare skin like plaster. It was in my hair, on my clothes, and I could even taste it. I washed off at a drinking fountain and then made lunch. After eating, I lay down on a picnic table and dozed off. When I woke up, it was even hotter, so I decided to leave my jersey off for the afternoon ride. I was about to get going when a couple rode up and stopped to talk. "Wow," said the man, "you've got quite a load. Are you doing the Canal?"

He looked to be in his late forties, stout, compact, and in good shape. He had sandy hair and an open, friendly face that broke easily into a quick grin.

"Yeah," I replied, "how about you guys?"

"Us too!" Said the woman, flashing a dazzling smile. She was the female version of her boyfriend, solidly built, fit, with dishwater-blond hair pulled back and held in place by a madras neckerchief. Her sleeveless jersey showed off her toned arms. She took off her sunglasses to reveal quick, intelligent eyes.

We made our introductions; her name was CJ and he was Scott. CJ was a nurse and Scott an engineer for AT&T. She was riding a beautiful new Salsa touring bike, and he had the polar opposite: an old clunker that he said he was going to replace soon. They were from Virginia, and this was their first big cycle tour. They had flown into Buffalo the day before and ridden into Canada over the Peace Bridge about the same time that I was crossing back into the USA. They had visited Niagara Falls and returned to the USA that morning. We decided to ride together for a while, talking as we rode. It had been a long time since I'd had a cycling companion, and I was really enjoying their company.

My plan had been to spend the night at a campground near the town of Medina, but CJ and Scott were pushing on. "You know, there's free camping at Brockport," CJ said. "I understand there are showers, too. That's where we're staying." It meant a few extra miles, but I decided to continue on. We reached Brockport around 6:00 that evening, and sure enough, when we checked in at the visitor's center, we were welcomed with open arms. "You bet," said the fellow manning the center, "you can set your tent up on the lawn." He handed me a key. "This is for the showers and laundry, and there's an electric hook-up by the campsite. And," he added, "there's free WiFi, too."

CJ and Scott stayed outside watching our bikes while I checked in. When I came out, they said they had made different plans. "It's just too damn hot to camp," Scott said. "We're going to stay at a B&B in town, but let's get together for dinner tonight."

We agreed to meet at a nearby tavern; then CJ and Scott left for their B&B, and I set up camp. The showers and laundry room were in the daylight basement of the visitors' center, and as my clothes washed, I turned the shower on cold and stepped into the spray. I had ridden most of the day shirtless, and when the water hit my skin, I recoiled in shock; I had sunburned my back and the water pressure from the shower hurt like the devil. Still, I wasn't about to pass up a free shower, and I managed to wash most of the stone dust off. When my clothes were dry, I held them to my face and breathed in. I had almost forgotten what it was like, and I took a few minutes to appreciate the simple pleasure of clean clothes. Now it was time to meet my friends for dinner, so I dressed in a clean jersey and long pants and headed for the tavern.

The Movie Star

In the days when the Erie Canal was the main thoroughfare between the east and Midwest, towns like Brockport were bustling centers of commerce. Today, those small villages are sleepy enclaves that live mainly off summer tourism. As in each little settlement, Brockport has a quaint bridge that spans the Canal and serves as the focal point of town. Clustered around the bridge are old brick, stone, and timber buildings that, in their prime, served the needs of travelers along the busy waterway. Today, they house tony restaurants, touristy knickknack shops, boutique bakeries and upscale watering holes. It was at one of these last that CJ, Scott and I met that hot, sultry July evening.

The Stonewall Bar and Grill sits cater-cornered to the bridge at Brockport, with an outdoor seating area and a view of the canal. We'd settled in at the bar and had barely finished our first brews when the host approached and told us our table was ready. We followed him downstairs to a low-ceilinged, heavy-timbered dining room crowded with suntanned tourists. In celebration of nothing in particular, I sprang for a good bottle of wine, which we drank heartily as we chatted and enjoyed dinner. I noticed that our waitress bore a striking resemblance to a popular actress, and when I mentioned it to her, she blushed. "Really," she breathed, "do you think so?"

"Absolutely," I said, "only prettier."

She smiled, rolling her eyes. "You know, a lot of people say I look like her, but my boss doesn't see the resemblance, and whenever anyone mentions it he gets irritated." She looked off, then back. A mischievous twinkle appeared in her soft brown eyes. "Would you like to play a joke on him?" she said, a conspiratorial tone in her voice.

"I'm always up for a good goof," I replied. "What do you have in mind?"

"Well, I'll keep an eye out, and when he's within earshot of your table I'll come over and you pretend to be a Hollywood mogul and mistake me for her!"

"It's a deal," I said.

It wasn't long before our waitress maneuvered her boss into position, and the play was on. She came by our table and started to make small-talk. I glanced at her, and then, as if suddenly becoming aware of her true identity, stood and took her in a theatrical embrace. "My God!" I said, loud enough for half the place to hear, "Mila, what are you doing here? Now don't tell me, you're researching a role! Why didn't you call me? Come on now, let the cat out of the bag, what project are you working on? Who's producing? Who's directing?" I blabbered on like that for a while, making no sense but putting on a show convincing enough to leave her boss slack-jawed and wide-eyed. CJ and Scott played along, gushing over our "movie star" waitress. We kept up the charade all through dinner and got more than a few inquiring looks from the other diners as we wound down the evening, still in character.

Aided by three glasses of wine, I slept soundly that night and woke the next morning rested. I got up and broke camp beneath a leaden sky. Dark clouds raced low overhead, promising rain. CJ and Scott showed up just as I was ready go.

"Looks like we're going to be in for it today," CJ said, glancing up. "Supposed to be raining by late morning."

"Well, I guess that's better than that heat wave we had yesterday," I replied.

"Couldn't we just have a happy medium?" Scott said. "You know, maybe something in the mid seventies and sunny?"

An Ad Hoc Repair

As we rode across the bridge and headed east, a light drizzle began to fall, then a steady rain. We stopped beneath some trees and donned storm gear. I had run short of food the day before, so when I saw a supermarket in the little town of Spencerport, I peeled off, promising to reconnect with CJ and Scott down the road.

When I came out of the store with my groceries, the rain had stopped. I stood for a few moments eating an orange, watching the clearing sky open to great patches of racing blue. CJ and Scott were up ahead somewhere, and I calculated that it would take me at least half a day to catch up to them, so imagine how surprised I was when, less than an hour later, I rounded a corner and saw my friends stopped at the side of the trail. CJ was standing on the edge of the pavement while Scott worked on his bike. When they saw me, they waved for me to stop.

"What's going on?" I asked.

"Scott's chain broke," CJ replied. "Looks like we're stalled."

"The damn thing just came apart," Scott said, looking up. "I figure I can just take out the bad link and reconnect it."

I knelt down and examined the broken parts. "Yeah, it'll be a few links short, but it ought to work."

"That's what I thought," Scott said. "Problem is, I can't get the pin back in."

"Yup," I nodded, "once the pin is out, you're cooked. The trick is to push it just far enough to break the chain but not all the way out."

CJ and Scott

Scott began to carefully work the pin out of the next link. Just then, some weekend cyclists rolled up. "Broken chain, huh?" one of them said. "Do you know how to fix it?

Scott was focusing on the chain, so I took on the job of crowd control. "Yeah, we've got it. Just putting things back together."

Now three more riders stopped. "You need pliers," one biker said, "to hold the link in place."

"You gotta squeeze the link," advised another. "Squeeezzze it!"

We were at a busy section of the trail, and more bicyclists gathered until there were half a dozen men standing in a circle around Scott and me, each one shouting out advice.

"You're never gonna fix it that way!"

"He's got the wrong tools!"

"Look at that chain! He needs a new one!"

"I'm going to call the bike shop, they can have a mechanic out here in half an hour!"

At one point, I had to physically restrain two overly helpful fellows who wanted to grab the chain out of Scott's hands. "Hey, thanks, guys, but let's let him do it," I said.

Scott looked up at me, intensity in his eyes. "Just keep 'em off me for a few more minutes," he pleaded. "I've about got it . . ." When the chain was repaired and back on, Scott flipped his bike over onto its wheels and a cheer went up from the crowd.

"I knew he could do it!"

"Good job!"

"Never had a doubt!"

Scott bowed deeply to a round of applause.

The three of us rode together until Scott and C.J. decided to stop for lunch. I sensed that they wanted to be alone, so I said I'd hook up with them down the trail, but I never saw them again.

Tough Guy

The sound of breaking glass roused me from my sleep. Shapes moved around out there in the dark, fleeting shadows and a low murmur of voices. Something inside told me not to move, to feign sleep until I could figure out what was happening. There was a floodlight in the parking lot next to my campsite, and I could make out four young men and one young woman standing not ten feet from where I lay. They were drinking beer out of paper bags. One of the young guys, a big brute in a sleeveless t-shirt, drained his bottle and threw it hard against the sidewalk. The crash made me jump.

As I watched the group's dynamics, I was able to sort out the pecking order. The big one in the sleeveless t-shirt was the leader; he was the biggest, rowdiest and loudest. He stood a bit over six feet, stocky, with a close-cropped, skinhead haircut. His face, mean enough I was sure in daylight, took on an even more gruesome appearance in the cold glare of the floodlight. It looked as if his nose had been broken. The woman, it was clear, was his property, and after breaking the bottle, he grabbed her by the arm and led her to the nearby glider swing. They sat in it and began swinging violently back and forth so that the sturdy steel poles rocked dangerously in their concrete anchors. After that got old, Sleeveless wandered over to the picnic table and began cutting into the top with a wicked-looking, long-bladed hunting knife. The other three men followed Sleeveless and stood around laughing at something he was carving into the wood. It took him a few minutes to finish; then Sleeveless grabbed a bottle from one of the other men, took a swig, and wiped his mouth on his arm. He was bored now and looking around for more mischief. His eyes seemed to lock onto my bicycle, lying on its side next to my tent. He stood up and looked right at me. A shudder ran up my spine. *Uh-oh*, I thought.

When I had arrived at the Newark Chamber of Commerce Center in Newark, New York, a few hours earlier, it looked like the perfect camping spot. There was a well-kept lawn, a picnic table, a gazebo, and even a quaint glider swing overlooking the canal. The place felt peaceful and safe. A few pleasure boats rocked gently at the dock. Besides the sailors aboard their boats, I was the only camper there. I'd checked in with the lockmaster and asked where he wanted me to camp. "Anywhere on the lawn," he smiled. "We're glad to have you, just sign in and I'll give you the key to the restroom and laundry room."

I was feeling pretty good about the Erie Canal, and the warm welcome I received at Newark made me feel even better. It was my second day riding the towpath, and so far I hadn't had to pay for a campsite. The riding was excellent, plus I got to take a shower every night, and I had clean clothes. The people I met were all generous and affable; I'd made at least five new friends since my start at Towanda.

After I'd pitched camp near the picnic table, I wandered down to the dock and talked with the people on the pleasure boats. There were two couples, both in their mid-forties. They had set up a small hibachi and folding chairs on the towpath and were seated around the glowing charcoal burner, sipping wine. "We saw you riding today," one man said. "I tried to keep up with you, but you were going too fast."

"Yeah," I said, "I was making about fifteen miles an hour."

"The State of New York frowns on drag racing on the canal," his wife said, "but Jim can't pass up a chance to rev his engine." She gave her husband a lascivious look and squeezed his hand.

"Aw, shucks," Jim said.

We talked some more, then I said goodnight and walked up the slope to my tent. I made a quick dinner and then settled into my bag. Feeling safe and secure, I was asleep in a few minutes.

That had been around 10:00 p.m. Now it was a little past 1:30 a.m., and I was wide awake and scared.

Sleeveless and his pals stood looking at my tent. He said something in a low voice to one of his gang, who listened intently and nodded. I still hadn't moved; for all they knew, I was asleep and would make an easy target. Were they working out a plan? I glanced around the tent for a weapon. I quickly ran through my options: I had a blade, too, a Swiss Army knife, but I knew I'd not be able to find it in time — man, they were within 10 feet! I kept a steel water bottle next to my sleeping bag; full, it would make a pretty good club, but against four men and that big, shiny knife? I remembered that I had a chrome-plated ink pen in a notebook that I kept in one of the tent's pockets. What if I sort of tucked the pen in my hand and pretended to have a gun? In the dark, would the barrel of the pen resemble the barrel of a small-caliber pistol?

As these crazy thoughts ran through my mind, the toughs started toward my tent at a fast walk. Sleeveless was in the lead, coming on with that jaw-jutting, shoulder-wagging, heel-digging swagger you sometimes see in aggressive young males. I jumped up, grabbed my water bottle, and got into a low crouch. When the time was right, I'd lunge out and take Sleeveless at the knees, try to get in a few good blows with the water bottle — it takes only six-and-a-half pounds of pressure to break the clavicle — and maybe I could cause enough confusion to get away. I can run pretty fast when the spirit moves me.

They were almost to my tent; any second now and I'd have to act. My heart was pounding. *Oh, God*, I thought, *this isn't happening...* Then Sleeveless was at the tent door. I prepared to spring, when at the last moment he swerved and he and his gang split into two groups and walked around past my tent, knocking up against it and laughing as they did. Their derisive guffaws drifted off into the night, and then they were gone.

I had the sudden urge to empty my bowels. I jumped up and ran to the bathroom and made it to a stall just in time. I washed my face, collected my wits, and then walked out into the night. The two couples from the pleasure boats were still sitting around the hibachi. From my tent, I wasn't able to see them, so hadn't been aware of their presence during my ordeal. I went over to where they sat. "Were those kids bothering you?" one of the men asked.

"I don't know," I said, "I think they were just being jerks." I tried to sound confident, but my voice came out shaky.

"Well," said the second sailor, "we were watching them for you. If there'd been any trouble, we'd have had your back. We were giving them the evil eye the whole time. When I saw that big Buck knife the one kid had, I went to my boat and got Old Betsy." He reached under his chair, and when his hand came out there was a big shiny revolver in it. "They finally got the message," he winked.

The Atomic Sunburn

My back resembled a sheet of bubble wrap. It was covered with a hundred fingernail-sized blisters all oozing gooey fluid. It had been ninety-eight degrees that first day on the Canalway Trail, and I'd ridden most of the time sans shirt. By evening, I'd known I was in trouble. My back had itched and burned, and even the gentle spray from the showerhead had caused pain, but I had no idea I would turn into something out of a medical encyclopedia.

It took several days for the blisters to form; I first became aware of them late in the afternoon after leaving camp at Lock 15, five days from the start at Buffalo. I had reached around to scratch my back and my hand came away wet. At first I thought it was sweat, but no, there was too much fluid. A closer examination revealed the blisters. Just touching one caused it to burst. I stopped, pulled off my jersey, and maneuvered my back to my cycling mirror. I reached around to touch my back and could see a blister break and ooze fluid. "That's it!" I said out loud, "I can't take any more of this!" I checked my map; I had covered more than sixty miles and was about ten miles out of Albany. It was late afternoon; I'd have to find a place to spend the night soon. I got off the trail to look for a motel. I just had to do something about those blisters!

The motel had a big sign that advertised LOW RATES • AIR-CONDITIONING, and was on a busy, four-lane road in what looked like a light-industrial neighborhood. I went in and asked about the rates. "It's sixty-four dollars," the young man behind the counter told me. "That includes continental breakfast, of course."

"Of course," I said. I checked in and pushed my bike to my room, stripped off my jersey, and stood with my back to the full-length bathroom mirror. Craning my neck around to get a good look, I was almost sickened by what I saw. My skin looked like the hide of a lizard. There were weeping blisters from my lower back to the tops of my shoulders. As I touched one, it burst and fluid spurt out, running down my back. I grabbed a towel and gently dabbed at the stuff, but even that light touch made the other blisters burst and emit their discharge. Finally, I gave up and rubbed the towel on my back, causing all the blisters to burst, and as they did, the dead skin tore off and left dark smears on the white towel.

I got in the shower and scrubbed at the affected area, sending most of the necrotic tissue down the drain. Now my back felt raw and tender where the blisters had been. When I looked at it again in the mirror, they were replaced by a pattern of small, lighter-colored areas where new skin was forming. I had a first-aid kit with a good supply of wound ointment that I rubbed on my back in gobs, covering it with a fresh towel and then lying gently on the bed.

The next morning, my back looked better. The spots where the blisters had been were tender, but it felt fine when I put my jersey on. I hadn't unloaded the bike the night before, so it didn't take long to get on the road. I pedaled through the bustling city of Schenectady, and before I realized it I was at the Hudson River. I had ridden the 400 miles in only six days! How was that possible? I went over each day and night in my mind thinking I'd missed something, but came up with the same total. When I started at Buffalo I'd thought it would take me at least a week, and probably more, to ride the whole Erie Canal, but I had cut days off my schedule.

Tony

I was now in the foothills of the Berkshire Hills, passing through the small town of New Lebanon, New York, when up ahead I saw an elderly man walking his dog. As I got within earshot, I called out, "Bicycle passing on your left!" The old fellow turned around, smiled and waved. I was going up a slight hill, so my speed nearly matched his pace, and as I passed, I asked him how he was doing.

"Just great!" he said enthusiastically. "Where are you headed?"

"Boston" I said over my shoulder, now a few yards ahead of him.

"Good luck!" he shouted, as I slowly pulled away and out of sight around a corner. A few miles later I stopped at a diner to get water, and as I parked my bike, a car pulled into the dirt lot and came to a sliding halt, kicking up a cloud of dust that momentarily enveloped the car and drifted off on the light breeze. The driver gave a toot on his horn and waved me over.

I was hesitant to respond. What if he was someone I'd made angry by my slow presence on the road, and who had chased me down? I stood holding my bike, getting ready to flee at the first sign of aggression, but when the driver got out, he was familiar and all smiles; it was the old gentleman who'd been walking his dog, whom I'd passed half an hour earlier. He shambled over to where I stood. "I'm buying you lunch!" he proclaimed, taking me by the arm and ushering me into the cafe, "I want to hear all about your trip!" His name was Tony, and he was in his mid-seventies, stout, with a wide, round face and a ruddy complexion that made his bushy head of white hair seem to glow. We sat at a table, and he insisted that I order something to eat.

"Well, let's see," I said as I perused the menu, "how about fries?"

"No, no," he said, "order, order, they have the best hamburgers in the county here."

"I think the fries will do," I said. "I'll have a Coke, too, with lots of ice."

"You're sure?" Tony said. "I know what cycling is like. I used to do a lot of it when I was younger."

He said that he wanted to hear about my trip, but I got very little talking done that afternoon. Instead, Tony entertained me with story after story of his long-distance bicycle trips up and down the East Coast and a hike he'd once taken on the Pacific Crest Trail.

"It was early spring," he said of his West Coast hike, "and the trail was buried in ten feet of snow. There was me and two other guys on this particular trip and one of the other guys was a geologist from Stanford University. This guy was amazing with a USGS topo map. You know, those elevation lines on those maps are a real devil to decipher unless you know your stuff. Well, this guy, the one from Stanford, he knew everything there was to know about route finding. Mind you, we didn't have GPS in those days, we had a compass and a map and that was all. Still, this guy, the one from Stanford, he guided us through the High Sierra without a hitch. Made it all the way in all that snow and never deviated off the trail by so much as an inch." Tony held his fingers close together. "Not so much as one little inch!"

I munched my french fries and ordered another Coke as Tony told me why he'd given up cycle touring all those years ago. "I was on a trip to Maine," he began, "riding not far from here. I'd just started out when a car came up from behind and ran into me." He shook his head. "I woke up in the hospital a few days later." He pulled back his shirtsleeve to show me an ugly scar running from his elbow to his shoulder. "Broke my arm in a couple of places, had a concussion and about a hundred bruises and scrapes. It was a young girl driving, I think she was sixteen, said she didn't see me. Once I was healed, I just couldn't get back on a bicycle."

"That's a shame," I said.

Tony smiled. "Oh well, that's life. Anyway, you're coming up on a big hill and there's a rest stop at the top. Don't stop there, it's a pickup spot for gay men."

I laughed. "Good to know," I said, getting up and putting my helmet on. "It's been great talking to you, Tony."

Tony stood up and shook my hand. "I wish I was going with you," he said. "Now where is it you're headed?"

Chapter Ten: Massachusetts

As I cranked up the hill, a woman called out to me from the front yard of an ancient semi-mansion. "Where are you headed?"

I glanced over. "Boston," I called back as I continued cranking. I was dead tired after a frustrating day of flat tires and Massachusetts traffic, and I knew that if I stopped, I might not get going again.

"Where are you coming from?"

I came to a wobbly halt. "Seattle."

Now the woman, who had been sweeping the driveway, put down her broom and came over to the neat white picket fence that surrounded the yard. It was the nicest thing on the property. "Well, what in the world are you doing on Route 20? It's the busiest road in Massachusetts."

"Tell me about it," I said. I made a cursory examination of the huge yard; I didn't want to be too obvious about it. "This your place?"

"No, I work for the owner." She looked me over and smiled; she knew what I was thinking. "I'll give her a call and see if you can camp here tonight."

"That would be great," I said. "I couldn't find a hotel . . ."

"It's cool," she said. "I've been there." She walked out of earshot and I stood watching as she talked on her cell phone. In a few minutes, she returned. "Well, the owner isn't comfortable with you camping on her property, but why don't you come home with me?"

"You bet," I said.

"Just let me pack up my tools and my dog and we can throw your bike in the back of my truck."

Her name was Mindy, and she was in her thirties, compact and powerfully built, with short dark hair. She had a jolly round face and almond-shaped eyes that seemed to change color as the daylight faded. I stood watching her clean up the work site, and then she helped me load my bike and panniers into the bed of her Toyota pickup. As we headed north, I learned that Mindy was a journeyman carpenter and had half a dozen projects going on in the area, including the duplex she owned in Holyoke. As she drove, she told me about the many bicycle trips she'd taken over the years, one in Alaska when she worked as a fishing guide.

"That's why I stopped you in the first place," she smiled. "Seeing you brought back a lot of fond memories."

We reached Mindy's place in half an hour. Her house was a two-story on a block of working-class homes. The lawns were dried out on that summer evening, but the streets were clean. We pulled into an alley behind Mindy's house, and she helped me stow my gear, then showed me to the spare bedroom. "You can sleep here tonight," she said. "Go ahead and charge up your phone and what-not, and if you need to get on line, I have WiFi."

"Mindy," I said, "you are a life saver. I don't know what I'd have done if you hadn't come along." I felt like hugging her.

"Oh," Mindy said, "it's nothing. I'm glad to help. I have to go into Barnes & Noble later on this evening. You can stay here or you can go with me. Why don't you take a shower and rest up. Then you can decide."

"Sounds good," I said, and started unloading my panniers. I sat on the bed, plugged in all my electrical gear, and then went into the kitchen where Mindy sat making notes on a yellow legal pad.

She looked up at me with an odd expression. "You're not going to kill me are you?"

I was stunned and stepped back. It was like a punch to the chin. "What?!" I said, "I . . . uh . . . gosh . . . I've never been asked that question . . . No, I mean, no, of course not." An uncomfortable silence ensued; then, "Look, Mindy," I said, "I understand you're having second thoughts about me staying here. After all, you don't know anything about me. So I'm just going to get my stuff and get going." I turned and headed back down the hall, Mindy following.

89

"I'm really sorry," she said, "I don't know why I said that, it just popped into my head, and before I knew it . . . I'd really like you to stay."

"I'll tell you what," I said, "I'll set my tent up on the lawn and sleep out there."

"No," Mindy said. "I really want you to stay in my house tonight. I have a roommate who's supposed to move in tomorrow. I'll call her and see if she can come over tonight with her boyfriend. That way everybody will feel safe."

I thought about it for a moment and said, "I think that will work."

I took a shower and put on clean clothes, and then Mindy and I drove into the city to a bookstore. In addition to being an ace carpenter, Mindy was also a writer of fiction. There was a little coffee shop in the bookstore where we sat and had a light dinner while she worked on a short story and I wrote an entry for my blog. When we got back to Mindy's house, her roommate and her roommate's boyfriend had arrived, and we sat around the kitchen table for a while chatting and sharing a bottle of pretty good red wine. I was used to being in bed by 9:00, and now it was past 11:00. I kept nodding off, and finally excused myself. "It sure has been swell socializing with you, but I'm going to turn in."

Mindy was up early the next morning and tapped on my door at 7:00 a.m. I'd been awake for a while and was dressed and ready to go. After we had breakfast, it was time for Mindy to go to work. "I can drive you back to Springfield," she said.

"Oh, no," I replied, "you've done enough already. I can just leave from here."

"It's kind of hard to find your way out of the city," she said. "Why don't I drive you out of town at least? That way you won't have to screw around getting lost." We loaded my bike and gear in her truck, and Mindy drove me out of the city and across the Connecticut River to a gas station near Route 202. We unloaded my bike, hugged, said goodbye, and promised to keep in touch.

Then Mindy drove off and I climbed on my bike and went looking for the start of my route.

One Continent Down, Two to Go

Morning came suddenly. I shot up straight like a jack in the box. I was wide awake now, dim sunlight filtering in through the closed curtains. I looked around — where am I? I wondered. Then slowly it all came back to me. After I'd left Mindy's, I'd had to make a long detour and had arrived at the campground after dark. When I got there, I discovered that the place was full and no amount of pleading could win me a spot. I'd had to push on into the night and wound up staying at an expensive hotel in Sturbridge, just a day out of Boston.

I got out of bed, took a quick shower, and shaved for the first time in a week. I wanted to be presentable; after all, I'd be meeting my friends, Ken and Mitzi, that afternoon. *No point looking like a bum*, I thought. As I packed, I reflected on the past ten weeks and still found it hard to get my mind around the fact that I had ridden across a continent, a damn big continent.

I looked around the room to make sure I'd not left anything behind. On the dresser, I had stacked the food I wasn't taking with me. There was a package of spaghetti noodles, two cans of tomato soup, two cans of tuna, half a loaf of whole wheat bread, and a bag of raisin bran cereal. I had thought about putting it all in the trashcan but hoped the maid might find use for the canned goods. The night before, I'd had to travel for a mile or so on the Massachusetts Turnpike. It had been a hair-raising experience. That evening, I'd consulted my map and plotted a route to Boston that retraced my journey back to Highway 9, a few miles north. Because I'd have to ride out of town on the Turnpike, I scheduled my departure for early morning to avoid heavy traffic. It was only 6:00 a.m. when I rolled out of the motel parking lot and onto the Turnpike.

I turned north when I reached the intersection with Highway

49 and rode back along the track I'd taken the night before. It was a glorious morning, sunny and bright and cool there in the thick woods that crowded up close to the edge of the road. I must have had a tailwind, because I fairly flew the nine or ten miles back to Route 9. I stopped at a convenience store and bought chocolate milk, a package of Hostess Ding Dongs, a bag of potato chips and some kind of highly-processed fruit Danish that tasted vaguely of cleaning fluid. As I sat on the sidewalk next to the bike, eating my junk food breakfast, I swore, as I did every morning, that this would be the last time I ate so badly. *For the rest of this trip*, I thought, I *will eat healthy!*

Route 9 started out as a pleasant alternative to the dreaded Highway 20. I rode through woods and past the occasional housing development or light industrial concern on a road with a good shoulder and light traffic. After a few miles, I reached the town of Spencer, where I stopped for a while at the bottom of the hill that Route 9 climbs on its way out of town. Spencer is one of those quintessential New England towns that, having passed through so many, I had gained a fondness for. Out west, where I had grown up, any building more than fifty years old was considered ancient. Here, in towns like Spencer, I was riding past homes built centuries before. I especially appreciated the practice each town has of listing its date of incorporation on its welcome sign. Spencer had been a town since 1753; it was twenty-three years older than the Declaration of Independence!

I pedaled to the city park and sat under a tree, people-watching and taking in the morning vibes. I could feel the day growing warmer. It was a little past 8:00 a.m., and the temperature must have already been in the mid-eighties. I got back on my bike and merged with the growing morning traffic.

Route 9 stayed rural until I reached the outskirts of Worcester, where it changed to the Boston Turnpike. As on Highway 20, I was again dodging and weaving amid heavy, inconsiderate traffic, pulling off every few miles to regain my composure and generally having a miserable time of it. But the Turnpike was the most direct route to Boston, and I was in no mood to get off and wander the maze of back roads.

The day wore on. I was nearing my goal now, and stopping often to check my map. I was forty miles away, then thirty, then ten. In the next hour, I would reach Boston, and I felt that I should do something special to mark the occasion. So I stopped at a convenience store and bought a can of Miller High Life, The Champaign of Bottled Beers.

I watched the miles tick off, and soon there was the sign: WELCOME TO BOSTON. Pulling off, I opened the can of warm beer, which fizzed and fumed and overflowed. Quickly, I put it to my lips and took a swallow. It tasted awful, and I coughed most of it back up. Beer spewed out of my mouth and nose. A car drove slowly past and a young woman in the passenger's seat saw me bent over puking beer and shook her head sadly. I smiled and waved.

The celebration had been a bust, but I'd made it across the continent, and that was all that mattered. It was hot now, and as I rode on, I felt like I was entering a state of heat exhaustion with neurotic complications brought on by Boston-Turnpike traffic. After one close miss, I pulled into a shopping-mall parking lot and stopped near the entrance to regroup. An old Rambler convertible with one brown fender and no muffler roared up behind me and the driver laid on his horn and gunned his engine, swerved sharply left, and stopped beside me. "Hey, you jerk," he yelled, "you're blocking traffic!"

I looked around. There were no other cars. I smiled "Yeah," I said, "you had to do this —" I mimed turning a car's steering wheel one-eighth of a rotation. He hissed obscenities, gave me the finger, and roared off in a haze of oil-thick exhaust.

I laughed and waved. "And you have a nice day, too, sir!" I yelled.

I'd reached Boston, but my friends Ken and Mitzi lived a few miles south in the town of Hingham. I'd have to cut rightwards soon and find my way to their house before dark. I rode along the Turnpike for a few more miles until the traffic became unbearable, then turned south. I rode through neighborhoods and small clusters of commercial establishments, finally arriving at the town of Rockland, to the west and slightly south of Hingham. Spotting a Subway Sandwich Shop, I parked my bike and went in. I ordered a cold drink, sat down at a table, took out my cell phone, and made a call. "Hey, Ken," I said when he answered, "I'm here!"

"You're in Boston?!"

"Well, not exactly, I'm in Rockland."

Ken laughed. "Rockland? What the hell are you doing way over there?"

"I don't know," I said, "I got off track somewhere."

"Do you want me to come get you?"

"No, I'm going to ride my bike right up to the Atlantic Ocean."

"Have it your way," Ken said. "When do you think you'll get here?'

"How far is it to your place?"

There was a pause on the other end. "About twenty miles."

"Yeah," I said without a moment's hesitation, "you better come get me."

Part Two: Europe

Chapter Eleven: England

"Well, have a good flight," Ken said, shaking my hand and giving me a slightly worried look. "Let us know when you get to London." He jumped back in his car and pulled away from the passenger drop-off at Logan International Airport's Terminal One.

I'd spent two weeks with Ken and Mitzi, and they'd treated me like a king. I had the chance to rest and do maintenance on my bike, and physically and logistically, I was all set to go. So why did I have butterflies? I watched Ken's blue Jag disappear into the evening traffic and almost hoped he'd come back and talk me out of leaving.

Sure, I was looking forward to riding through Europe, but now there would be an ocean between home and me. Moreover, I knew I'd have to face a whole crop of additional cultural and linguistic challenges. A lump formed in my throat, and my heart kicked up a few beats. I leaned against the handle of the baggage trolley, causing the stack of cardboard boxes that represented all my worldly possessions to tumble to the ground. I stood looking down at the jumble of cartons. I bent over, wrestled them back onto the trolley, hoisted my backpack, and trundled off toward the International Departures Desk.

Day 86, Trouble at Heathrow

The English customs inspector glanced at my passport and waved me through to baggage claims, where I waited for my oversized parcels to slide out of the chute.

The flight across the Atlantic had been uneventful. The plane, though crowded, was relatively quiet, and I even managed to doze for a few minutes out of the five-plus-hour trip. Soon after I reached the baggage carousel, I spotted the rest of my stuff. Finding a spot out of the way, I tore open my bike box and removed the wheels, fenders, racks and saddle. The last thing to come out of the box was the frame, and after a quick inventory, I was pleased to find that everything except my cycle computer had made the trip in fine condition.

I dug out my multi-tool, a handy little device that combines a number of hex wrenches, screwdrivers and other assorted spanners into one compact unit. The front fender went on with little trouble, but as I was turning a bolt to attach the front rack, the multi-tool came apart and tools fell to the floor, scattering all about. I thought I saw one bounce beneath the baggage carousel.

It was the first day of the 2012 Olympics, and Heathrow was a beehive of frantic activity. Throngs of people milled shoulder to shoulder, vying for a position near the carousel. I stared into the crowd. I had to get my tools! I dropped to my hands and knees. "Excuse me, pardon me," I mumbled to startled travelers as I crawled along at their feet, gathering up wrenches and screwdrivers.

"What the . . . ?!" one lady exclaimed as I crawled past her legs. She gathered her skirt and shied away, bumping into a man holding a small child, who began to wail.

"Hey there, you, mate, what are you doing?!" another man demanded as I scurried by.

I looked up and smiled. "Lost my tools . . . just need to get over there . . . if you could just move a bit . . ." I finally made it to the spot where I thought I'd seen a wrench bounce beneath the carousel. Getting down on my belly, I peered underneath. Sure enough, there in the dusty bowels of the machine lay my six-millimeter Allen wrench. I reached in and grabbed it, then back-crawled and stood up, to find myself in a circle of people who had made room and were now regarding me with caution. I smiled and held up the wrench. "Got it!" I announced, and threaded my way back through the crowd.

It took another thirty minutes to reassemble my bike, pack the panniers, and load them onto the bike. I was finally starting my European trip!

My New Friend, Sally

I had made arrangements for overnight lodging through the Web community Warm Showers, which is a virtual gathering place for bicyclists looking for places to stay. My host for that night was Sally, who lived in Southeast London and had a house with a spare room. I had her address and a map that I'd downloaded from Google and loaded onto my iPad.

I had learned from a kiosk that the bike trail from the airport led through a tunnel and then onto London's surface streets. It took a while and a few backtracks, but eventually I made it out of the airport and into the madness that is London traffic.

It was a short fourteen miles to Sally's house, but it took me almost four hours of winding through the rabbit warren of London's narrow streets to reach her neighborhood. I knew I was close, and I'd stopped at the side of the road looking at my map when a car pulled over and a young man hopped out. "You must be Darby," he said as he approached.

I was dumbfounded. "Uh, well, yes, I am, how . . ."

He laughed, "I'm Sally's son, Gregg. She asked me to keep an eye out for you, and when I saw you ride past with all that stuff on your bike, well, I figured it had to be you. Come on, follow me, our apartment is just up the street."

We arrived at Sally's place in five minutes. It was a mid-century brown brick row house with three narrow stories and a basement garage. "You can stow your bike here," Gregg said as he undid the padlock and opened the garage door. "My mum's away right now, and I have to go to class, but make yourself at home." Gregg gave me a quick tour of the place before hurrying out the door. "Mum should be back in about four hours," he said over his shoulder as he jogged down the steps to the sidewalk. "There's clean towels, and help yourself to whatever you want from the fridge."

"Gee, thanks," I said, and waved goodbye as Gregg sped off in his small red car.

I had been given the TV room on the ground floor. It opened through sliding glass doors onto a small, lush garden, and the myriad flowers, now in full-summer bloom, gave the place a cheery feeling. I took a long shower, then collapsed on the couch and soon fell asleep. It was late afternoon when I awoke. I could hear stirrings on the floor above, and when I climbed the stairs, I found Sally busily putting groceries away in the pantry.

"Welcome," she beamed, and shook my hand. "It's wonderful to meet you." She had short red hair and a broad, open face with gray eyes that lit up when she smiled.

I was still a little groggy, and I tried to rub the sleep out of my eyes. "It's great to meet you, too," I said.

"Would you care for a cup of tea? Just the thing to put the spring back in your step."

"I would love a cup of tea," I said. "I'm afraid I'm still a little jet lagged."

"Never you mind," Sally said. She was standing at the counter now, turning on the electric teakettle. "After tea I'll take you on a bicycle tour of our little town."

An Olympic bicycle race had been held on the streets of her Richmond neighborhood the day before, and all the racecourse markers and flags were still in place. We finished up the day's ride with a visit to Sally's favorite pub. "You left too much for the tip," she said as we sat sipping beers at a window table overlooking the Thames.

"I'm still not used to the pound thing," I said.

"Bianca Jagger lived in an apartment next door," Sally said. "Mick lived there, too, for a while."

It was getting hard to follow the conversation. The travails of the day and the warm beer had caught up to me, and I remember looking out the window and wondering how that polar bear could be riding a motorcycle . . .

"Darby, wake up," Sally said, giving my shoulder a gentle shake.

I jerked awake and looked around frantically. "Wha . . . what the . . . ?"

"I went to the loo, and when I got back you were out, with your head on the table. I think I need to get you home."

Across England

It would take two days to ride from London to Dover, where I'd catch the ferry to France, and that evening, Sally helped me plan a route. We had breakfast together the next morning and said our goodbyes, and with Sally's handwritten map in hand, I set off for my first full day of riding in England. I rode east through the towns of Mitcham and Croydon, New Addington, Otford, and West Mailing. Once, I accidentally wandered onto the A20, England's version of a superhighway, but I was able to backtrack onto the less trafficked but equally dangerous surface streets.

Most of that day's riding was through dense urban landscapes, but there were rural stretches, too. I went into one quaint village pub across a narrow road from what looked like a dairy farm to ask directions and found it so charming, and the people so welcoming, that I took time to have a beer with some of the locals.

The traffic in London and the surrounding environs was some of the worst I encountered on my trip. It seemed that the English drivers had it in for me. They would speed past mere inches away, going ten miles an hour over the limit. More than a few times, I swear drivers tried to hit me, and I would wind up having to make emergency maneuvers to keep from getting squashed. England is an old country, and there are so many roads and intersections that staying on route was hard. I constantly got lost, so even though I had only forty-five miles to cover, it took me most of the day to reach Maidstone.

Dusk found me on the outskirts of that town, tired and, as usual, lost. I pulled into a parking lot and called my Warm Shower hosts for that night, Sue and Andy. Sue answered. "Where are you?" she said. "We can't wait to meet you!"

"Well," I said, trying to keep the fatigue out of my voice, "I'm not sure." I looked around for a landmark. "I'm in the parking lot of a Hilton Hotel, I don't know the address . . ."

"Never mind," Sue said, "I know right where you are. Do you want us to come and pick you up?"

"No . . . yeah . . ." I stammered, "I don't know." I was too tired to make a decision.

"Okay," Sue said, "We'll be there in ten minutes."

I leaned my bike against a hedge and sat down on a parking block. God, I was tired! I'd left Sally's place that morning hoping to reach Maidstone early in the day, but just getting through London had taken me until early afternoon. By the time I cleared the city and got to the country, it was evening and I was thankful that Sue and Andy were coming to my rescue.

They soon arrived, and we put my panniers in her car. Andy brought his bike, and though I was tempted to accept Sue's proffered ride, I opted to cycle with Andy. Andy leads a busy life as an electrical engineer, but he finds time to ride a lot and is one of those natural athletes who could probably give a racer a go. But he dialed it back and rode at my pace. With Andy in the lead, we wound up through hilly neighborhoods for forty-five minutes. I was about to call for a break when Andy looked over his shoulder. "Here we are," he said, pointing to a handsome, two-story, mid-century house situated well back from the street.

Never did a light in a window look so good.

Sue met me at the door with a cold beer that I gulped down, and then led me upstairs to show me my room. After a leisurely shower and a change of clothes, I went back downstairs where I was greeted with a dinner table overflowing with sumptuous victuals. Who said the British can't cook?

I lingered over dinner, savoring each bite and talking pleasantly with Sue and Andy. Sue is a teacher and one of those people who are natural-born nurturers. She couldn't do enough for me. She kept my wine glass filled and made sure I got enough to eat.

"I know what it's like to bonk," she said, smiling. "Nothing like a little nourishment to recharge the spirit!"

"It was a rough day," I said.

Andy had been listening attentively and spoke up. "I read on your blog that you are going to Dover tomorrow."

"Yup, that's where I'll catch the ferry to Calais. I'm a little worried about route-finding though, based on how badly I got lost today."

Andy smiled. "We have that covered," he said. "Sue is going to ride with you tomorrow and show you the way."

I was dumbfounded. "Wow, really? You don't have to go to all that trouble . . ."

"Nonsense," Sue said, "I'm looking forward to showing you my country." She smiled a wry smile. "I don't want you to form the wrong impression."

We chatted on through the evening, and before I knew it, it was after 10:00 p.m. and time for me to turn in. I slept a deep, dreamless sleep and was awake and feeling rested and ready to go by 7:00 a.m. I took a shower and went downstairs, where Sue had a real English breakfast waiting. There were fried eggs and fried potatoes, orange juice and tea, fried bread with butter and jam and slices of fresh tomatoes.

As I tucked in, Andy laid out the plan for the day. "Sue is going to ride with you to Dover and I'm going to meet you guys there. I'll drive over after work and bring Sue home."

"I don't know what to say," I said. "I sure didn't expect such VIP treatment."

"It's going to be fun," Andy mused. "I sure wish I could take the day off work and go with you."

"Me too," I replied. "The first beer in Dover is on me!"

We started out at 9:00 a.m., with Sue leading the way along narrow, rural lanes, through quaint villages and past miles of farmland, hedgerows and woods. The weather was pleasant, though there was one short rain squall that we sat out in a pub.

In contrast to the previous day's ride, I didn't have to figure out where I was and where I was going; all I had to do was pedal. I was happy to leave the route-finding to Sue, and the day passed in a happy blur. Then, far too soon, we arrived at the outskirts of Dover. Andy was waiting for us at the agreed-upon pub, where we had Lager Shandys, which are half beer and half lemonade. I was hesitant to try one since I prefer beer-flavored beer, but after two or three, I decided they weren't bad.

We sat outside at a table and talked and laughed until late afternoon; then it was time for us to part. We took pictures, hugged, and promised to keep in touch. I helped Andy load Sue's bike on the car, and an awkward silence ensued. It was an ordeal I had endured far too often. It was hard to part with my new friends, but it was getting late and I still needed to find my way to my Warm Showers host in Dover. So after another round of hugs, I mounted my bike and started out.

The Deserted Hospital

I had his address, but when I found the street, the numbers didn't match. I finally phoned. "I'm sorry, Antony," I said, "but I can't find your place."

"Never mind, mate," Antony said, "I'll come get you."

"But I have a big, loaded touring bike and a ton of gear," I said. "It might not fit in your car."

"Don't worry about that," Antony said, "I'll see you in twenty minutes."

Half an hour later, a big white moving van pulled up and a man got out and approached. "I'm Antony," he said, shaking my hand. Then he hooked his thumb back at the moving van. "Think your bike will fit in that?" he asked with a laugh.

As it turned out, I was many miles from Antony's place. We drove for twenty minutes before pulling up in front of what appeared to be an abandoned hospital. It was a 60's-era, one-story, dull red brick building on a dead-end street. The windows and doors were covered with plywood, and weeds had taken over the lawn. A wheelchair with one bent wheel sat crookedly on the cracked concrete sidewalk. "Well, here we are!" Antony said, smiling.

"You live near here?" I said hopefully.

"I live HERE!" he said.

"G-g-great!" I stuttered.

Antony helped me unload my bike and my gear, unlocked the double glass doors, and led me inside. It was dark and musty. Steel beds, wheel chairs, stretchers and all kinds of hospital equipment were piled ceiling-high in the foyer. Antony led me along a narrow path that had been hewn through the junk to another set of doors, which he unlocked with a key hanging from a ring of about a dozen others. A sign on the door said, "MEDICATIONS IN PROGRESS." Pushing my bike through, I found myself in a large room lit by ceiling-mounted neon tubes. At one side of the room were a sink, counter, cupboards, stove and refrigerator. In the middle was a dining table, and off to the side were a couch and a TV. The far end of the room opened onto what had once been a garden but was now choked by waist-high weeds. The proportions of the room were somehow off; the ceiling seemed low, giving the room a cave-like feeling.

Antony offered me a chair at the table, and I sat down. "This is an old nursing home," Antony said cheerfully. "I'm the caretaker. I keep the bums and neighborhood toughs out. In turn I get to live here for free."

I had no doubt that he was more than capable of guarding the place. Antony was a big guy, standing well over six feet and weighing around 180 or 190. He had deep-set, dark eyes and close-cropped, jet-black hair. He looked tough, all right; I doubt many "neighborhood toughs" would challenge Antony.

Antony was also a world-class bicycle tourer. He had been around the globe twice and had plans in the works for another long ride. As he cooked dinner, he told me of his adventures. "I was in South America," he said as he stirred carrots into the stew, "Brazil, I believe it was, and I had been riding on a road for days. Well, about the third day, I came to an impasse; I tell you the road just ended in dense jungle. It was mental! I had read my map wrong and had to backtrack three days! Can you imagine that?!"

"I did something similar," I said, "along the north shore of Lake Erie in Ontario. But I had only to backtrack a few hours. Still, I wound up sleeping in a ditch!"

We spent the evening in pleasant conversation, comparing notes and swapping stories; then it was time to call it a night. Antony led me down a long dark hallway to what had once been a patient's room. It was about what you'd expect: a steel bed, steel side table, a chipped, green steel lamp, a worn linoleum floor, and a red fire extinguisher hanging from the wall. A piece of plywood was nailed over the single window.

"I have to leave here by eight tomorrow morning, does that work for you?" Antony asked.

"Sure does," I said. "I'll see you bright and early."

Aside from a few visits during the night by ghosts rattling chains, I slept well.

Chapter Twelve: France

It was a short ride from the nursing home to the Dover docks, and I arrived at the ferry terminal early the next morning. Big ships lined the piers, each boat displaying the livery of a different steamship company. I bought my ticket and was directed to a numbered lane that led up a ramp and into the bowels of an eastbound ship. Stowing my bike on the auto deck, I climbed the stairs to the upper-level cafeteria, where I spent my last few pounds on dry hash browns and rubbery scrambled eggs, all washed down with watery orange juice. Out on the deck afterwards, I watched the White Cliffs of Dover recede in the distance as we set out across the English Channel. We made the crossing in fine weather on calm seas, and I rolled off the ferry in Calais, France, in a good mood. I was on the Continent!

As I headed north toward Dunkirk I could see another biker up ahead, so I picked up the pace. *Maybe he's a local*, I thought. *Maybe he knows the way.* After five minutes, I pulled up alongside. "Hey, how you doing?"

He was riding a beat-up mountain bike with ragged panniers and an old plastic shopping bag tied to the rack. He wore a threadbare polo shirt and Beastie Boy shorts, sported a three-day growth, and was missing a few teeth. It looked as if he'd had a rough life. He was broad in the shoulder, with big hands that looked like they'd seen a lot of hard work.

"Well, hello, mate," he said, sounding cheerful. "Fine day for a bike ride, what?"

Some Brits, I'd found, were almost impossible to understand, but not Archie (not his real name). He was articulate, smart, and even philosophical. "I've 'ad me some tough 'appenings this past year," he told me after we'd ridden together for an hour. "Lost me dad, and me mum's not well." He looked off across the wheat field we were passing. "But then that's life, ain't it?"

Archie, a Londoner in his mid-fifties, had been retired from the maintenance business for a while. "I take the ferry from Dover and ride up to Belgium a couple a times a week to do a little business," he said, giving me a knowing wink. "I buy cigarettes at a discount and resell 'em in England for a small profit. The few quid I get helps to make ends meet." We stopped for a rest break and I asked him for directions to my next Warm Showers host's home. "Yeah, sure, I know right where this bloke lives," he said after I'd shown him the map on my iPad. "Just follow me." After a few hours of pleasant riding, we rolled into the outskirts of Dunkirk, and Archie signaled for a stop beside high bushes next to a canal under a bridge. "Let me see that map again," he said.

I was beginning to worry. I was thinking that I probably shouldn't have shown him my expensive iPad. I'd just met Archie, and I knew he was involved in small-time crime. What if he decided to rob me? I pulled to a stop. "I have his address, you want to see that?"

Archie gave me a look. "Naw, mate, let's have a look-see at that fine gadget o' yours."

I opened my pannier, dug out the iPad and handed it to Archie. He looked at the screen, tilting it to one side, then back, really giving it the once-over. Was he trying to eliminate the glare or figuring what it'd fetch on the black market? "Hmmm," he said, "you know what I think, don't you?"

I tensed up.

"I think we passed it." He pointed back the way we'd come. "Head up there," he said, pointing at the roadway, "take the first left, and you should be right on top of it." He handed back my iPad. "Sorry to leave, you mate." He shook my hand. "I've 'ad a lovely time bikin' wi' you this fine afternoon. But I 'ave to break off here."

I watched Archie ride away. As he rounded the corner, he turned and gave me a hearty wave. "You be safe on your journey," he called with a smile, "and best o' luck, mate."

Boy, did I feel like a jerk!

Captain Zargo

Thanks to Archie's unerring route-finding, I arrived in Dunkirk several hours before my scheduled rendezvous with my Warm Showers host, Zargo. It took only a few minutes to locate his house, after which I found a McDonald's and had a cold drink. I tried to use the restaurant's WiFi, but McDonald's in France has a weird process whereby one of the cashiers has to send a code to your cell phone, which you can then use to log in. Unfortunately for me, the French McDonald's texting system was incompatible with my phone, which still had an American chip.

To kill time, I rode to the seashore and wandered around the wharfs until it was time to meet my hosts. I knocked on the door and was greeted by a bear of a man.

"Velcome!" Zargo said, "Please to come in!"

Zargo, I learned, was from Croatia. He'd spent most of his life on the sea as a captain of ocean-going ships and was now retired, living with his French wife in a two-story house near the beach. She spoke no English, so I got to try out my college French, and we mostly just laughed at my abuse of the language.

"I vill ride wit you to Oostende tomorrow," Zargo told me after dinner. "Is very nice to travel along beside ze coast. I give you history along ze vay."

After dinner, my hosts took me for a walk and showed me the place where the British Army was evacuated during World War II. What was once a bloody battlefield is now a glittering line of tourist-crowded shops, hotels and restaurants. The next morning, we rode out of town early. By 8:00, we were on the canal heading north. As we drifted along, Zargo shared with me his philosophical views of life. "Zo many people killed in var for vhat reason?" he asked. "Is part of man to vant to make var but makes no sense." We stopped at a boulangerie and had second breakfast; then Zargo asked if he could take my bike for a test ride. He had never ridden a loaded touring bike and was anxious to give it a try. He wobbled around the parking lot a few times, then stopped and got off. Handing back my bicycle, Zargo grinned. "Is very heavy!" he laughed. "Very hard to steer!"

Later, we stopped at a small graveyard and Zargo led me on a tour. "Ze Germans, French, British, zey are all buried here togezer." He gave me a look. "Okay, I understand is var, but such a vaste."

I was impressed by the way people view World War II in that part of the world. We are blessed in America in not having been occupied by a hostile army, so we don't pay the same kind of homage to our war dead as they do in Europe. In this part of France, they were not so lucky. The reminders of the horror are all around. You couldn't miss them if you tried.

Zargo rode with me all the way to the Belgian border. Then we said our goodbyes, and he turned around and headed back to Dunkirk while I continued on toward Oostende, farther up the Belgian coast.

Chapter Thirteen: Belgium

The North Sea was on my left, and on my right were sand dunes with the occasional World War II German gun emplacement. The road was narrow but had little traffic, and what traffic I encountered was considerate of cyclists. The weather was fine: sunny but not too hot. Before I had ridden many miles, I saw up ahead another cyclist. It looked like he or she had a full set of panniers, and I thought, *Hot dog! Another tourer!* I sped up and soon overtook the rider. "Hello!" I said as I pulled up alongside.

"Hello," said the young man, in a British accent.

"Where are you headed?" I asked.

"Oostende," he replied.

"Cool," I said, "I'm headed for Oostende, too, mind if I tag along?"

"It would be my pleasure," he said. "My name's Peter."

I introduced myself, and we chatted as we rode. Soon, we reached Oostende and slowly threaded our way carefully through the throngs of tourists that crowded the glitzy boardwalk.

Peter told me he had come across from Dover on the ferry just as I had, and was combining a work conference with a cycling vacation. After the conference in Oostende, he planned to ride farther up the coast and then return to his flat in London. We stopped on the promenade, and I got Peter to take a few photos of my bike and me with the North Sea in the background. Peter had to check into his hotel, so we parted ways. I rode to the center of town, the zentrum, which, as in most old European cities, is a pedestrian square surrounded by old, ornate buildings draped in colorful flags and banners. I leaned my bicycle against a low fence that encircled an open-air restaurant, but was quickly run off by a waiter. He waved his hands and shouted at me in French, shooing me off as he would a stray dog. For some reason, I found him funny and had to laugh, which didn't go over well. He gave me a dirty look. "Americans," he muttered disgustedly under his breath as he turned and stormed away.

I love chocolate and had promised myself that once I got to Belgium, the center of the world of chocolate, I would treat myself to the ultimate chocolate experience. So I found a chocolate shop and ordered the most ornate truffle they had, a chocolate croissant, and a cup of cocoa. Sitting down at the table, I got ready for heaven. The truffle was something to write home about, and yes, the croissant and cocoa were good, excellent even, but I didn't experience the epiphany I had hoped for. But later, in a grocery store, I noticed something called sucre waffles. They're sugar-coated waffle cookies about the size of a small pancake and are delicious. I got hooked on them, and all the while I was in Belgium and Holland you could find a pack of sucre waffles in my handlebar bag.

I had arranged to stay that night with another Warm Showers host outside Oostende, but it was early yet, and I had time to kill. I wandered around the narrow streets and, after an hour or so of sightseeing, found myself back at the zentrum. As I was sitting on a bench people-watching, a young man approached and struck up a conversation. It turned out that he was an artist, too, so we had a lot in common. When I mentioned that I was heading to Bruges the next day, he invited me to stay with him and his girlfriend at his apartment there. He gave me directions to his artist's stall in the town square, where we agreed to meet the next evening. I was glad to have scored free lodging for the next night, but later, as I was riding to meet up with Henk, my host for this night, I ran into my young friend. He flagged me down and explained that he'd phoned his girlfriend and she had nixed the idea. "I'm very sorry," he said, "but perhaps we can find other accommodations for you."

"That's okay," I said, trying to hide my disappointment, "but thanks for making the effort." It looked like I'd be paying for a room in Bruges after all.

I reached the neighborhood where my host's house was, but as usual, I got lost trying to find it. So I gave Henk a call, and he rode to where I was and led me to his house, a modern, nicely-furnished, two-story bungalow with a spacious garden. Since it began to rain almost as soon as we arrived, we had our barbecue on the patio beneath an awning. After dinner, we sat around the living room and chatted. Henk and his wife were planning a trip to Seattle and intended to ride south through central Oregon.

"I want to see a bear in the wild," Henk told me. "Have you ever seen a bear?"

I smiled. "Sure, there are a lot of them in the mountains where I come from. In fact, I grinned a griz to death once!"

Both he and his wife traded confused looks. I guess they don't get Davy Crockett in Belgium.

"Would you like a beer?" Henk asked.

"Sure," I said.

Henk went to the kitchen and returned with three big bottles of Duvel beer, a Belgian brew that poured like molasses and formed a thick, foamy head. It sure looked good, and after the first glass they insisted I have another. After the third, I could barely stand up. Henk and his wife giggled and poked each other in the ribs. I had no idea they were serving me what is known as "nen echten duvel," "a real devil" because of its 8.5% alcohol content.

In Bruges

It was a short ride from Oostende, and I arrived in Bruges early enough to spend the day wandering around town, visiting the tourist sites, buying fresh fruit, and going to the tourist information center, where I rented a small room in the attic of a boarding house. It was a cool little garret on the top floor with a view of the rooftops of Bruges. Being in such a bohemian environment made me feel a little like one of those romantic expat American artists from the thirties.

The next morning's ride, from Bruges to Antwerp, where my next Warm Showers lodging was to be, was only a hundred kilometers, so I figured I'd make the trip in seven or eight hours. And

I'd have done it too, if I hadn't gotten lost halfway, near the town of Zelzate. Despite several stops to check my map, I couldn't find the road I was looking for. Eventually, I stood at a dead end where my road should have been; I knew I'd made a wrong turn, but I was damned if I knew where. After backtracking several times and winding up in the same place, I stopped to ask an elderly woman for directions. She smiled and indicated with a shrug and a wave of her hand that she didn't understand. She went into her shop, and in a few moments reemerged with an elderly man who I thought was her husband. They discussed the problem in Dutch for five minutes; then the man turned to me and in broken English asked, "Now, wheere ess eet you vant to go?"

I told him, and he nodded. He turned to his wife and they carried on a conversation in Dutch. There was much hand-waving and excited utterance; clearly they disagreed about which way I should go. I glanced nervously at my watch. I had a long trip ahead of me, and it was already early afternoon. If I was late, I might have to spend the night on the street, or worse yet, pay for a room. The old man finally began to give me directions, but before he spoke ten words, a passerby who had stopped to listen interrupted him, and they too began to argue.

Now the old woman joined in, and a heated, three-way debate ensued. I stood there for a while, then got on my bike and rode back the way I'd come, leaving the Belgians to their little dust-up. They were still going at it when I left. I don't think they even noticed I was gone.

Escalator to Hell

The Scheldt River flows through the heart of Antwerp before it empties into the North Sea, and a pedestrian tunnel runs underneath it. There's an old wood-trimmed escalator leading to the tunnel, and I stood at the top looking down the long dim tube, which seemed to go and on. The escalator was so narrow that I wasn't sure my bike and I would fit. But I saw no alternative, so

I got a firm grip on the handlebars, maneuvered around behind, and carefully rolled the front tire onto the first step. My bike took off with a violent jerk, catching me by surprise, and I hung on for dear life, dragged along behind like Goofy in a Disney cartoon. It was all I could do to keep my bike from tearing loose from my grip and plummeting down the steep escalator. By the time I got to the bottom of the thirty-meter drop, my nerves were as tightly wound as the high E-string of a guitar. As I pushed my bike through the tunnel, I fretted about how I was going to handle the "up" ride. Somehow I managed it, though I was sweating bullets when I came out on the far bank. Henning, my host for the night, was waiting for me with his own bike, and when he saw me emerge, he shook his head in disbelief. "You took your bicycle on the escalator?!" he said in amazement. "Why didn't you use the elevator?

"There's an elevator?" I said. Boy, did I feel dumb.

Henning shook his head and smiled. "Well you made it. I guess that's all that matters. Come on, let's go." I followed him as we sped through the crowded streets of Antwerp to his second-floor apartment on a narrow lane in the heart of the city. After stowing my bicycle in a garage at street level, we schlepped my bags up to his flat. Henning was a hardcore ice climber; we compared notes about the various mountains we'd climbed, had a few beers, and then I grabbed a quick shower and we hit the town. Antwerp has an excellent public bicycle system. We went to the nearest kiosk, got bikes, stopped to pick up a friend of his, Li, a Chinese grad student, and they took me on a nighttime tour of the city. We dined in a restaurant located in an old church courtyard, and then rode back to his digs.

After a quick breakfast at a nearby bakery the next morning, I said goodbye to Henning and made my way out of the city. I wish I had spent more time in Antwerp; it's a beautiful city, but I had arranged to spend that night with another Warm Showers connection in Breda, and I had promised to be there early.

Chapter Fourteen: Holland

Around noon, I crossed the border into the Netherlands, and by 2:00 p.m. I had reached the outskirts of Breda. As the streets were under construction I got lost, so I asked a pedestrian for directions. He looked at my map, thought a minute, then said, "Follow me," and walked me nearly all the way to my host's door.

At first, I thought I had the wrong address. The number matched the one I had in my notebook, but the place was grand! Six stone steps led up to an ornate wooden door a good eight feet tall. The building looked like something out of a coffee-table book on baroque architecture. The small, perfectly-manicured yard was enclosed by a fancy wrought-iron fence and tall, stately shrubbery. In my shabby clothes I felt uncomfortable in such a tony neighborhood, but I screwed up my courage and knocked on the door. It opened, and Frans, my host for the night, stood there smiling. Extending his hand, he said, "You must be Darby," and clapped me on the shoulder. Frans's appearance was as meticulous as his home. In his late fifties, he had a neatly-trimmed moustache and close-cropped salt-and-pepper hair, and was dressed impeccably in dark tropical wool slacks and a light v-neck cashmere sweater. I noticed that his fingernails were manicured. "Come on," he said, "follow me." Frans led me down the street and into an alley behind his house. We parked my bike in his garage, and he helped me carry my panniers through his garden and into his kitchen. There, I met Eveline, his wife. She was petite, with fine features and a gentle countenance. She wore jeans and a light cotton pullover. Eveline was as casual as Frans was formal.

"Would you like a beer?" Frans asked as we settled into the plush chairs arranged around the sun room.

"You bet!" I said.

Eveline produced cold glasses of Duvel and a bread-and-cheese plate. We spent the rest of the afternoon chatting amiably, sipping cold beers and munching on a seemingly inexhaustible supply of goodies. The conversation finally got around to Frans and Eveline's home, and I discovered that the block of houses had been built to billet officers of the Dutch Army. Frans and Eveline had bought theirs many years before at a bargain price. I shudder to think what such a grand home would be worth today. Later, Eveline showed me to my room on the third floor. I took a shower, caught up on my e-mails, Web-chatted with my daughters, and had a short nap. When I awoke, it was dark. Heading downstairs, at the second-floor landing I detected an aromatic scent: dinner was on the stove, and the smell got my digestive juices to roiling. Eveline stood over the burner of her massive range, stirring a pot. "Well hello," she said, smiling brightly. "I was just going to come up and get you."

"Something smells good," I said.

I wish now that I had made a note of dinner, because though I can't remember exactly what was served, I know it was one of the best meals I'd ever had, and I wolfed it down shamelessly. After dinner, we sat in the drawing room and had aperitifs and chocolates. I learned that Frans and Eveline were avid cycle tourers and had travelled in Asia and Europe. They had not been to America, but it was on their list. They planned to leave soon for a bike trip to Australia that would last six months. I stayed up as late as I could, but by 10:00 I was nodding off, so I made my apologies and stumbled upstairs, where I collapsed on the bed and didn't move till morning.

The Knooppunt

I awoke early, had breakfast, and then Frans and Eveline took me on a bike tour of Breda. We visited the moat-encircled Breda Castle, and Frans insisted I try a local delicacy: raw sardines garnished with onions. Later, they showed me a monument honoring the liberation of Holland from the Germans by the Polish Army. I asked Frans about the numbered signs I'd been seeing along the trail. "That's the Knooppunt," he explained. "Knooppunt means literally, knot point. You simply go from point to point or knoot to knoot. Each number corresponds with a knoot. You ride from knoot to knoot until you reach your final destination. It's really simple."

My next destination was Rotterdam, and Frans scribbled down a list of knoots for me to follow. I said goodbye to my hosts at a knoot in a forest outside town, and armed with Frans's list that, in theory at least, would get me to Rotterdam, I set out.

Now I went from knoot to knoot, and soon I was riding along an elevated towpath beside a canal. The canals are raised above the level of the surrounding countryside, which I assume is below sea level. I pedaled past ancient windmills and through quaint villages, past fields and through stands of woods and around 11:00 stopped at a small café and sat at a table outside in the warm sun to enjoy a pastry and hot chocolate. An old fellow sat in a folding chair nearby, fishing. His pole must have been ten feet long; after musing on the purpose of such a grand instrument, I asked him about it. He shrugged, replied in Dutch, and went about his business.

I reached Rotterdam late in the day and sought out my Warm Showers host. Her name was Kathy, and she lived in a small, neat-as-a-pin house in a middle-class neighborhood. Over dinner, she mentioned that she would be leaving on a bike trip herself in a few days. She and her sister were going to ride the Elbe River trail to Prague. My plans took me as far as Amsterdam, but I didn't know where I'd go after that. As Kathy described the route, I thought it sounded pretty good, so I decided I'd give the Elbe a try, too. But first, I wanted to see Amsterdam. Kathy planned a knoot route for me and printed it out that evening. So the next morning, I was on the road to Amsterdam.

Most of that day was spent riding through rural countryside, but toward early afternoon I began to sense that I was nearing a metropolis. First, there were suburban neighborhoods; then I entered a more commercial area. As I neared the sea, the canals got bigger. At one point, I had to take a ferry across. Now I was riding past tony restaurants and bars, and though I was tempted to stop and have a pint, I was anxious to reach Amsterdam. I picked up the pace, and soon my diligence was rewarded: I arrived in Amsterdam! I rode through a sea of bicycles, cyclists crowding all around and occasionally bumping up against my overloaded bike. The typical Dutch cyclist rides an upright commuter bike with front and rear racks, headlights, and taillights. Everybody in Holland rides a bike, and I often saw two people on the same one with the passenger sitting sideways on the rear rack. I couldn't help but smile: These were my people!

Amsterdam street scene

I had promised myself a good meal and a cold beer when I reached Amsterdam, so I pulled over at a sidewalk restaurant next to a canal and ordered fish stew and a Deuval, and sat people-watching. The place had WiFi, so I sent an e-mail to my daughters letting them know I'd arrived safely. While online, I searched for a place to settle down for a few days. There was a campground a few kilometers outside Amsterdam in Zeeburg; I paid my tab, climbed on my bike, and plunged into the late-afternoon bicycle rush-hour traffic.

Camping Zeeburg

Somewhere a few tents away, a drug fiend emitted a high-pitched, hysterical laugh. A pigeon strutted in under my rain fly, saw me, and tried to take off, but instead hit the tent and fell to earth, fluttering around in blind panic and then stumbling out again.

The scent of marijuana permeated the air; it was everywhere and served as an olfactory baseline for daily life at Camping Zeeburg a few kilometers outside Amsterdam.

The tents were jammed together like sardines in a can, with barely enough room to walk between them. When I awoke that first morning I discovered that a new neighbor had camped so close I had to climb out the other door. The sea of multi-colored tents filled the grassy meadow right up to the edge of the water, some as big as small cabins, others, tiny one-person models shoehorned into every available space. I made my way carefully through the maze, tripping over guy lines and walking between campers sharing breakfast. I saw all kinds of people there, young Europeans, Africans, Americans, also a good cross-section of older family types. Camping in Holland is a civilized affair, simply a cheap way to get out of the house for a few days or weeks. There's no pretense about it being a wilderness experience. At Zeeburg, you can order dinner and drinks at the restaurant, buy supplies at a grocery store, rent a bike, hear live music, use the laundry and showers.

This was the first time I'd camped in Europe; all the other nights had been spent with Warm Showers hosts, and I was amazed at the difference between European campgrounds and the more spartan American versions. Here, there was an automated bakery where I bought fresh bread, and the pain au chocolate was better than anything I could get in the States. I walked around that first morning getting a feel for the place. I had breakfast in the common area and then gathered my clothes and did a load of laundry.

Dressed in my best street clothes, jeans and a t-shirt, I walked across the bridge to a station where I caught the train into Amsterdam. It was modern, fast and spotless. The commuters were courteous to a fault, and after a pleasant fifteen minutes, I arrived at the Amsterdam metro station, the building from which, each morning, thousands of people emerge and descend on the old city. Joining the throng, I walked past a massive construction site, across a street crammed with cyclists, and down the broad boulevard that is one of Amsterdam's main arteries. The crowd was shoulder to shoulder. For a few steps I walked beside a woman eating french fries; she would dip one in a glob of mayonnaise and daintily nibble at it like a rabbit eating a carrot. Soon, I spotted an intriguing alley and left the crowds behind as I wandered past small shops, restaurants and bars. Tables lined the narrow passage, and at times I had to turn sideways to shuffle past diners.

I emerged onto a broader street that ran parallel to a canal. Glass-topped cruise boats jammed with tourists plied the waterway. On the banks, vendors sold tulip bulbs out of booths. The streets had long ago been taken over by bicycles and motor scooters, and cars were a rarity. The pedestrians outnumbered the pigeons, and in places spilled over the sidewalk into the street. Ancient buildings with ornate facades were wedged in between more modern, severe architecture, and this diversity of style, along with the throngs of people, gave the city a sense of eclectic vibrancy. Every few blocks, I'd come out of a narrow street into a broad public square. Usually some form of street entertainment could be found in these gathering places. In one square I watched while a shirtless, bearded escape artist struggled without success to free himself from the chains and padlocks draped over his body.

It felt at first, at least to my American sensibilities, that in Amsterdam, "anything goes": dope, whores, live sex shows, mayonnaise on french fries — there seemed to be no end to the debauchery. Near the central train station, I saw posters for a torture museum. Later, I watched cops gang-swarm a young man in the middle of the street. He struggled and screamed for help from the passersby as the officers beat him into submission and dragged him off in manacles.

A Plan

Planning a route ahead was the first order of business, so I sought out a bookstore where I could purchase a set of maps that showed bicycle routes across Holland and Germany. I also bought a guidebook for the Elbe River. Back at the campground, I perused my maps and planned a route that would take me from Amsterdam to Dessau, in Germany; from there, I'd head up the Elbe River to Prague. I wasn't sure where I'd go after that, but I wasn't worried, I'd ride off that bridge when I came to it. Bicycle-touring in Europe is more complicated and harder than in America. In the USA, I would get up in the morning and ride hell-bent-for-leather all day. I had left Wenatchee, Washington, on May 6th, and barely made a turn until late June. With a few exceptions, navigating was easy: just head east. In Europe, there are a lot more roads, and each time I came to an intersection (which happened far too often) I would have to stop and check my maps. All that stopping and starting took a lot more energy than simply tearing along at a steady pace, and though I thought I was strong, I was getting more tired than usual. I couldn't ride as fast or as far as I had back home. One morning, for no reason at all, I fell off my bike beside a canal and nearly went for an impromptu swim.

I stayed in Amsterdam longer than I had originally planned. The stress of life on the road in these foreign lands had worn me out, and I sorely needed time to unwind and acclimatize to my new surroundings. It was four days before I felt ready to pack up and get back on the road.

Several days east of Amsterdam, I had a hard time route finding; I couldn't locate the next knoot and had to retrace my tracks back to the previous one. As I stood looking at my map and scratching my head, another cyclist stopped to help.

"Vere are you going?" he asked. I pointed to the day's destination on my map. "Ah yes," he said, "I know exactly vere dat is! I vill take you zere, just follow me!" Just then, his wife pedaled up, and we made introductions all around. Sonya and Paul were locals out for a day of riding. They knew the country well, and after a brief description of the route we'd be taking, they sped off down the road with me in tow. It was hard keeping up with my guides; they were really flying. Soon, we left the pavement and pedaled through a forest on a dirt path, bouncing along at high speed, twisting and turning through a tangle of trails so that I began to lose all sense of direction. The forest closed in and blocked the sun. I knew that if I lost sight of Sonya out there in the middle of the forest, I would truly be lost. I had no idea where we were or how we got there; we just kept going deeper into that unknown place.

Now we were riding on a winding, narrow, single-track dirt trail fit only for mountain bikes. Every kilometer or so there was a cattle guard, and though Paul and Sonya negotiated them with ease, I had to grit my teeth and hang on for dear life as my heavy bike shimmied and shook across each grating. The turns were sharp and sudden, and I nearly went off several times. On one arched bridge I was going so fast that both my wheels flew off the ground. For just a moment, I was completely weightless as I sailed oh-not-so-gracefully through the air, then hit the earth with a clanking and clunking so loud that it startled a flock of birds to flight.

Soon we emerged from the deep woods into a sun-dappled clearing where there was a restaurant and bar. It was the turning-around point for Paul and Sonya, so they made a map for me on a cocktail napkin, and after a beer or two, we parted ways.

Chapter Fifteen: Germany

Since the establishment of the European Union, there's not much to mark the transition between countries in Western Europe anymore. As with most countries in Europe, the border region between Holland and Germany is sketchy. There are a lot of dingy and vacant buildings, and I saw quite a few rough-looking individuals lurking in alleys and under bridges.

I was following the R1 across Germany now, which is a network of bicycle routes that meander through the countryside on narrow farm roads and surface streets. Unlike the Dutch Knooppunt system, it's pretty fast, and I still got to see the little villages but could roll up miles while doing it. Back in Holland, near the ocean, the temperatures had been comparatively mild. But now, I was three days east of Munster, deep in northern Germany, and it was getting hotter the farther inland I rode. I spent the morning climbing a long ridge, passing through quaint villages under a bright sky. Most of the riding was on narrow, paved farm roads that doubled as bicycle trails and wound up through forests and farmland alongside creeks and small rivers. I reached the top of the hill in the afternoon; then it was an enjoyable race down the other side. I hardly turned a pedal in ten kilometers. As I swooped through one village I passed a half-timbered pension, jutting out from which was a deck filled with happy bicyclists feasting on heaping plates of delicious-looking food and drinking good German beer. I was tempted to blow my budget and join the merrymaking, but I resisted and flew past the congregation with a smile and a wave.

The descent into the Weser River Valley seemed to go on forever. My map showed a campground at the village of Hoxter, but when I got there, I found a big paved parking lot filled with RV's. Sunburned Germans in workout suits lounged in lawn chairs, drinking beer. It didn't seem to be my kind of place (except for the drinking beer part), and since it was only another ten kilometers to the next campground at Holzminden, I decided to go the extra distance to make a nice, round 120-kilometer day. I rolled out of Hoxter on a trail following the Weser River on its journey to the North Sea. Though the sign at Hoxter showed the trip to Holzminden to be quick, nine kilometers, at twelve I still hadn't reached the town. I began to worry that I had somehow missed the turnoff — could it have been that small bridge I'd raced past? As I studied my map, a woman rode up and struck up a conversation. She appeared to be in her forties, with short blond hair and a fair Teutonic complexion. She said something in German, and I replied that I only spoke English. "American," I said, shrugging.

"Ah, American!" She broke out in a broad grin, "you come from America to Deutschland?"

I nodded. "Seattle, Washington."

"Yes," she said, her features lighting up. "Seattle, I have never been but I know of it!" Then turning more serious, "Are you lost?"

I showed her the map. "I'm looking for the camping platz," I said. "It's supposed to be around here someplace, but I fear I've missed it."

"No," she said, smiling, "you are going the right way. Come, follow me, I will show you."

We rode along together making pleasant conversation, she helping me to fill in a few blank spots in my German lexicon. Then, before I knew it, we were there. "I am glad I met you and I hope you have a pleasant journey," she said.

I was hoping she'd take more than a casual liking to me and invite me to stay at her place that night, and I prolonged the goodbye, turning the Old Roach Charm on high, but I guess I wasn't her type. After an awkward hug she pedaled off, throwing me a casual wave over her shoulder. I shrugged and walked my bike to the office, where I checked into the campground and set my tent up on a grassy swath on the riverbank. From my tent I had a view of the village, the bridge across the Weser, and Holzminden's cathedral, all for just three and a half euros! I slept well, and the next morning dawned bright and clear.

During my ride across North America I had developed the bad habit of stopping at convenience stores and eating junk food for breakfast. I had promised myself I would eat better, and now that I was in Europe where there are more wholesome alternatives, I had been keeping that promise. Now, instead of Ding Dongs and Cheetos for breakfast, I had fresh fruit and fresh-baked goods from the outdoor markets that grace every small village. There was always a wide selection of fruit and pastries, but I didn't know the names of the baked goods, so I would point to the ones that looked good. Sometimes I'd be disappointed in the flavor, and once in a while I'd discover some kind of cured meat lurking inside a fluffy pastry crust.

I found the market in Holzminden and was going to buy breakfast, but when I checked my funds I discovered that I had only a few euros, so I went looking for a cash machine. It was Sunday and the German banks were closed, so I rode around and around and up and down every street, but there wasn't a cash machine to be found anywhere. Finally stopping, I asked a lady on the street, who directed me to the post office, which in Germany is also a bank with ATMs. Sure enough, I was able to draw out several hundred euros, and I rushed back to the farmer's market and had a feast.

Kaltem Vasser

The ride out of the Weser River Valley was spectacular. After climbing up from the village on a single-lane bike path through a recently harvested wheat field, I looked back at the village, the river, and surrounding forest and farmland. The sun had not yet climbed very high in the sky, and the light gave the wheat stubble a golden, almost ethereal glow. It was a color not in any palette I had ever seen, and it made me laugh out loud to be in such a fantastic place.

By late morning the weather had turned hot, and I stopped

often to drink and find shade. I was in the Harz Mountains now, and most of the day's riding was up hill and down, through villages and fields with little shade. I was really suffering in the heat.

In a small village at the bottom of a climb, I stopped to drink from my water bottle. As I stood eying the hill ahead, a stout lady in a print dress came out of her house and pointed at my water bottle. "Kaltem wasser?" she asked.

Chateau, Elbe River

I didn't need an interpreter. "Cold water? Ya!" I replied enthusiastically. She'd seen me through her kitchen window as I drank what she knew must be lukewarm water. She grabbed my water bottles, went back in her house, and emerged a few minutes later with both sweating-cold bottles. I drank one bottle dry, which she happily refilled as I worked on the second. Once I'd drunk my fill, I began pouring water over my head and down the back of my neck. The woman burst out in laughter and joined in the fun by pouring a bottle of kaltem wasser over my front. Now we were out of water again, so she ran back in the house and in a moment reappeared with both bottles filled. Her husband had followed her outside to see what all the commotion was about. "Kaltem wasser!" the woman and I kept shouting, "ver goot!" We stood laughing and taking turns dousing me until I was completely soaked and cooled off.

Red Riding Hood

No longer a country of bad haircuts and ill-fitting suits, this former satellite of the old Soviet Union looked like one of the nicest and most prosperous parts of the modern unified Germany. This is where the Harz Mountains get serious, and the Germans flock here for their holidays. It's also where many of the Brothers Grimm fairy tales are set. Legend has it that witches gather atop the Brocken, the highest mountain in the region, each October 30th for the German version of Halloween.

I rode on narrow cobblestone lanes that meandered past well-tended fields and through deep woods and storybook villages. I found nothing quaint, though, about the tractors with which I was sharing the road. They were big suckers, the size of our diesel trucks, and when I saw one speeding around a blind corner at thirty miles an hour, I got out of the way fast.

It was a slow, easy ride that day. I made only forty kilometers before I stopped at a camping platz in the town of Thale. It was on the grounds of an old monastery with ancient rock-and-brick walls adorned with Christian iconography. I had to wonder what the ghosts of the monks who wander those halls must think of the tourists defiling their sanctified ground.

The town of Thale lies right in the heart of the Harz Mountains. According to the pamphlet the clerk at the front desk gave me, there were lifts farther up the canyon: a gondola and a double chair.

I pitched my tent next to a small stream beneath a big oak tree. Later that afternoon, a gorgeous young woman rode in and set up camp next to me. Her bicycle, panniers, tent, even her cycling clothes were a bright red. We chatted, and I discovered that she had ridden from Sweden and was heading to Venice. She was the first long-distance cycle tourer I'd met in Europe.

The next morning, a hospitable German couple invited me to their trailer for tea. We sat in the sun and talked, and before I knew it, it was almost 9:30. It was a pleasant way to spend the morning, and I was sorry to leave. The weather was cool, and stayed that way all day, which made for good riding. For the first time since I'd been in Germany, I had a tailwind, and I made ninety kilometers almost without trying. I had hoped to reach Dessau that day, but it wasn't in the cards. I made it to Bernburg and camped along a river with two other long-distance tourers, a man and a woman from Bavaria who had ridden around the world. They were riding Koga Miyata bicycles, which are Dutch-made, and very high-tech and expensive. Alongside them, my battered, vintage Trek 520 looked shabby, but I had no complaints. It had been a good bike.

I studied my maps and saw that I should reach Dessau and the Elbe River the next day. From there, I'd follow the river to Prague. I arose early the next morning with a sense of happy anticipation. All through my career as a graphic designer, I'd heard about and studied the Bauhaus, the design school where the modern design movement began. Originally located in Weimar, it moved to Dessau and then to Berlin, where the Nazis closed it, calling it decadent. After decades of decline under Soviet rule, the Bauhaus has been restored to its original condition, and I couldn't wait to see it.

The Elbe River

I got up early and made good time, and by 1:00 p.m. I reached Dessau and found my way to the Bauhaus. It was a thrill to see where all the design greats once resided, Gropius, Albers, Bruer

. . . the list goes on. The buildings had been designed with right angles in whites and grays, and are modern looking even though they're almost a hundred years old. It was late afternoon now, and I didn't have time to spend touring the Bauhaus, so after a quick ride-by, I went looking for a campground. I located the little tent icon on my map, but it gave only the general location. It looked like the camping platz was on the Elbe, so I found a road that ran parallel to the river and followed it back west. The route started out nice enough, with a good paved road, but soon deteriorated into a muddy, rutted track in thick forest. After a few kilometers of wrestling my bike through that swamp, I turned around. I had learned that getting lost was just part of bicycle touring. I got angry with myself the first twenty or thirty times it happened, but by now I was used to it. After a few more aborted attempts, I wound up in a small village of half-timbered houses and narrow streets. I wandered around for a while and finally stopped to ask a pedestrian, who turned out not to speak English. At first he just shrugged, but after some coaxing, he got the idea and directed me to a turnoff a block away. Sure enough, I saw a road sign with the welcome tent symbol, and I followed the arrows to a lake, upon the shores of which was the camping platz.

The Bauhaus

People were swimming in the little lake, and I discovered an odd habit the Germans have of changing in and out of their swimming suits in public. One elderly man whipped off his bathing suit right in front of me. Man, what a sight! I was legally blind for fifteen minutes!

I set up my tent with the door facing the water and watched as groups of Germans in long wooden boats raced up and down the lake. My stove had been acting up, and that night I could barely coax enough heat out of it to boil water. I had rebuilt it in Minneapolis, but I guess I'd done something wrong because now it was on the fritz again. I wanted to find a camping store in Dessau the next day; maybe someone there could fix it properly. But the big event would be the Bauhaus.

The sound of rain awoke me at 5:14 a.m. I sat up and peeked outside; it wasn't that bad. The tent acts like a big drum and magnifies sounds so that even a light drizzle can seem like a downpour. I rolled over and went back to sleep for what seemed hours. When I looked at my watch again, it was nearly 8:00 a.m. It had been raining for three hours. A storm like that is unusual in these parts; usually, it would rain for ten or fifteen minutes and then clear up. But it seemed today was to be different. *Oh well*, I thought, *I've ridden in the rain before.* By the time I'd packed, the rain had stopped and a nice breeze blew through camp. I loaded my bike and headed for the gate, only to find that it was closed. "What the . . ." I checked my watch; it was 7:45. I'd misread it before and was getting a really early start.

I rode back to the Bauhaus and checked the hours. The doors opened at 9:00 a.m., which gave me time to visit a market and buy fruit and pastries. Later, sitting on a bench in the Bauhaus courtyard as a light rain fell, I ate my breakfast, soaking up the ambience and imagining the great artists and designers who had trod this hallowed ground. After breakfast, I went in and looked around, had a seat in the Marcel Bruer Lounge, and caught up on my e-mail. The Marcel Bruer Lounge is nothing special, except that it's in the basement of the greatest design school that ever was, and oh yeah, there's a full bar. I visited the permanent exhibition, wandered around, and poked my nose in here and there, hoping to catch a glimpse of Walter Gropius's ghost, but he didn't show. The tea I'd had was going through me, so a trip to the WC was in order. As I stood at the porcelain facility, I thought, *Gosh, Joseph Albers might have taken a leak in this very same urinal!*

I had originally planned to spend the day at the Bauhaus, but after a few hours I felt I'd seen enough. The manager at the campground had given me directions to a camping store, and after a lot of riding around in circles, I finally found it tucked into a small storefront on a busy street. The proprietor spoke English, but though he was able to sell me gas, he didn't seem to know much about fixing my stove. I'd have to make do.

Singing With Willy and Michael

I had been following the bike trail south up the Elbe River from Dessau for two days now. It's a nice paved trail that runs on the west bank, but I got turned around and wound up on the east side. As I stood studying my map, a fellow rode up and asked if I needed directions. His English was good, and soon we were riding along together chatting. "If you want to get a beer," he said, "follow me." We turned down a side road and rolled into the courtyard of what looked like a farmhouse.

"This is a bar?" I asked.

Michael smiled, "More like a club." Soon, we were seated at an outdoor table enjoying a local brew with the proprietor, Willy. The campground where I planned to spend the night was on the other side of the river, a dozen kilometers farther on, and I was anxious to get there and set up camp. I finished my beer and went to the restroom. When I came back, there was a fresh beer at my spot. *What the heck*, I thought, *one more can't hurt*. We sat for a while longer, and then I got ready to leave. "Why don't you camp here tonight?" Michael said. He and Willy were old pals, and Michael had arranged for to me to set up my tent in the garden.

"Well, sure," I said, "that'd be great. It started to rain, so we moved indoors. A few beers later, a local couple showed up who had immigrated to the USA in the 60's but still had roots in Germany. We sat and talked about America, drank another beer, and then Michael, who is a blues musician, took down a guitar from the wall, and he and Willy began to sing. They sang German songs, so I didn't understand the words, but Michael was such a great guitarist and Willy had such a good voice that it really didn't matter. It wasn't long before we all joined in. I hummed the tunes until we began singing American rock 'n' roll, folk, and Beatles, and then I really got into it. I think I might have even danced.

Willy spoke no English, so Michael interpreted for me. We'd all had quite a few beers by then, and we started telling jokes. I'd tell one, everybody but Willy would laugh, then Michael would tell the joke to Willy in German. After a few more beers, things began to get fuzzy. I told a joke, which Michael then "translated" for Willy, except he forgot to tell it in German and simply repeated what I'd said in English. I didn't notice the mistake and blurted out, "Hey, I can understand German!"

Willy disappeared into the kitchen for a while, then emerged with a heaping bowl of scrambled eggs. We ate and sang and drank until after midnight. "To heck with camping" Willy said, with Michael interpreting, "I have an apartment you can use tonight."

Finally the party wound down and Willy showed me to my room. I took a long hot bath and slept in until past 7:00 the next morning.

Dresden

I left Willy's shortly after 7:30. Everyone was still asleep, so I left a thank-you note and headed for the trail. It had rained during the night, and the fresh air was invigorating. Since it was only seven kilometers to Riesa, I arrived before the shops opened. Michael had told me the night before that I could poach free WiFi at a certain street corner, so I went there, but all the networks were password-protected. As I stood scratching my head, a young woman approached and asked if I needed help. This had happened to me often, both in the USA and in Europe; I guess I just have that look. She directed me to a T-Mobile store, where I bought an hour of WiFi for five euros. What a bummer! I couldn't even send e-mails. I'd run into this problem a few times in Europe and could never figure out why. I suppose it had something to do with incompatible technologies.

We'd had a serious conversation at Willy's the night before

about Germany's checkered history. The residents of the old East Germany held great animosity toward the Russians, but didn't seem to resent Americans despite the War. The saturation bombing of Dresden during World War II was still a touchy subject, though, and Michael had talked about how the ancient Dresden Frauenkirche, the 18th-century cathedral, had been blown to bits by American and English bombers just a few weeks before Germany's surrender. "When you get there," Michael told me, "notice that most of the stones are light-colored, with just a few dark ones here and there. The building was restored in the 1980's using as many of the old blocks as possible. Those are the dark ones, blackened by the fires that engulfed the city during the bombing. A few singed stones were all that was left."

Chapter Sixteen: The Czech Republic

I'd been on the road four months, and the old self, the one used to the comforts of home and family, was fading, making way for a new personality more suited to life on the road but whose nature was, as yet, as indefinite and malleable as that of an embryo. There seemed to be a connection, though, between who I was becoming and the people I met, the hardships I endured, the joys I experienced and the landscapes I passed through.

Near the Czech border, less than a day's ride from Dresden, the Elbe River Valley changes dramatically. The broad flood plain gives way to a narrow gorge hemmed in by towering rock formations. High atop one of the cliffs looms an ancient fortress, the Konigstein Castle, built by the princes and kings of Saxony. The Nazis used it as a prison, and it's now a military museum. Lower down, the villages along the river have a medieval feel, and a ride up the Elbe is a journey back in time. The bike path hugs the river and runs along at water grade all the way to its point of origin just north of Prague. Colorful commercial tour boats filled with merrymakers ply the slow-moving river, while more sedate tourists sip the local estate wines and watch the action from pension and café patios.

With all the positive vibes in the air, it was easy to feel good. The Elbe Cycle Route, Elberadweg in German, is perhaps the quintessential example of what cycle touring should be. It is flat, scenic, and varied. There are great expanses of open farmland, narrow rock canyons, small villages, and big cities. You have your pick of cheap nicely-appointed campgrounds placed at just the right intervals.

At one campground on the Elbe, I pitched my tent on a grassy meadow overlooking the river. Next to me were two young men dressed in military uniforms. They both slept in a small tent not half the size of mine. For a few days I leapfrogged with two young women who I believe were German. We camped at the same campgrounds each night and would wave when we passed on the trail. I met one couple who, in their mid-seventies, were on their second ride around the world.

In between camps, I would pedal through two or three quaint villages a day, as well as big cities such as Dessau, Dresden and Wittenberg. It looked as though the trains run daily along the river, and though I didn't check them out, I imagine you could catch one if you didn't feel like riding. I enjoyed every minute of riding the Elbe River Route. I ate and slept well and was on a high the whole time. I went slow, dragging the trip out.

And This Too Shall Pass

Crossing the Vltava River

I entered the Czech Republic, my sixth country since leaving the USA, around 10:00 in the morning. The only indication that I had crossed an international border was a small coat of arms on a sign in the center of the trail. I got off at Decin, the first town I came to, and found a grocer where I bought fresh fruit for second breakfast. Trouble started when I got to the checkout and discovered that the Czech Republic doesn't use the euro, which was all I had. There was a tense moment that lasted until I produced my debit card, which, luckily, they were able to swipe.

Later that afternoon, I stopped at a little grocery store to buy more provisions. I wasn't yet used to the Czech monetary system, so when the tab came to 271 kopecks, I was confused. I pulled out my wad of cash and started flipping through bills, looking for the right denominations while simultaneously trying to convert from kopecks to euros and then to dollars. The total didn't seem right; I was holding off paying, but the clerk became impatient, grabbed a 500-kopeck note out of my hand, and shoved some change at me.

Over the River & Through the Woods

It was my third day in the country. I'd spent a rainy rest day at a campground and was itching to get going; I guess I had become addicted to motion. I hated standing still, and even twenty-four hours of sedentary life put me in a lousy mood. So at first light I set out at a brisk pace beneath an overcast sky. It had been raining for a full day, and it looked as if I might get wet before this day was over, too. From Melnik, the trail leaves the Elbe and follows the Vltava River to Prague. After an hour, I arrived at the little ferry that crosses the river. With the help of the ferryman I loaded my bike aboard, and we pushed off. There was no motor; the ferry was equipped with an ingenious series of lines and pulleys that harnessed the river's current and powered the ferry across. A quarter of an hour later, I was on the far bank. Another stretch of pavement gave way to a crumbling, once-cobbled road, which soon turned into a narrow, rocky and winding path that snaked along through dense woods a foot from a three-meter drop into the murky waters of the Vltava River. There was just enough room for me to slip between the forest and the river's edge. My nerves aren't steely enough to ride under those conditions, so I got off and pushed most of ten kilometers.

Prague

The rest of that day and the next were smooth sailing. I had sunny, warm weather and good trails, and I sped along, reaching Prague in the afternoon four days after crossing the border. I rode the trail until it dead-ended under a freeway overpass. Stopping to consult my map, I discovered that there were several campgrounds nearby. I wanted to spend a day or two playing tourist in the city, so I backtracked, found a campground, and set up my tent. This part of the river turned out to be something of a vacation destination. Engineers have diverted a section of the Vltava into narrow channels that parallel the main watercourse, and whitewater enthusiasts come from all over to test their mettle against these man-made rapids.

I was the only cyclist at the camp, and as I unloaded my bike, a kayaker came over and struck up a conversation. "You are coming from where?" He said in stilted English.

"I am originally from Seattle," I said as I stowed gear in my tent. "I'm attempting to ride around the world."

"Ah, yes, Seattle," he mused, "a fine city, but I think you will find Prague much to your liking. Yes, I think so."

We chatted as I put my camp in order, and he filled me in on what sights I should see. I looked forward to soaking up the sophisticated ambience of Prague, but I had business to take care of first. So the next morning, I made the short ride to the heart of the city and went looking for the maps I would need to continue my journey. Somewhere along the way I had decided to visit Rome. After that? Who knew? But for now, I needed maps to get me through the rest of the Czech Republic and Austria, and then to the Alps, where I'd cross into northern Italy. I had no luck at the three or four big bookstores I tried, but I stopped at a tiny shop in a narrow winding side-street near the center of town not far from the grand old Hotel Europa. To my surprise, the young woman who worked there had what I needed. I bought a bicycle guidebook to the Czech Republic titled *S Cyklotrasami*, and later, as I sat at a sidewalk café, I plotted my next move.

According to the guidebook, there were mountains to the south, but if all went well, I'd be over them and in Austria in a few days. With a firm grasp of the route ahead, I spent the rest of the afternoon wandering the streets and taking in the sights. I was struck by how stylish the people of Prague appeared, and I felt shabby in my worn travelling clothes. Prague may not have the grandeur and scale of Paris, but it certainly rivals the City of Lights in sophistication and haute couture. It has an excellent public transportation system, and the streets are bike-friendly.

Prague struck me as a very open and liberal city, but until recently it was a part of the Soviet Bloc. The Czechs chafed under Russia's authoritarian rule and reacted with reforms. That didn't sit well with Moscow, and in August of 1968, the Soviet Union invaded, ending the Prague Spring. As I strolled past fashionable boutiques and hip watering holes it was hard to imagine that, not long ago, these same streets were a savage battleground where Czech freedom-fighters slugged it out with Soviet tanks.

I spent the next day sightseeing — riding across the iconic Charles Bridge, hanging out in the Old Town Square, and walking around the Prague Castle. It was nice to take it easy for a change, but by afternoon I was getting the old travelling bone. My obsession with motion made me think of the shark that has to keep moving or drown.

I got up early the next morning, and by 9:00 a.m. I was well south of the city. I was no longer on the Elbe River Route, and even with my guidebook, route-finding proved to be a challenge. At one point, I wound up on a freeway on-ramp. It had happened to me before, outside London, except that time there had been a nice wide shoulder and I was able to turn around.

Not today, thank you very much. There was no shoulder, and

no way to turn around. To my right were a Jersey barrier and a drop-off to the cloverleaf below. To my left was merging traffic. Luckily, the cars and trucks were traveling slowly and making room for me by swerving out of the right lane. Still, I was apprehensive. Who knew when someone would get impatient or be talking on their cell and do something stupid? I mean something stupider than getting stuck on a busy freeway on a bicycle. I couldn't stand there all day. I had to do something, but I had no idea what.

The most frightening thing of all is when you're in a tight spot and your frontal lobe runs all the data and returns an error message. That's when the limbic brain takes over. The limbic brain is the second oldest part of our brain, and it's where emotion lives. Love, compassion, jealousy, hate, fear. Fear. Fear is an auto-cannibal. It feeds on itself. The more afraid you are, the more afraid you become. There's no reason, just primal instinct, and when fear is calling the shots, your odds of actually doing the right thing are about one in twelve — roughly the same as drawing to an inside straight. I call it luck.

With nowhere to go but forward, and trusting to luck, I pedaled as fast as I could to the top of a slight rise, and there, thirty meters ahead, I spied a pedestrian walkway and made a beeline for it. When I reached it, I was dismayed to find that the walkway was separated from the road by a thirty-six-inch-tall combination Jersey barrier and guardrail. Now I was almost on the freeway proper, with traffic bunching up behind me. Some of the cars were pulling out and gunning past the more courteous drivers.

I reached down, grabbed the bike, and using every bit of strength I had, I picked it up and tipped it over the guardrail. I dove after it, and the bike and I landed together in a tangled heap. A few new scratches and dents aside, both the bike and I were still operable, and I soon found a road that led in the right direction.

Over the Hill

The guidebook led me up into the mountains south of Prague. The hills are more wooded than the flats back on the river, forming a rugged and rural land with isolated villages tucked into valleys or clinging to steep mountainsides. After the festive environs of the river, this place seemed gloomy and joyless. I came upon a few forlorn farms carved out of the forest where goats and cows peered at me with anxious and haunted eyes from within ramshackle pens. They seemed to be pleading, "Take me with you . . ." A gray-muzzled old dog limped along behind me for a while and then was gone. I spent endless hours climbing up and down through second-growth forests on bad roads. I rode through a patchwork of back lanes and farm roads, some little more than cow paths. It was lonely, too. Down lower I'd always been surrounded by people, but here in the deep forest, it was rare to see more than a few stoic farmers or woodsmen during the course of a day.

While the condition of the roads varied from bad to awful to barely navigable, the one constant was the hills. It wasn't that they were big hills. I don't think any one of them had an elevation gain of more than two hundred meters, but climbing half a dozen of them every day was wearing me down. At night, I would collapse in my tent, sleep restlessly, and awake tired. I could tell that my stores of energy and positive humor were dwindling. I was way down from the almost 200 pounds I'd weighed at the start and was now so thin that I had to be careful to keep food in my stomach to avoid fading.

I'd been plodding through this unfriendly landscape for what seemed like forever when one morning I awoke to discover the peanut butter I had counted on for breakfast had gone sour. I had to start the day with just a few crumbs of bread and an orange. It was late morning, and I'd just pushed my bike up a steep hill on a rocky path when I had my meltdown. It had been a tough climb; it had taken all I had to make it to the top. When I reached the summit, I leaned my bike against a tree, my legs like rubber and my stomach growling. I hung my head and cradled my face in my hands. I was so damn tired. And not just tired of these hills, but tired of eating meals in parking lots, tired of my musty sleeping bag, tired of being tired. I had to be honest with myself, I was tired of this life. Raw enthusiasm had gotten me over the rough spots when this trip was shiny and new. But now, this was just my life, and when I hit the low spots I landed hard. What was I doing here, anyway? Had I really been looking for answers, or was I just bored? In time, would I find this life boring, too? If so, what would I do then? It all seemed pointless, and I couldn't think of a single reason to go on. I decided right there that I would quit. I'd get to the nearest city and fly home.

I was amazed at how easily I had made up my mind. I'd thought that if I ever made the decision to quit, it would be after a long, well-thought-out consideration of all the facts, not on a whim at the side of the road in the middle of nowhere.

But I did feel better, and with the decision made, it seemed that a great burden had been lifted, and I found a measure of solace in defeat. I rested a while longer, then mustered what little strength and resolve that remained, got back on my bike, and slowly soldiered on. I rode for hours, and as the miles passed, the country took on a new character. I had left the deep woods and shotgun shacks behind. The hills were not as steep, the roads were in better shape, and the farms I now saw looked prosperous, with well-kept houses and outbuildings. Fat cattle and rotund sheep with fleece like clouds grazed peacefully in bright, open meadows. That afternoon, I reached a campground on a lake in a high mountain valley where there was a little store.

After a big dinner and a beer, I crawled into my bag and slept for ten hours.

I awoke to a brilliant, blue-sky morning, and I took my time making breakfast. The big meal of the evening before and a good night's sleep had improved my mood, and after I gorged on eggs and potatoes and a few cups of tea, I felt more like myself and anxious to get back on the road.

I rode along through pleasant woods, and as I topped out on a gentle rise, I stopped to admire the view. The road cut across a ridge above a wooded valley, and off in the distance, brown and white cattle grazed in an emerald pasture. At the edge of the woods was a neat, half-timbered farmhouse, and next to that, a big barn. I could see the road twisting down the ridge ahead; it looked like I'd have ten or fifteen minutes of effortless gliding. My mood was as bright today as it had been dark the day before. I was happy just to be where I was, and I decided to stick with it a while longer. I could always quit later.

Chapter Seventeen: Austria

There's a sense of freedom that comes from being lost. I'd been wandering the hills of the southern Czech Republic for days, so I can't say exactly where or when I crossed the border into Austria. I might have crossed it several times; the frontier is jagged there. I had abandoned the guidebook I'd bought in Prague and was simply roaming around on secondary roads. I was tired of schedules and objectives and quests and had decided to drift for a while. When I came to an intersection, I chose the road that looked most interesting. If you had asked me to point at my location on a map, I wouldn't have done it if I could. I simply didn't care. I travelled in a generally southerly direction, but with no particular destination in mind.

I didn't know where I was, exactly, but I felt no angst, just relaxed and unhurried as I pedaled over gently rolling hills through groves of old hardwoods. I was being pulled toward something, and I gave myself over to the road and let it take me where it wanted.

I camped by a lake in deep woods and awoke to brilliant sunshine. Instead of getting an early start, I lingered over breakfast and had a second and third cup of tea as I watched the lake mist evaporate in the morning sun. I knew I would have to get back on schedule eventually, but for now it was good to be off the clock. I was in no hurry to get going, and I spread my gear out on the small beach to air. I was carrying a lot of equipment; I got to wondering if it was time to send some things home, but I saw nothing I didn't need. Still, it seemed like an awful lot. I wondered what Tom Stevens would have to say about it.

Tom Stevens was the first person to ride a bicycle around the world. He did it on a single-speed Columbia 50-inch, penny-farthing. *His* gear consisted of a raincoat that doubled as a tent and bedroll, spare socks, and a revolver. He left San Francisco on April 22, 1884, and finished on December 16, 1886. He must have made some of the same discoveries I was making and felt some of the same feelings as I. I bet he understood the importance of getting lost now and then.

Bad Leonfelden

I rode out of the mountains one afternoon into the village of Bad Leonfelden. I got out my map and discovered that I was in Austria. The trees up in the hills were shedding their leaves, and I knew my happy-wanderer days were over; I'd have to make it over the Alps before the snows set in. But right now, I needed a place to sleep. The map showed a campground and hostel, but when I asked the locals, they shrugged and told me they'd never heard of them. I finally found the address of what was supposed to be the hostel, but when I rang the bell, no one answered. I hung around and peeked in the windows, but it looked like a private residence, so I left.

It was late in the day, and with no other options, I checked in to a hotel in town. It wasn't a bad deal: thirty-five euros, and I got breakfast in the morning. My clothes were getting pretty dirty, so I did a wash in the tub. As I lay on my bed, I pored over my map of Austria. The Inn River was a hundred kilometers to the west. Like the Elbe, the Inn has a trail that follows its course, and like the Elbe, it's mostly flat, running along the border between Austria and Germany. It looked as if the trail crossed between countries here and there. I plotted a course, and the next morning, instead of heading south toward Italy, I pointed my handlebars west toward Germany. It would take me a day or two to reach the river and then another three or four to get to Innsbruck. From there, I'd cross the Alps via the Brennerpass, then ride to northern Italy, and eventually, to Rome.

The weather was fine and the country was beautiful. I rode through small hilltop villages and beside rushing streams, past dairy farms, pastures and hay fields. Houses, barns and fences looked immaculate, and everything was neat as could be. Even the hay bales in the fields were arranged on a grid, and the cows grazed in close-order drill. The roads were in great shape, there was no litter, and the few drivers I encountered were courteous. My route kept me on back roads, and I enjoyed the ride.

Around noon one day, I dropped down from a hilltop to the Danube River and rode beside it for an hour or so. A fellow pulled up beside me on a mountain bike, and we started talking.

"Is this the way to Linz?" he asked. I couldn't quite place his accent.

"Uh, yeah, I think so," I replied, not used to being asked directions; it was usually the other way around.

"Going to Vienna," he said. "Where are you headed?"

"Innsbruck. Then I'm going over the Brennerpass."

He nodded. "You Canadian?"

"American. You?"

"Brazil. I flew into Istanbul, rode down through Greece and up through Italy. Boy, that Tuscany, she's got some damn hills. All the towns, they're up on top of mountains one or two kilometers high. But, boy, is it pretty! Rode down in the Greek Isles, beautiful but hot."

"I'm going to some of those places."

He looked at my bike with all its gear, then up at me. "You riding a long way, huh? You long-distance man?"

"Yup," I smiled. "I'm riding around the world."

"Figured it was something like that," he said, a wry grin on his face. "You win the crazy contest!" We rode along chatting and trading notes, but soon our ways parted.

I reached the Inn River midafternoon of the second day. Now I was headed south again. It was 225 kilometers to Innsbruck, and I figured I could get there in two and a half days.

The Apartment

I couldn't have been going more than three or four kilometers an hour when I swerved to miss the lady and her baby carriage, hit a parked bicycle, and landed in a heap on the sidewalk. I could feel the angst welling up inside. This was just the latest thing to characterize a day that had started out all wrong. I had planned to make a hundred kilometers, but by 1:00 in the afternoon, the rain was coming down so hard I could barely see. When the rainstorm turned into a mini-hurricane, I abandoned the Inn River trail and headed for Waldkraiburg, the nearest town that looked like it might have a hotel. It was while I was looking for a room that I had my accident.

I picked myself up and wrestled my bike upright.

"Heavy load," said the man. He was sitting beneath an awning at the nearby sidewalk cafe.

"Yeah," I mumbled, "heavy. Hey, do you know if there's a hotel around here?"

He thought for a moment. "I'm sure there is, but I'm not sure where."

"Okay, thanks," I said, "I'll just ride around till I find one." I rode down the street, then turned and was a block over when I heard someone shout. It was the fellow from the coffee shop. He caught up to me, saying, "You look beat, why don't you come with me? You can spend the night at my daughter's and my apartment."

I didn't hesitate. "You bet!" I said, and introduced myself. His name was Hans, apparently in his mid-forties. We walked a few blocks to the building where he and his daughter lived, where he fixed us a dinner of steamed soya beans, carrots and tofu. It was delicious. He explained how I could make the same recipe and gave me a bag of soya beans to take with me. I had a hot shower and laid my sleeping bag out in their spare room. It was the first time I'd been dry all day long.

I got a late start out of Waldkraiburg the next morning. As I needed to pick up supplies, Hans helped me do some shopping. I'd been looking for powdered milk but could never find it in the European stores. Hans said it was not something Europeans commonly use and suggested baby formula, so I bought a box. We had tea at a bakery and talked a while; then I glanced at my watch and saw it was past 10:30. Saying goodbye to Hans, I split, and then circled around the area for an hour getting good and lost, so that it wasn't until nearly noon that I found the correct route and was really on my way again.

Fall had arrived and the day was cold and windy. The trees were shedding their leaves, and I could see my breath. The September days were getting short; night came on quickly, and it was dark by 8:00 p.m. It wouldn't be long before snow began to fall in the Alps. I'd have to get a move on. I sure didn't want to get caught in another blizzard!

Innsbruck

I rode south along the river, passing through Rosenheim, Kufstein, and Schwaz, covering the 160 kilometers from Waldkraiburg to Innsbruck, in two days. It took me some time to find the campground, but I finally stumbled upon it and set my tent up on a grassy spot at the base of a tall cliff. I had decided to take a rest day before I tackled the Brennerpass. Though it's the lowest pass in the Alps, it's still over 4,000 feet high, and I wanted to be good and rested. Besides, it was Innsbruck, a genuine Olympic site! You can see the ski jump from the bahnhof. The next morning, I buttoned up my tent and rode into town, where I stopped at a pastry shop and had a cup of tea and a croissant. The weather was sunny and clear, but cooler here than it had been lower down. I had researched the Brennerpass and learned that there was a bike trail most of the way up. There was only one short section of about five kilometers where cyclists had to ride with traffic. It sounded like a fine trip, but just for fun, I thought I'd stop at the train station and see what a ticket over the Alps cost.

"For you and your bicycle, ten euros," the lady behind the desk said. "The next possible departure is at 12:40.

"Oh, I don't want a ticket," I laughed. "Just curious." I thanked her and left.

The bahnhof in Innsbruck is a main terminal for rail and bus traffic between northern and southern Europe, so it's busy even on a Sunday. It's set up like a mall, with all kinds of stores, shops and fast food joints. I wandered into a bookshop thinking I might pick up a map; I'm always on the lookout for good maps. I couldn't find one I wanted, but I as I browsed, a big poster caught my attention — a photomontage of a road leading up through the Alps. Huge, glacier-clad peaks towered all around, and in the foreground, a mountain climber stood draped in alpine climbing accoutrements looking very stout and brave. He had what looked like a dueling scar below his right eye. *Boy, those mountains sure did look steep.* It got me to thinking, and I left the bookstore and went back to the ticket counter. I stood in front of the same blond lady. "I'm just wondering, you know, but could you . . . uh . . . tell me how long the trip is from . . ." She must have remembered me from before, because she didn't let me finish.

"From Innsbruck to Brenner at the top of the pass?" she said.

"Uh, yeah, that," I mumbled.

"Fifty minutes. But you must go by bus; the tracks are being repaired."

"Oh, bus, huh, then they probably won't be able to take my bike and all my gear."

"Is not a problem," she said, "there's plenty of room."

"Well, it really doesn't matter, because like I said before, I'm just curious. You see, I'm going to ride up the pass."

She was doing something on her computer, studying the screen, and she glanced up and gave me the once-over. I'm pretty sure I saw her shake her head. She returned her attention to her computer. "Do you want that ticket for today or tomorrow?"

"Let's make it tomorrow," I said.

She began tapping keys. "I'll book you on the afternoon departure."

Chapter Eighteen: Italy

I learned long ago not to get my hopes up. I knew that few experiences live up to expectations, so I should have realized that I was setting myself up for disappointment. I had read about the region and was looking forward to a profound historical experience. After all, the Brennerpass is one of the oldest pathways between northern and southern Europe. It's been in use since prehistoric times, and the Romans, who controlled the area until the fifth century, built the first road over it 300 years before that. That's over 1,800 years ago. As I bounced along in the bus, I conjured up visions of Roman legions marching over this same ground on their way to quell an uprising of the Germanic tribes of the far north.

At around 4,500 feet above sea level, it's the lowest, and most coveted, of the trans-European Alpine passes. It has been under the rule of the Romans, the Austrians, and the Italians. It's where Adolf Hitler and Benito Mussolini met to celebrate their Pact of Steel. With all the important things that had happened there, I was sure that the town of Brenner, at the top, would be a historical treasure trove, and I planned to spend some time immersing myself in its rich heritage. Boy, was I mistaken. Instead of ancient ruins and museums, I found an eclectic mix of modern businesses where you can get anything from souvenir lederhosen to a pizza. There's even an outlet store. There are a few traditional buildings, but I saw nothing that looked older than a few decades. What a letdown.

But what the town itself lacks, the setting more than makes up for. Wooded mountains rise dramatically from the narrow valley, and a beautiful bicycle trail winds its way from the pass down through the Italian Alps.

The Descent

The bus let me off in the center of town. There was one other cyclist onboard who turned out to be an American, about my age, and traveling as light as I was heavy. As we got to talking, I found that Bob was from the San Francisco Bay area and was in Italy for a two-week tour. Since the town turned out to be a bust, I decided to join Bob and head down the pass right away.

The Brennerpass bike trail

The bike trail took us on a winding, high-speed descent into Italy. We rode beside tumbling streams, through wooded glens, and past steep hillside fields where workers raked hay by hand. The trail seemed to follow a course that intentionally provided the steepest descents and tightest corners. Covered in ice, it would have made a good bobsled course.

Bob was in front, and I watched as he drifted around a tight left-hand sidewinder and out of sight. I braked for the turn and leaned into the hill, then let it run on the straightaway. As the bike went faster and faster, I got that oh-boy-here-we-go sensation in the pit of my stomach. I was afraid to take my eyes off the trail long enough to look at my speedometer.

It was late afternoon when we coasted into Sterzing Vipiteno, a medieval village with a cathedral, clock tower and narrow, cobblestone streets. Sterzing Vipiteno is a tourist town, and we had to dismount and walk our bikes across the crowded town square. It was then that I noticed my rear wheel was rubbing. I had broken it in Germany and bought a cheap replacement that had given me problems from the start, and now it was so bad that I couldn't continue. Bob had to go on, so we said our goodbyes; then I unloaded my bike and overhauled the wheel in the village square while tourists watched, pestered me with questions, and snapped photos. By the time the repair was complete, it was early evening. I found the tourist information center and got directions to a campground a few kilometers south of town.

I awoke the next morning to find everything coated with a thin glaze of frozen dew, so I wore a windbreaker for the first few kilometers. With the exception of a few short climbs, the several days it took me to reach the lowlands were spent gliding effortlessly down through the Italian Alps. The weather was clear but not too hot, and the riding was pure bliss. But the nights were cold, and I spent a few hours each morning shivering in the chilly air. I found I was having fond thoughts of those scorching, hot days I had spent in Germany, and I was looking forward to more of the same along the beaches of the Mediterranean.

The Beach

It was as though I had my own private resort. I had a tiki bar and a white sand beach all to myself. I waded out fifty meters into the warm Mediterranean, and the water came up only to my waist. It was mid-September now; summer was over, and the resorts along this stretch of the north Italian coast were practically vacant. I sipped my beer and watched as the last sliver of the Great Magnet sank beneath the horizon.

Just a day before, I'd been riding in a torrential downpour.

High winds and chill temperatures made riding not only miserable but dangerous. The fine weather of the first few days in the Alps had deteriorated, and it rained steadily. I rode through the first day, but five or six hours into the second day, I could feel the warning signs. My hands and feet were numb and my muscles reacted sluggishly. I'd toughed it out long enough. It was time to get in out of the weather.

I had left the scenic Alps behind and was now riding through the agricultural, industrial, residential and commercial areas of far-north Italy. As I neared the outskirts of Trento, I got lost and wound up on a rural road that dead-ended after fifteen kilometers. It was disheartening to have to backtrack, and by the time I reached the main road, I was in a dark funk. I rode back to the last intersection, a four-way, and stopped and stood in the driving rain, trying to decide which branch to take. There was a lot of traffic, and each time a truck passed I got doused with road slush.

I picked a road and began pedaling. Soon, I reached a freeway on-ramp and had to turn around. Now I stood at the same intersection again. I was getting frustrated. Would I just keep going around in circles all day? Well, there was only one option left; if it turned out to be a dud, I didn't know what I'd do. A few kilometers along, I spotted a gas station and pulled in. There were two fellows standing just outside the door talking, and I asked one of them for directions. His English wasn't good, and my Italian was nonexistent, but we were able to communicate well enough that I found my way into town.

Planning to find a cheap hotel or hostel in Trento, I rode through the centro keeping my eyes peeled for a likely place. As I pedaled slowly along, another bike tourer pulled up beside me. "Hey," he said, "are you the American?" He sounded German.

"American?" I said, "I'm *an* American."

"I was riding with some guys yesterday who said there was an American on the trail who's riding around the world. Is that you?"

It all came back to me. I'd ridden with three cyclists the day before and we'd stopped and had a soggy lunch together. I suppose they'd told him about me.

"Yeah," I said, "I'm the crazy bastard, where are you going?"

He smiled. "I'm getting the train here in Trento. I came from Munich and I've had enough of this crappy weather. Two days of rain is enough for me. I'm quitting!"

The train sounded like a good idea. Besides, it would be a way to get out of the rain for a lot less than what a hotel would cost. We found the train station and watched each other's bikes while we bought tickets. His train was on a different track, so we said so long, and after a short wait I wrestled my bike onto a train bound for Viareggio, on the coast. I changed trains four times that day and arrived at the Mediterranean coast about 10:30 at night. At a cabstand where I stopped for directions, I found that it was only a few kilometers to the nearest campground. I found the place, checked in, and set up my tent. It was still wet and musty from the foul weather up in the Alps, but it soon dried out nicely in the warm Mediterranean climate, and so did I.

Life of Leisure

She was standing at the side of the road in a wide spot with room enough for just one car. I didn't see her at first. It wasn't until she called out to me that I noticed her breasts were exposed. When I finally looked her way, she crossed her arms over her chest and gave me a coy smile, then said something in Italian that sounded like a come-on. I was past her before it registered. Then, *Jesus*, I thought, *she might have been a prostitute!* A few meters farther along, there was another, and in a few more meters, another. I was incredulous. These women were plying their wares on the side of the highway five kilometers or more from the nearest town. I guess they went back in the woods to deliver their services, but I just couldn't believe anyone would actually pull their car over and trot back into the bushes to have congress with a hooker. Was I in for a surprise. Later, along a similar stretch of wooded countryside, I saw four or five empty cars parked in wide spots with well-worn paths leading into the forest.

I'd been slowly making my way down the Mediterranean coast from Valparisio to Tirrenia to Vada and Livorno. I had my choice of campgrounds and seemed to pass one every few kilometers. The weather was perfect, sunny but not too warm. I had spent the night at a campground, Camping Tripesce, just south of Livorno. When I was leaving the next morning, the owner called out to me to stop. *Crap*, I thought, *what did I do this time?*

"Where are you going from here?" he asked.

"I'm riding around the world," I told him.

"You rode here from America?"

"Yup."

"Come with me, I have something for you."

I followed him to a storeroom, where he rummaged around and produced a beautiful cycling jersey with the Camping Tripesce logo. "Here, this is for you. Send me a picture when you get far away!" I thanked him and promised I'd send him a photo from somewhere.

The route I was riding hugged the coast, rarely out of sight of the sea. There was only one hill worth mentioning, and that only two or three kilometers long. It was near Piombino, and at the top, that I was rewarded with a spectacular view of the Mediterranean Sea. Off in the distance, I could see big cargo ships, and beyond lay mountainous Corsica. While I was stopped, I checked my map and saw that I was not too far from the Isle of Elba, where they exiled Napoleon the first time. From near Piombino, the road took me inland, and I soon left the sea behind. Now I was riding through farm country and becoming a little worried about finding a place to camp. But as if on cue, I rounded a corner and saw the familiar tent sign that indicates a campground. When I arrived, I thought I'd gotten lost again because the place looked more like a farm than a campground. It turned out to be both. I'd seen something similar in Holland when I stayed at a campground that was also a dairy farm. Since this particular farm/campground was a vineyard, I bought a bottle of their estate wine and had it with my dinner that night.

In Rome

My bike was getting in worse and worse shape. The back wheel gave me the most trouble. I would have to stop several times a day, unload everything, turn the bike upside down, and spend half an hour truing the wheel. Though the wheel was the worst, there were other things wrong, too: The chain and gears were so worn that the chain constantly skipped, and it would get stuck two or three times a day. All that roadside maintenance made for slow going and a lot of frustration. It seemed as if my hands were always covered in grease. I was still 190 kilometers from Rome when my bike quit all together. The wheel was so beat up that I could no longer make it straight enough that it didn't rub. Limping into the town of Grosseto, I bought a train ticket to Rome.

I'd decided I'd like to spend the winter in Rome. One of my goals has always been to live in a foreign city, so for weeks I'd been perusing the Rome room-for-rent ads. I even posted an ad of my own on Craigslist Rome and got a few interesting offers, but not the kind I was looking for. I don't speak or read Italian, so when I got a response, I'd ask an English-speaking waiter or clerk or cop to translate for me. Some of the messages were of a sexual nature, and their translations afforded a few awkward moments. Solicitations aside, by the time I unloaded my bike in Rome, I'd still had no offers. I found a hostel a few blocks from the train station and checked in.

It was a bare-bones place with cement floors. Steel-framed bunk beds with thin mattresses and sagging springs lined the walls. Next to the entrance was a row of metal lockers with flimsy doors. My gear took up two lockers, and I had my bike locked to a railing downstairs. It felt a little weird to be separated from my meager possessions, but it felt good, too. I sat on the bed and scoured the want ads, but every room for rent was far out of my price range.

I gave my bike a close inspection and made an inventory of the parts I would need to make it roadworthy. The chain and gears were all worn, the main steering bearings were shot. My bike needed a complete overhaul, and getting it back in shape would take a lot more time and money than I had bargained for.

I was physically beat, too. It seemed that I couldn't sleep or eat enough. I was thin as a rail, and I gorged myself on Rome's wonderful street pizza several times a day and took naps.

I thought about pushing on to Greece or Turkey, where the rents were cheaper, and wintering there, but I knew the bike couldn't make another five miles, let alone 500. I also knew that I was in no shape to tackle another big ride. I needed rest as badly as my bike needed an overhaul. With my bike out of commission, and no prospect of getting it fixed, I was stuck in Rome. Okay, Rome's not a bad place to get "stuck," but I didn't have the money to live there. There was only one thing left to do: I would fly home to Seattle, rebuild my bike and rest, and then come back and pick up where I'd left off. But before I boarded a plane, I wanted to see Rome. I also needed time to pack my belongings and find a box for my bicycle. Booking two more nights at my hostel, I split my time between playing tourist and rounding up supplies for packing.

Rome is not a bicycle town. Most people get around on motor scooters, so there aren't a lot of bike shops. I located one, and on a bright, sunny morning, I walked the five kilometers to the place. Though no one there spoke English, I got a heavy-duty cardboard box, that a new bike had been shipped in, for free. I couldn't lug it back to my hostel, so the store owner agreed to hold it for me until the following day; I'd get a cab and come back for it then. However, talking with one of my roommates that evening I discovered that there was a bike shop a few short blocks from my hostel. *Hot damn!* I thought, and I made my way through the dark streets. When I arrived at about 9:00 p.m., I was delighted to find the shop still open, and in front, stacked up with the other trash, was the most beautiful cardboard bike box I'd ever seen. One of the shop mechanics was on the sidewalk working on a customer's bike, and I asked him if I could have the box. "Yes," he said, "help yourself."

When I started to remove the other cardboard scraps that had been stuffed inside the box, he stopped me. "No!" he said firmly, "you must take it all."

Ruins, Rome

There was at least twenty pounds of recycling in the pile. What was I going to do with all that cardboard? "But I'm on a bicycle," I protested.

He shrugged and scowled. "All or nothing," he insisted. What was I to do? I turned and walked away, glancing one last time at my beautiful bike box.

Now it was the day before my departure, and I had a lot to do to get ready. I hired a cab and picked up my box, hauled it and my bicycle up two flights to the luggage room, and got to work. As I was taking off the rear rack, the desk clerk came back and stood watching me. Finally he spoke. "So you are going to . . . ?"

I was sitting on the floor turning a wrench. "I'm going to disassemble my bike and put it in that big box over there," I said, smiling. "Then, I'll take it to the airport for shipment to the USA."

He looked at the bike and the various tools and parts scattered on the floor, then back at me. "It will all fit?" he said.

"Sure," I replied, "I do it all the time."

He paused and looked around. "Well, could you do it as quickly as you can?"

I grinned. "I'll hurry up every chance I get."

With everything packed, I got a good night's sleep, rose early, and had breakfast at a sidewalk cafe not far from the Coliseum. I'd arranged for a cab the night before, and at 11:00 a.m., I headed for the airport. The taxi let me off at the wrong terminal, and when I tried to board the shuttle bus with all my gear, the driver refused to let me on. Some of the passengers offered to help, but the driver was adamant, and shut the door in my face. *Great*, I thought, *now what am I going to do?* I went to the information desk and inquired. The lady there made a call, and in a few minutes, two uniformed guards appeared, picked up my luggage and bike box, and escorted me to the bus stop. The bus pulled up, and this time the driver never said a word. One of the guards gave him a dressing down and apologized to me for the inconvenience. The guards rode with me to the terminal and helped me navigate through customs, staying with me up to the gate. It was a fine farewell to Italy.

A day later, I was home in Seattle. My daughter Brittney and her husband, Marty, who were house-sitting for me, met me at the airport and drove me home. For the first time in five months, I was again sleeping under my own roof.

Chapter Nineteen: Intermission

I suppose it's time to talk about my bicycle. It didn't make it to Seattle with me; the airline had lost it, and it took them several days to locate it. But finally it arrived on my doorstep, and I set about making repairs. It had been in bad shape when I purchased it from a second-hand shop in Seattle a few years before. I had rebuilt it from the ground up and thought I had a pretty solid platform for riding 'round the world, but when put to the test, many of the components wore out prematurely, broke, or just weren't up to the task. I'd learned a thing or two about what makes a good tourer, and this time I was determined to put together a machine that would meet the challenge.

The basic bike was still good. Though I'd put a few dents in it and the paint had taken a beating, the frame, a high-quality, steel Trek 520 touring model, needed little attention. But just about everything else would have to be rethought.

I started by having wheels built with sturdier rims, designed for bicycle polo. The shifters had worn out in the Czech Republic and were held together with glue and good intentions, so I bought a new set of bar-end paddles. The gears were barely functional and had to be replaced as well. Both derailleurs, the steering bearings, tires, and pedals all got upgrades, and I splurged on a new, bigger handlebar bag. I had the frame rust-treated and added generator-powered lights. It took two months to finish the job, but by December it was done, and I spent the next few months fine-tuning and making adjustments. I took a lot of multi-day tours to test my newly-outfitted bike, and by February, it and I were ready go.

East to West

I had decided that instead of returning to Rome, I'd reverse course and go from east to west. My plan was to ride through Southeast Asia, across India, and north to Nepal. The USA was still engaged in a war in the Middle East, and I felt it would be imprudent to try to ride there, so I would skip that part of the world for now and fly from Nepal to Turkey and on to Rome, where I'd finish my trip.

Part Three: Asia
Chapter Twenty: Vietnam

Saigon

On February 20th, I boarded a plane for Vietnam. I had talked my good friend, Mike, into accompanying me for the first two weeks, and we met at a hotel near the train station in Saigon the next day.

I'd never been to Asia, and the culture shock hit me the minute I walked out of the Saigon airport. A crowd of at least a thousand milled around in front; most of the people wearing surgical masks and conical bamboo hats called non la's. I hired a cab from the taxi hustler, we loaded my gear in back, and plunged into the late afternoon rush hour traffic. I was amazed at the abandon with which the Vietnamese drive their motor scooters. The streets are choked with them and the locals zoom them in and out of traffic with seemingly little regard for their own wellbeing. Instead of regular motorcycle helmets, most Vietnamese scooter riders wear a kind of polo helmet. The flimsy lids don't provide much protection, but they are the height of Saigon style nevertheless.

Mike and I had decided to take the train north to Hue and then ride our bikes back down the coast. We spent the first two days in Saigon sightseeing, and on the third morning headed to the train station to buy our tickets. But we ran into trouble when the man running the freight depot refused to accept our bikes. We tried to explain that we'd need them to ride back down Highway 1, but it seemed that no amount of gesturing and phrase-book pleading was going to get our bikes on that train; he sat placidly behind his desk and refused to budge. It wasn't until one of the workmen motioned for us to detach the panniers from the bikes that we finally got things straightened out. "I guess we have to take our baggage with us on the train," Mike said with a shrug, as two workmen rolled our bikes away into the darkened recesses of the cavernous freight hub.

It was a short walk from the freight depot to the passenger terminal, but loaded down as we were with bulging panniers, it was a hot, uncomfortable 200-meter schlep. We made a pitiful sight as we struggled through the crowds, dodging motor scooters and jitneys. The locals pointed and laughed. They seemed to find our plight hilarious.

Through the Jungle

We shared our four-birth cabin with a young British couple who were headed for the beach at Na Trang. The train left on time, and it wasn't long before I was lulled to sleep by the rhythmic rocking and click-clack-click of the old train's northward progress. I slept soundly that night, and bought hard-boiled eggs the next morning from a woman pushing a cart down the aisle. Not being used to Vietnamese money, I gave her too much. Instead of change, she made up for the difference with extra eggs. At noon, we had rice and boiled cabbage.

Near the end of our trip, the old locomotive pulled us up through lush mountains, our already unhurried pace slowing to an even more casual fifteen to twenty miles an hour. As we ascended higher, we were awarded spectacular birds-eye views of the rough, surf-carved cliffs far below. The jungle crowded in even closer than it had lower down. Soon we reached the summit, where thick fog limited vision to a few ghostly meters. The ride back down to sea level and the outskirts of Hue was shrouded in mist and a steadily-falling rain. When we reached Hue, around 4:30 in the afternoon, we were greeted by an unpleasant surprise: our bikes wouldn't arrive until the next afternoon, which meant we'd have to spend an extra day there.

We gathered our baggage, hailed a cab, and checked into our French-colonial hotel a few blocks from the Hue train station. At a small street-side restaurant a short walk from our hotel, we had a dinner of soba noodles and shrimp, squeezing our oversized bodies into plastic chairs that in America would be more fitting for a kindergarten than a restaurant. Since we were waiting for our bikes to arrive, we spent the next day sightseeing. There were Communist propaganda posters and billboards everywhere. Most showed images of Ho Chi Minh. He's the George Washington, Abraham Lincoln and JFK of Vietnam all rolled into one, and his picture is on everything, even the money.

Hue was the scene of an epic battle between U.S. forces and the North Vietnamese during the Tet Offensive nearly forty years before. The U.S. Marines spent weeks fighting block by block to retake the city. One of the most ferocious battles was for the provincial capital located in an ancient complex known as The Citadel. We crossed the bridge over the Perfume River to the north side of the city and had a look at where all the fighting had taken place. It was a sobering experience.

The next day, our bikes arrived and we spent what we thought was our last night in Hue preparing for the trip south down Highway 1. We arose early and started out, but soon ran into trouble. An hour outside Hue we had stopped at a wide spot so I could investigate a rubbing fender, when Mike made an observation. "Looks like your steering is loose," he said, twisting the forks out of alignment to demonstrate. He was right, and I was giving the bolt a few degrees of a turn to tighten it when I heard a snap and the bolt spun freely. I had broken it.

"Son of a . . ."

"That didn't sound good," Mike said. We traded knowing looks.

My heart sank. There was no way to steer the bike now. It was out of commission until a new part could be found. And we sure as heck weren't going to find it out here in the middle of rural Vietnam.

As I fretted and fumed, Mike removed the stem and held up the tightening bolt. "Yeah, you stripped it alright. This bike isn't going anywhere except in the back of a truck." He went over to a nearby road sign and took a picture of it with his iPhone. Then I could see him making a call. Walking back to where I stood, he said, "It's all taken care of. "I got ahold of our hotel in Hue and sent them a picture of our location. They're sending a cab."

When we got back to our hotel, the manager took the broken pieces to a machine shop, where a new part was fabricated. I reinstalled it, and the next morning we really were on our way.

The coast of Vietnam is home to a spectacular mix of breathtaking ocean and mountain views, ancient villages and tranquil farmland. Highway 1, the thin ribbon of pavement that cuts through this bucolic scene, is an ugly scar. Trucks, busses, scooters and cars rocket along the road at breakneck speed, passing sometimes three abreast and always with a heavy hand on the horn. To see the Vietnamese drive, you'd think they were the rudest people on Earth. But off the road and out of their vehicles you'd be hard pressed to find kinder, more generous people. Mike got a flat tire the first afternoon as we rode through a small village. Within a few minutes, half the tiny hamlet's population showed up to help.

There was no hesitation, the townspeople simply saw what needed to be done and they pitched in.

We spent the first night on Highway 1 in an old colonial hotel and were treated to dinner at the little restaurant next door. The cook came out and asked what we liked, and whipped up a seafood-and-rice plate to our order.

Our rooms were adjacent, sharing a common wall that stopped just below the ceiling, leaving a twelve-inch gap at the top. The building was a leftover from French-colonial times and had high ceilings, ornate windows and doors, and a brass-and-bamboo-bladed fan that hung lifeless above the bed. Everything was damp from the humidity; it wasn't unusual to spot small green lizards clinging motionless on the walls and ceiling.

We knew that the next day's ride would involve climbing Hi Van Pass, the highest road in Vietnam, but the next morning, the hotel proprietor, whom we knew only as "D," suggested that we skip pedaling up it and ride in his cousin's truck instead. It wasn't yet 8:00, and the day was already sweltering. We decided to take D's advice and hitched a ride to the top, where there's an old French fort that was taken over by the Americans during the war. It has a big parking lot, and what was once a military outpost is now a tourist trap. Stalls line the dirt lot, and peddlers hawk their wares to the throngs of camera-toting Western tourists that pile out of an endless line of busses. D and his cousin helped us unload our bikes, and we attached our panniers, made sure everything was secure, thanked D, and started down the south side of the pass.

That highway is steep, and soon we were flying along at better than thirty miles an hour. I was in the lead, following a motorcycle, when suddenly and without warning the motorcycle rider's helmet came off, bounced down the road, and headed straight for me. I slammed on my brakes, swerved, and nearly crashed into a ditch at the side of the road. After retrieving the helmet and returning it to the motorcyclist, we took a break and mused about what a strange occurrence we'd just witnessed. Little did we know that it would be one of the least strange things we'd see in Vietnam.

From near the summit, it was a terrific six-mile plunge down to Da Nang and then another twenty-five-mile ride in a scorching headwind to the small riverside resort town of Hoi An. We rented rooms with balconies overlooking the Thu Bon River in a new hotel that had just opened that week. Maybe because we were the only guests, the lady who ran the place hovered over us like a mother hen. There were fresh towels every day, and the dining room was open early and late. It had a good bar.

Going With the Flow

Traffic in Vietnam is beyond hectic. Scooters swerve in and out of lanes, zipping past trucks and busses with only a hair's width to spare. It's a kind of orchestrated madness, and a sane person would have no part of it. But we had the day off from bicycling, so we decided to rent scooters and head to the beach. We gassed up at an ancient, hand-crank pump, donned helmets, twisted the throttles back, and plunged into eastbound traffic. Ever since Saigon, I'd wanted to get my hands on one of these suicide machines. I'd been watching how adept the Vietnamese are at riding them and thought I had a handle on the strategy and technique. I'd had a dirt bike as a kid and fancied myself a pretty good moto rider; a scooter should be easy. The idea of jumping on a sixty-horsepower, 500-pound street rocket and ripping through the unfamiliar, narrow streets like a Harlan County moonshine runner had a certain bent appeal, and I was convinced that no trip to Asia would be complete without the experience. It was a blast! It took only a few minutes to master the various maneuvers, and soon I was speeding, tailgating and lane-switching with the best of them. We rode to China Beach, a main R&R site for GI's during the war, and had lunch at a seaside restaurant. We drank a pretty good bottle of Vietnamese white wine and watched the fishing boats ply the waters of the South China Sea.

A Gracious Host

That evening, we decided to splurge on dinner and asked a doorman at a swanky hotel if he could recommend a restaurant. He gave us directions, and we wound around back streets until we found what we thought was the place; we could see the lights from the road. Walking our bikes down the long path, we settled in at a large table. In a flash, a man approached. "Do you speak English?" I asked.

The fellow smiled. "Of course," he replied.

"Well," I said, "do you think we could have *menus*?"

The man gave me a questioning look, paused, and then, "This is my home," he said, ". . . but you are certainly welcome."

Mike and I traded astonished looks. Instead of finding the restaurant, we'd stumbled into a private residence!

We were embarrassed, of course, and apologized profusely, getting up to leave, but the man would have none of it. "No, please stay," he said, "it would be my honor to serve you." We sat with him for a while and had tea, met his family, and bounced his young children on our knees. The only member who was less than enthusiastic about our presence was the matriarch, who sat placidly nearby and kept an eye on us.

The next day we left Hoi An and soon were again on Highway 1 heading south toward Saigon. I had read that the Vietnamese were expert bargainers, and I was anxious to test my Yankee horse-trading skills against these accomplished wheeler-dealers. We had stopped at a kind of farmer's market at the side of the road in a big dirt lot. I'd made my selections and was at the cashier with my groceries. "Fifty thousand," said the woman. She held up a bill to show what she meant. "Fifty thousand," she repeated and started putting my purchases in a plastic bag. I shook my head,

"Too much," I said. I crossed my arms in front of my chest and assumed a defiant expression. "Thirty," I said, and held up three fingers. I pointed at the three boxes of cookies I'd selected from among the piles of packaged foods, gizmos and assorted gimcracks jammed onto a small table in this crowded market. All around me, commerce was going on at a furious pace. Every imaginable fruit, vegetable, mineral and animal, alive, dead, butchered, boiled and sautéed, was being bought, sold, traded and bartered. Strange, intoxicating and exotic scents mingled in the smoky air. "Thirty," I repeated, and held up some bills.

Now another woman jostled for position, edging the first woman out of the way. "Ok, thirty," she smiled, and nodded as the first woman handed me the bag. This was my first attempt at bargaining with the Vietnamese, and it had been a total success. I paid and thanked the woman, all the while congratulating myself on my shrewdness. I guess my smugness showed, because as I was leaving, the woman I'd been dealing with gave me a knowing grin and held up two fingers. "Twenty," she said, "you could have got it for twenty."

Highway 1

Vietnam's coast and Highway 1 are a study in contradictions. It's not uncommon to see a truck passing a bus, passing a car, passing a motor scooter, passing a water buffalo all at the same time and bearing down on oncoming traffic at sixty miles an hour, horn blaring. At the same time, you're likely to view a quiet pastoral scene, a family at the communal dinner table, or a solitary worker, her white, conical bamboo non la in stark relief against the dark green of a rice paddy.

Unlike in the cities, out in the "bush" bicycles seem to be one of the main modes of transportation, especially with the young. We often found ourselves among groups of school children dressed in their smart, crisp uniforms, riding two and three to a bike. They would see us and smile, shout out greetings, and wave happily. Many times I feared for the children's lives as huge trucks and busses sped past on the highway mere inches from where they rode.

Camping was not an option along Highway 1; there were just too many people and very few unoccupied spaces where we could set up a tent. That meant we had to stay in hotels, which were clean, safe and cheap; we rarely spent more than eight dollars U.S. per night. We usually had breakfast at the hotel, but lunch was a variable option. Often, it consisted of whatever we could find at one of the ubiquitous food stalls or truck plazas, where I once had a garlic-flavored ice cream cone and some kind of ginger-tasting peanut brittle stuck to a disc of hard rice bread.

School kids, Highway 1

But neither of us was prepared for the withering heat and energy-draining humidity of coastal Vietnam. We would make good time in the early mornings, but by 2:00 in the afternoon, the wind had usually picked up, the heat set in, and we slowed our pace and stopped often for shade and water. The last ten or twelve miles were taken at a leisurely pace, and we would start looking for a hotel by midafternoon. We'd check in to our hotel and then seek out a place to eat. Dinner would be a rice or noodle-and-broth dish with bread and a Tiger beer. Back in my room, I'd grab a quick shower, watch Vietnamese TV, and then, by 8:00 p.m., be in bed, and asleep by 9:00. For breakfast, we'd have fried eggs, sliced cucumbers, rice and tea, all for about twenty-five cents U.S.

We never knew what strange sight would greet us around the next corner. It was not uncommon to see scooters zipping by loaded down with all kinds of merchandise. I saw scooters hauling TV's, small refrigerators, once even three full-grown hogs. I'd thought I'd seen everything until I saw two fellows speed past on a scooter with a six-foot canoe. No, really, an aluminum canoe. They were wearing it like a hat!

Every conceivable form of commerce takes place along Highway 1. Rows upon rows of narrow, tin-roofed, concrete stalls about the size of small one-car garages line every village street. None are more than ten feet wide, and all are open to the road. Usually, the whole family works there and lives above in a small loft. We saw farmers pedaling the morning's produce and fishermen selling their catch. Machinists and metal smiths were banging and grinding and cutting and welding, sometimes producing goods, sometimes disassembling them and turning them into something else. Once we came upon a stalled semi truck half-blocking the southbound lane. As we pulled alongside, we were amazed to see the driver lying beneath the engine making a repair with an arc welder. Sparks flew everywhere, and we feared that the fuel that had spilled on the road would catch ablaze at any moment. As we passed by stalls, we could see motorbikes and bicycles being repaired, and fans, refrigerators, wire fencing, sheet metal, shovels, scythes and myriad other gizmos, whatchamacallits and thingamajigs hanging from the bamboo rafters of the shanties. One whole block of stalls sold nothing but caged birds.

We could sometimes find an English speaker, but most people in the bush spoke only Vietnamese, or maybe French. Usually, I could make myself understood, but things took a strange twist one day. We had stopped at one of the little food shacks you see everywhere along Highway 1. There were a few tables and a counter where elderly Vietnamese women were grouped. I'd had a big breakfast a few hours before, and now I desperately needed to use the restroom, but I couldn't make the ladies understand. It seemed that no amount of phrase-book pleading could communicate my urgent need to the wise-looking old woman who was running the place. I had tried everything short of mime. Finally, her frustration clearly matching my own, she handed me a piece of chalk and pointed to the cement floor, nodding and poking her finger emphatically at the ground. The other women smiled and nodded and pointed, too. Whatever it was she wanted me to do, the rest of the women were in enthusiastic agreement. I was confused; was she instructing me to draw a target on the concrete and grab a squat right there in front of everyone? I'd never been to Vietnam, maybe that's just how they did things here. I looked at Mike, who had interpreted the exchange the same way I had, and we both burst out laughing. It took us a few moments to realize that she wanted me to write my request. With great relief, I scrawled "WC" on the cement, and the old woman smiled and directed me to the water closet around back.

Night Train to Saigon

We continued down the Vietnam coast at a leisurely pace, covering sixty to eighty kilometers a day. It soon became clear that we wouldn't make it to Saigon in time for Mike to catch his plane back to Seattle, so we decided to take the train from Dieu Tri. When we got to the station, we discovered that there were no sleeper cars available, so we bought tickets on the night train in what was called First Class. Boarding the train late that afternoon, we found our seats in a broken-down car that looked a hundred years old: It was dirty and crowded, and our seats had worn springs and sagging backs. Boxes, cages of animals and bundles of produce were stacked in the aisles. The cabin lights, the ones that worked, at least, flickered and buzzed, and that, along with the crowded and generally down-at-the-heels ambience of the place, made it impossible to sleep. The train stopped often, and it would take the old engine half an hour to get back up to twenty miles per hour. Then it would be time to stop at the next village, and the whole process would be repeated. The trip took forever.

We arrived at Saigon in the early morning hours well before sunrise. There was no announcement, the train just stopped and people began exiting. We got off and walked a few tens of yards along the tracks until we reached the front of the train and the Saigon station. We had reserved rooms at the hotel where we'd stayed the first few nights, and we walked the three or four blocks and checked in. I took a nap, and around 10:00 a.m. went downstairs to help Mike disassemble and box his bike for the flight home.

On the Town

Later that night we visited Saigon's tourist district, hailing a cab that let us off on a bustling, brightly lit avenue. When I'd first arrived in Vietnam, crossing the street was an adventure. My first attempt found me frozen midstream. Scooters, jitneys and cabs jostled for position like skaters in the Lower East Bay Roller Derby Semi-Finals. I'd stood wide-eyed as vehicles sped toward me, swerving out of the way at the last second. After a few near misses, I finally figured out a strategy for dealing with Saigon's manic traffic. I would look upstream into the confused mass of speeding metal and scan for patterns to emerge. Narrow lanes would appear for a few brief moments before being swallowed up. But it was enough: I would chart a course through the ever-changing rhythm of traffic, stopping momentarily to reconnoiter. When the opportunity presented itself, I'd sprint into one of the temporarily clear zones and watch for the next one to materialize.

After a while, I got into the flow and rhythm of the thing, so that by now, my last night in Saigon, I crossed the busiest street almost without thinking.

Walking past "nail salons" where scantily-clad young women beckoned us to come in and "get the works," we wound up in a street bar and drank Singapore Slings while watching the rich flow of humanity pass by. A woman approached us and sold me two pirated books: *Catcher in the Rye* and *Zen and the Art of Motorcycle Maintenance*.

Mike had a midmorning flight to catch the next day, so we had a few drinks and then retired to the hotel.

In the morning, we grabbed a cab to the airport, and I saw Mike off. I spent one more night in Saigon, and early the next morning loaded up my gear and headed west toward Cambodia.

Solo

The ride out of Saigon in the Monday-morning, rush-hour traffic was insane. But I had picked up a smart phone with GPS while I was in Seattle and used it to navigate to the edge of the city, getting onto a side road without much trouble. Unlike Highway 1 on the coast, the route I rode that day was nearly traffic-free as it meandered through rural villages and past upper-middle-class homes. I guess it was the Vietnamese version of suburbia. I stopped at a stall for breakfast, and since there was no place to lean my bike, I laid it on its side. When I went to pick it up later, some Vietnamese fellows passing by pitched in to help.

It was hot and humid as usual, and I had to stop several times to get cold drinks. At one stall, the waitress noticed my overheated condition and filled a plastic bag with ice for me to put on my head. I would soon cross the border, and I would miss the Vietnamese. I hoped the people in Cambodia would be as friendly.

Chapter Twenty-One: Cambodia

Though the U.S.-Vietnam War first comes to mind for most Americans, this part of the world has a long history of conflicts. Southeast Asia has been the theatre for revolutions, coups and, more recently, superpower proxy wars. One little-known war, to most Westerners at least, was the one between Vietnam and Kampuchea. Vietnam invaded Cambodia (Kampuchea) in 1979, tossing out the ruthless "Killing Fields" Khmer Rouge government and occupying the country for ten years. That war is in the living memory of many Southeast Asians, yet I sensed no bad blood between the people of the two nations. I guess when just getting by is often a struggle, grudges are an unaffordable luxury.

I thought I was getting used to the Asian culture. I'd seen a lot that looked strange, but nothing prepared me for what I was to encounter when I crossed the border at Moc Bai. I arrived late Monday afternoon, tired and a little weirded-out from the heat. I guess it showed, because the border officials, both Vietnamese and Cambodian, couldn't have been nicer and rushed me right through. After crossing the border, I went looking for a hotel with air conditioning. Instead of the usual bare-bones lodging I was used to, I was surprised to find a whole slew of glitzy, Las Vegas-style casino hotels lining both sides of the dusty road that ran through Krong Bavet, Cambodia. There must have been five or six of them, and what a strange sight they were! It was as though a section of The Strip had been plopped down in the middle of the jungle, flashing lights, gaudy colors and all. Yet somehow it worked. It was just one example of how adept many Asian cultures are at assimilating exotic constructs and making them their own. I was beginning to think I might have to spend the night in one, but I kept pedaling and soon found a nice guesthouse across from a market.

I got a late start the next morning, and it was crazy hot by the time I hit the road. The day before had taken a lot out of me. I'd ridden a hundred kilometers in the heat and humidity, and I still wasn't recovered. Even though it was flat, and I had a tailwind, I was soon too tired to go on. I stopped early in Svay Rieng, just twenty miles from Krong Bavet.

I had a wad of cash when I'd left that morning, so I didn't start to worry until I paid for my room in Svay Riegn. It was only seventeen dollars U.S., but when I counted up my bankroll afterward, I discovered that I had about two dollars left. That sure wasn't going to get me very far. The ATM around the corner, the only one in town, took only Visa, and I had MasterCard. I had 140 kilometers to go before reaching the next big town, Phnom Penh, where I was told I might find an ATM that would take my card. It was a terrible feeling to be so far from home and broke. I skipped dinner that night, reserving my money for the water I'd need to buy the next day.

In the morning, I filled every bottle I had from the hotel tap and started out at first light. It was cool for Cambodia, probably in the low eighties, and for several hours I clocked along at a fast twelve miles an hour. I would try to make Phnom Phen before dark, find an ATM, and get a room. A hundred and forty klicks, about seventy-seven miles, isn't an outrageous distance. I'd had some ninety- and one-hundred-mile days back in the USA, but because of the heat and humidity here in the jungle, my mileage was much less than that. Making it to Phnom Phen would be a challenge, but what choice did I have? I'd heard that the monks in Cambodia would put up travelers for free, and I decided that if I had to, I'd go begging at one of the many temples I'd seen along the road.

I was drinking a lot, and by 9:00 a.m. I was down to one bottle of water. About 11:00, thirsty and hungry, I rolled into the Mekong River town of Neak Leoung, which sits about halfway between my starting point and Phnom Phen. It was mistakenly bombed by a US B-52 in 1973 and almost destroyed, but today it's a bustling little place, and as I turned the corner on the main drag,

I spotted a bank displaying the MasterCard logo. I was saved! I took out an extra hundred dollars, vowing that thereafter I'd always have a C-note tucked away. At the hotel I found, I splurged on an air-conditioned suite.

A market springs up around the Neak Leong ferry landing every day, with all kinds of vendors selling everything from jelly-filled baguettes to live chickens. The place wasn't yet in full swing when I bought my ferry ticket the next morning; the sun wasn't up, but in the predawn light I could see farmers and fishermen arriving with their wares. I skipped breakfast, thinking I'd grab something at the market, but on the way to the river I spotted a woman with a plastic bag of whole pineapples balanced on her head. Through hand motions I indicated that I'd like to buy one. She took a pineapple out of the bag, whipped out a machete, and started chopping away. In a few moments, I was feasting on the freshest, sweetest pineapple you can imagine.

The river crossing took only a few minutes, and I rode off the ferry in a good mood, with a full stomach. The western side of the river was greener than the country I had been riding through since crossing into Cambodia. The road was good, and I made excellent time as I pedaled through villages of rough wooden huts teetering on tall supports and past colorful, ornate temples. I could see the red-robed priests going about their daily routines in the courtyards. Every few kilometers, I heard the singsong chants of acolytes broadcast over loudspeakers. I sped along in a happy mood, and before long I entered the outskirts of the capital, Phonm Penh. As I crossed the Baasac River on a modern bridge, I stopped in the middle to snap pictures of the many boats and ships that ply those waters. I went looking for a place to spend the night and stopped at an upscale hotel to check the prices, but I was buttonholed by a fellow before I could get in the door. "Are you looking for a hotel, sir?" he said.

"I am," I replied. "What's this place like?"

"Very expensive," he responded, shaking his head. "I have a

very fine place of lodging with air conditioning and an excellent restaurant for only twenty-five American."

"Lead the way," I said. "Let's take a look."

The hotel was a few blocks away and looked pretty good, so I checked in. Later in the day, I went walking along the manicured banks of the Mekong as it wound through the city. At a café where I stopped for a cold drink, the fellow behind the counter, noticing that I was American, asked if I would mind paying with U.S. dollars. I had a few bucks tucked away, so I obliged. But when he saw that the five-dollar bill I offered him was a bit worn, he said he could not accept it. "The banks here take only pristine American bills," he said. I shrugged and paid with Cambodian riels; it made no difference to me. While I was in Cambodia I tried many times, just for fun, to pass that fiver, but each time it was rejected.

Phnom Penh was a ghost town during the rule of the dictator Pol Pot, but today it's a vibrant, modern city, though much of the old French-colonial buildings still stand and the Royal Palace near the river is a fantastic vision of Khmer architecture.

I had met a fellow bike tourer outside Phnom Penh the day before who had just come from the city, and when I mentioned that I planned to visit the Angkor Wat Temple District, he recommended that instead of trying to ride my bike there I take the bus. "The road north of Phnom Penh is in terrible condition," he said. "Pretty much unrideable."

Back at the hotel that evening, I booked passage on the Golden VIP Bus line to Siem Reap, the staging area for trips to the Angor Wat Temple District. It would leave the next evening at 8:00 p.m. and arrive sometime in the wee hours of the morning. As the departure hour neared, I flagged down a tuk tuk and had the driver take me to the bus station, where I loaded my bicycle in the bowels of the bus and took my place on the upper deck. I had two seats all to myself and a panoramic view the whole eight hours. Taking the bus to Angkor Wat turned out to be a good decision. Just as I'd been warned, the road was a mess, and the bus bounced and swayed all over the place. We achieved zero G several times when it went airborne over big bumps.

Sometime during the night I woke up and noticed that the bus wasn't moving. A few people still dozed in their seats, and I could see other passengers milling around outside. We had stopped at a little roadside restaurant for a break. I got off and bought a boiled egg, eating it at a table near the edge of the jungle.

Angkor Wat

It was 3:00 a.m. when the driver let me off. I unloaded my bike and gear and the bus drove away. The few passengers who had disembarked with me melted into the night. I was alone. I looked around. Strange sounds drifted from the jungle. The air was humid and thick, clinging to me like something alive. It was dark as the inside of a cow, and I had no idea where I was or in what direction I should ride. I had reserved a room in a hotel somewhere in the city, and I could see dim, mist-smeared lights off in the distance; *was that the town?* I flicked on my headlight, keyed the address of the hotel into my phone, and, guided by the dim glow of the small screen, plunged into the darkness of that moonless night. Soon, I reached the heart of the city. Though it was early morning, music still blared from inside colorful, neon-lit nightclubs. Bleary-eyed merrymakers spilled out the doors and stumbled along the sidewalks, yelling and hooting as I pedaled by. Smiling nervously, I waved back. I rode and rode, but after a few dozen turns I was lost. I had given up on my phone's map and trusted to luck.

I was now in what looked like a residential neighborhood, with no streetlights. My generator lights had failed, and the feeble glow from my battery-powered headlight was next to useless. As I rode down a narrow dirt alley, two snarling dogs rushed out from behind a fence and gave chase, and it took all the adrenaline I had to outrun them. Later, I rode past a multi-story building with a security guard sitting in front smoking a cigarette, legs propped up on a table and drinking a beer. Littered tables and overturned chairs filled the small courtyard; evidently there had been a party not too long ago. He was the only sign of life, so I stopped to ask directions. When I showed him the address and name of the hotel I was looking for, he nodded and indicated that yes, this was it. I suspect that the true nature of my inquiry was lost in translation, and I doubted that I had in fact miraculously stumbled upon the right place, but it was a hotel, and I was prepared to settle for that. Trusting my bike to the guard, I went in, and to my dismay saw that dozens of people were sleeping on the lobby floor; I had to step over and around them to reach the front desk. But when I got there, the clerk told me to go away and come back in the morning. The owner had died, she explained, there'd been a wake, all the beds were filled, and the overflow simply slept on the floor.

I had no choice but to go looking for someplace else to spend what was left of the night. I tried to retrace my route to the heart of the city; surely there'd be someplace to sleep there, or at least an all-night bar where I could hunker down till daylight. A few blocks from the center of town, I passed a decent-looking building that I thought might be a hotel, so I rolled my bike across the patio and roused the fellow sleeping on the floor behind the front desk. He wasn't too happy to be awakened at such an hour, but he grudgingly rented me a room on the second floor.

Anyone Can Get You Anything

One of the appealing things about Asia is that, unlike in the Western world, boundaries between types of businesses are blurred and it often seems that anyone can get you anything. Nothing is written in stone. In America, it would be folly to try to rent a motorcycle at, say, a grocery store. But in Asia, such a transaction would be commonplace. If the proprietor didn't have a scooter to let, he would know someone who did and would arrange to have it delivered to your hotel with a helmet, gloves and a full tank of gas within the half hour. I bet I could have bought a goat from a dentist.

I had come to Siem Reap to see the temples, and as I lay in bed the next morning I fired up the Internet and looked for a guide. My search producing a confusing slew of options, I went downstairs to ask the desk clerk for advice.

"Oh, sir," he said when I inquired, "there is no need for you to go to any bother. Please help yourself to breakfast in our fine restaurant and your guide will be waiting for you at your leisure." Sure enough, when I'd eaten and showered, Than, my guide, was sitting in the lobby. When he saw me, he jumped up, grabbed my backpack and escorted me to his tuk tuk parked in front of the hotel. Such service! I felt like King Farouk!

Dancers, Angor Wat

We drove the dozen or so kilometers to the temple district, and Than let me off near an open-air restaurant where I had second breakfast. "Take as long as you want," he told me, "I'll meet you over there under that tree when you're done." I walked around the Hindu temples first; it took me an hour to see all I wanted to see. I know these centuries-old ruins should have enthralled me, but by noon I was ready to go home and soak my feet. The temples were worth seeing, but I've found that it's usually more interesting to knock around the common places where the locals go, such as cafes, markets, street kiosks and bookstores, and to avoid the usual pre-packaged tourist attractions.

I spent one more night in Siem Reap, got up before dawn, and rode the first half hour in the dark. I had to make 107 kilometers to reach the next town, Sisophon, before nightfall. As it was, I made excellent time and reached my destination in the late afternoon. I found a cheap hotel, checked in, took a shower and a nap, and around 6:00 p.m. was awakened by the sound of rain. Downstairs in the lobby, I found that a mini-typhoon was blowing outside. The wind howled and the rain fell in buckets. The street flooded and the electricity went off as a collective "Ohhh" rose spontaneously from the small crowd gathered in the lobby. The day turned suddenly dark. Lightning flashed, followed immediately by the crash of thunder. Damn! It was right on top of us! The big picture windows rattled in the gale. Outside, we could see a lone woman on a scooter, her head bowed into the wind, fighting her way up the flooded street. Now came a gust so powerful that it blew an aluminum awning off the roof and threw it across the street, crashing it against the side of an adjacent building. Then, as quickly as it started, it was over. The sun broke through, and soon the streets were dry. Though there was no juice for the fan, the rain had cooled things off, and I slept well.

Chapter Twenty-Two: Thailand

The man next to me nudged me with his elbow. "I've never seen them do that before."

"Do what?" I said.

"Go over an American passport the way they're going over yours." We could see the border guard examining it through the window; he would flip through the pages, look at my photo, then at me, then back at my photo. He passed it around now, and each official went through the same routine. They had found something interesting, and I was starting to worry.

I gulped. "That's not good."

The man, who looked to be an American expat, gave me a grim smile. "Well, good luck." The Cambodian border guard handed him back his passport. "You might want to give the American Embassy a call before they take your cell phone away," he added.

"Right," I said — then, "Wait, what?!" I looked around, but he had vanished into the throng of humanity streaming across the Cambodian border into Thailand.

The border guard crooked his finger at me. I leaned in the window. "Wait over there." He indicated a spot out of line next to a high chain-link fence. Several soldiers standing nearby, their rifles at the ready, looked my way.

"Uh, is there something wrong?"

The border guard pointed. "Wait over there."

I did as I was ordered and tried to appear calm, but my heart was beating in my chest like something trying to get out. There were four or five lines of people waiting to cross the border. There must have been close to a hundred people in the crowd, and they all seemed to be looking at me. I felt exposed, singled out for . . . what? What was going on? Was there something wrong with my passport? Some flaw? Or maybe they had me mixed up with someone else? Was it a case of mistaken identity? I was sweating bullets now. I glanced around; the border guards were eyeballing me, I was sure of it. I had heard stories of Westerners who had run afoul of Cambodian law and simply disappeared for reasons that no one could properly explain. I'd seen the movie *Midnight Express*, and I conjured up visions of prison and torture. They'd throw a net over me and drag me to some filthy jungle pit. My family would never know what had happened. The Thai border was right over there, not fifty yards away. *Could I make a break for it?*

And the day had started out so well. It was only a few hours ride from my hotel in Sisophon, Cambodia, to the border-crossing with Thailand here in Paoy Paet. It had been a nice ride, with a fine tailwind and milder temperatures. I'd been in a particularly good mood, feeling in control . . . until now. I stood with my back against the chain-link fence. I felt closed in and cut off.

Ten, twenty, thirty people were processed, and still I waited. I could see the guards looking intently at my passport through the smoked-glass windows. Soon, the station chief got involved. I watched him inspect my passport; he'd look at it, then at me, then at my passport again and flip through the pages. One last glance at my photo, and he raised his eyes and motioned for me to approach.

The other guards were dressed in plain olive-drab, but The Chief was decked out in an elaborate uniform. Gold braids hung from his shoulder epaulets, filigree adorned his tall visored cap, and a slew of medals ornamented his chest. I could see my nervous reflection in his Saigon-mirrored sunglasses. He was about my age and short by Western standards, maybe five-foot six or seven, and clearly in charge.

"Where did you cross into Cambodia?" he asked.

"Moc Bai," I said.

"And how long have you been in my country?"

"Uh, well, let me think, uh, nine or eleven days, I guess."

He tapped my passport with his finger. "You have no entrance stamp," he said.

"Entrance stamp?" I said, "I need an entrance stamp?"

"There's no entrance stamp," he repeated. "Did you see them stamp your visa?"

I shrugged. "No, I just gave them my papers. I don't know what they did, they just waved me through . . ."

"I can't let you leave the country without an entrance stamp," he said. He looked at me for a few beats, then said, "For all I know, you have overstayed your visa."

A Cambodian visa is good for two weeks if you enter by land, thirty days if you come in through an airport. I'd heard of the Immigration Department making sweeps of tourist hotels and arresting foreigners who'd overstayed their welcome. They'd been imprisoned, heavily fined, and then deported. I knew the Cambodian Government had no sense of humor when it came to these kinds of things, and once you were plugged into The System, you were screwed.

The Chief turned and said something to one of his subordinates, who looked at me and then hurried off. Now I was really scared. Was I about to be arrested too? I glanced around nervously, half expecting to be gang-swarmed at any moment. I started talking, stalling for time: *Maybe if I explain my situation.* "You see, I'm trying to ride around the world," I said. "No good reason, I guess it's just that . . . well, it's kind of hard to explain, but I felt that there should be more . . . not that there was really anything wrong . . ."

I was nervous, and it all came out in a confused jumble. What was I doing half a world away from my home and family? I looked at The Chief. He returned my gaze with no interest. I wasn't getting through to him. I shook my head, my whole body sagging in resignation, and I looked down at the ground. What was the use trying to explain something I myself didn't understand?

Maybe I should just stick to the facts, I thought. "See, I rode across America and I've been through Europe and I wanted to see this part of the world too," I said. "I just flew into Saigon with my pal, Mike. We rode down from Hue as far as . . ." Then I had a thought. I put up a finger. "Wait a minute," I said, "I might have something." I started digging in my wallet . . . *If only I could find it . . .* I pulled scraps of paper out and examined each one — the lottery ticket I'd bought from a street vendor in Saigon, *no that wasn't it,* a bar tab from a restaurant in Hue, *nope, still no good,* then, there it was: my train ticket for the trip from Dieu Tri, Vietnam. *Eureka!* It had a date on it and was proof that I hadn't been in Cambodia for more than two weeks. "Here," I said, "will this do?" I passed the ticket through the slot, and The Chief gave it a cursory glance. He didn't seem impressed. He looked past me at my beat-up, overloaded bicycle. It looked like something out of *The Grapes of Wrath*.

"Let me understand," he said, "you're trying to ride around the world on *that*?"

"Well, uh, yes . . ."

A small smile creased his stern countenance. He looked off, then back, peering at me over the top of his sunglasses. He seemed to be trying to make up his mind. Finally, he gave a little shrug and stamped my passport. "Just go," he said, "and . . . good luck."

Bandits

I had only a general idea of what route I'd take through Southeast Asia once I finished with Vietnam. Back home in Seattle, I'd planned to ride north through Cambodia and cross the border into Laos, then follow the Mekong. But I'd met a fellow who ran a bike shop in Saigon who, when I told him my idea, warned against it. "There were some cyclists attacked on that route not too long ago," he said. Having made it a practice to rely on local knowledge, I took his word for it and decided to bag Laos, instead heading for Bangkok and then flying to Kolkata in India. I would buy a ticket online a week or ten days in advance and hang out in Bangkok for a while.

From the Thai/Cambodian border it would take me four or five days to reach the city. I followed the main highway, Route 33, toward Sao Kao and then cut off onto Route 359, heading in the direction of Bangkok. The road was in good shape, with new pavement and a good wide shoulder. The country was much the same as what I had seen in Cambodia: lots of farmers' fields carved out of the jungle and wooden houses sitting atop tall supports. I suppose they were built that way so they would survive the monsoons, and also as a kind of natural air conditioning.

Thai stilt house

As I got farther east, I noticed something strange: ninety percent of the cars I shared the road with were the same make, model and vintage. I've never seen so many 1995 Toyota Camrys! And what made it even weirder was that they were all the same dark-gray color. I was never able to come up with a satisfying explanation for this oddity, but pondering the mystery kept my mind occupied as I slugged along in the sticky heat.

I passed an occasional village, but most of the riding took me through rural farmland. Small stands popped up every three or four kilometers along the highway, little shops that were nothing more than a few sticks of wood knocked together with a palm frond or tin roof. I kept seeing rows of jars and pop bottles filled with a golden-yellow fluid for sale at these little shacks. At first I thought it was tea, or maybe some kind of fruit juice, but I finally figured out that it was how gasoline was sold in this part of the world.

Refrigeration, as a rule, is nonexistent, and the Cokes and beers I stopped to buy were tepid. At one bustling rural crossroads, though, there was electricity, and I when I saw the ice machine I thought I had died and gone to heaven. Pulling in, I leaned my bike against a pole. The little restaurant was open-air, with the ubiquitous palm-frond roof and dirt floor. I ordered a Coke, and the woman running the place popped open a can, poured it into a plastic bag half filled with ice, stuck in a straw, and tied off the bag with a wire twisty. I'd never seen a soft drink served that way.

Since there aren't a lot of bicycle tourers in that part of the country, most people I passed would stop what they were doing and wave and shout a greeting. It seemed they were genuinely pleased to see me, and it gave me a warm feeling toward the Thai. But one day, two young toughs on a scooter pulled up alongside and slowed their pace to match mine. I looked over and smiled. "How you doing," I said.

"Where you from?" the one on the back asked.

"America," I said.

"Where you go?" asked the driver.

"Bangkok."

"You stop," he replied, pointing to a wide spot a few yards ahead.

I gave them the once-over. They were in their late teens or early twenties, and I could tell by the way they looked at me that they had nothing good in mind. There wasn't a lot of traffic; we were at a place where the jungle closed in on either side of the road. *The perfect place for a mugging*, I thought. I got the unmistakable sense that they had done this before.

"No can do," I replied, "

"No, no, you stop," the one on the back insisted. "Facebook, you got Facebook? Just want to be friends. You know, practice English."

"Sorry," I said, "I'm on the clock."

They continued to pace me as they conversed in hushed tones. The one on back whispered something in the driver's ear. He listened for a few moments then nodded. "You like buy cigarette?"

"Don't smoke."

"How 'bout gum. You like gum I tink."

The driver inched his scooter a little closer. *Was he trying to run me off the road?* He was only a few centimeters away now, he could easily reach out and touch me, but I held my line and didn't budge. The only way they were going to stop me was to ram me. The passenger fumbled in his pocket for something and produced a pack of gum. He tapped out a stick, reaching across the span between us. "Gum?" he said, smiling.

I shrugged, accepted it, unwrapped it with one hand and popped it in my mouth. He grinned. "Fifty baht," he said, "you stop, you pay now."

I laughed. "Take a hike," I growled, "go find another sucker."

The driver looked at me and glared. He slowed the scooter and fell back a few yards. Then, in a flash, they were past and speeding down the road, getting ahead no doubt to set up an ambush. I kept my eyes peeled for them for the rest of the day, but I never saw them again. This episode put me on guard. Up to that point I had been feeling safe and secure, but now . . . I didn't know. So it was with the greatest relief that the next day my faith in humanity was restored. The set-up was much the same as when I'd been approached by the two toughs, except this time there was only one. He was young, also in his late teens or early twenties, and he pulled up beside me on his scooter. Just as the day before, I smiled and said hello, only this time my greeting was returned with heartfelt sincerity. We rolled along at the same pace for a few kilometers having a nice conversation, which consisted of me answering his questions about where I was from and where I was going. He finally asked politely if we could stop up ahead; he would have to turn off soon and wanted to know more.

I needed a break, so I said, "Sure," and pulled over.

I learned that he was a college student and that he lived with his parents, whose house was nearby. He wanted to know all about America and my family, so I pulled out my photo album and showed him pictures of my kids. "You have such a beautiful family," he said, flipping through the pages. "You must be very proud."

"I've been lucky," I said.

He looked off toward the jungle, then back. "I would consider it an honor if you would come to my home and meet my parents," he said. "They would be very impressed to see that I have such an important American as a friend."

I had to laugh. "I would like that very much," I said, "but I'm on a tight schedule. I have to make it to Bangkok to catch a plane."

"Oh, but we have a very fine place, and you would be welcome to stay with us. My mother will fix us a very fine meal." He was such a nice, polite kid that I could tell it would have meant a lot to him, so I was tempted to accept his offer. But I had been in a groove for a couple of days and didn't want to break the spell, so I let him down as gently as I could, made my apologies, and pedaled off feeling much better about life.

One Night in Bangkok Makes a Proud Man Humble

The Thai/Cambodian border was four days behind me now, and I was passing through a small town when I saw a train station. On a whim, I pulled in and inquired about a ticket to Bangkok. I had less than a hundred kilometers to go, but the heat and humidity were really getting to me that afternoon, so I decided to catch the first train headed west. I had ridden trains with my bike in Europe, and through trial and error had come up with a way of getting my gear onboard in a hurry. The first several times, I had pushed my bike up the steps from behind, causing the front wheel to flop around and the panniers to get stuck. I finally figured out that if I pulled the bike on backwards, the front wheel would naturally follow. It made getting on and off trains quick and easy. Unfortunately, this particular train's door was too narrow, and I wound up taking all my gear off and tossing it on board, then wedging the bike through the slim opening. It worked out, though, because unlike the European trains, Thai trains stay in the station longer than a few minutes.

Tuk tuk, Bangkok

I arrived in Bangkok in the late afternoon and went looking for a hotel. Outside the station, a throng of tuk tuk drivers swarmed around me.

"What hotel you going to?" the first one asked.

"Oh, I don't know," I said, and tried to push through the crowd.

"The I Don't Know Hotel!" one driver shouted gleefully. "I know where that is!"

Though they were insistent, they were a friendly lot, and I succumbed to their pitch and agreed to let one of them take me to a hotel. In a flash, a dozen hands grabbed my bicycle and were busy strapping it to the back of the nearest tuk tuk. The tuk tuk is the Asian taxi, and it's a ubiquitous sight on the streets of most Southeast Asian cities. It's basically a three-wheeled motorcycle with a partially-enclosed passenger compartment with room for three or four Asians or one or two Westerners. The driver sits up front at the narrow end and steers with regular motorcycle handlebars.

My bike was now strapped to the back of the tuk tuk and my panniers were piled beside me in the passenger seat. As the driver revved the engine, we roared off in a cloud of blue, oily exhaust. We careened through the busy streets of Bangkok, swerving and braking, darting in and out of lanes and squealing around corners at such high speed that I had to hang on for dear life. Soon, we screeched to a stop in front of a nondescript storefront and the driver jumped out and headed for the door, motioning for me to follow him inside.

He pulled a chair up for me and then turned to leave. "I wait outside," he said, "I watch your gear. You come out when you finish, I take good care of you, yes, you bet!"

"Wait," I said, "is this a hotel?"

"No, no worry, I take good care of you!" he said as he dashed out the door.

In a moment, a woman appeared from somewhere in back and introduced herself. "You are looking for a place of lodging?" She asked.

"Is this a hotel?" I asked.

She smiled, "No, but I will be happy to find a fitting place for you to stay."

It turned out that the tuk tuk driver had taken me to a kind of travel agency. I suppose he had a deal with the woman to funnel customers to her door. I wound up renting a room in a pretty nice hotel for seventy-five dollars a night, which was way over my budget, but I figured it would only be for three days. And after all, it was Bangkok; I could afford to splurge a little.

My room in the Swan Hotel was small, but it was in an interesting part of the city, and there was air conditioning and a pool. The staff couldn't have been more helpful, even going to the length of calling bike shops around town to find a box to pack my bike in. I got to know one tuk tuk driver, and he would always be sitting outside my hotel whenever I needed to go somewhere. I spent three days wandering around the city sightseeing, sampling the food, and getting ready for my flight to Kolkata, near the Bay of Bengal. It would be a four-hour flight across the Indian Ocean to northeastern India. I was sorry to be leaving Southeast Asia, but I was ready for a new adventure, too.

Chapter Twenty-Three: India

Ridley Scott's science fiction film, *Blade Runner*, imagines a world where overpopulation has left the planet almost unlivable. The air, water and earth are polluted, and most people lead a hardscrabble existence huddled among the husks of once-great cities. Scott's tale takes place in future Los Angeles, but it could just as well be set in contemporary Kolkata.

Street bathers, Kolkata

I landed at the Netaji Subhash Chandra Bose International Airport in Kolkata late in the afternoon and hired a cab to take me to the Heera Holiday Inn Hotel, where I'd reserved a room. The neighborhood kept getting shabbier the farther we went. "Okay," I said to myself, "it'll be okay if it doesn't get any worse than . . ." I looked around for a building that would meet my Western standards, but they all looked pretty bad. We rumbled down the rutted pavement, dodging throngs of people spilling over the sidewalks and jamming the street. Tuk tuks wove in and out of the mad rush as beggars tapped politely on the cab's window. I looked straight ahead and pretended not to see them. I'd thought the poverty in Southeast Asia would brace me for India, but I was unprepared for what I was seeing. It was dark now, and the cabbie had to pull over several times to ask directions. We finally came to a stop halfway down a dark alley in front of a dilapidated building with peeling paint and a crumbling façade. A sign reading "Heera Holiday Inn" hung crookedly over the front door. My heart was in my throat. "Oh crap," I mumbled.

Back in Bangkok, I'd scoured the Internet for a hotel in my price range. I'd finally settled on a place that, from the photos, didn't seem too bad. And though it was more than I wanted to pay, I had made reservations at this thirty-five-dollar-a-night hotel anyway. "Here we are," the driver said cheerfully, and jumped out before I could tell him to hit the gas and take me to a Westin or a Hilton, anywhere but this hovel. A group of hotel attendants appeared, the cab door opened, and they grabbed my bicycle and my luggage. In a moment, everything I owned disappeared through the door and into the crumbling old building. I got out of the cab and went into the lobby. What a surprise: it was bright and clean and attended by a staff of six or eight well-dressed men in crisp, wine-colored uniforms.

The manager came out from behind the desk and greeted me with a bow. "Yes, Mister Roach, we have your room all ready. We will store your bicycle in our garage and our security staff will guard it. Please let me know if there is anything I can do to make your stay more enjoyable." Two porters grabbed my panniers and led me upstairs through a maze of dimly lit halls to my room. It was cramped, old, and worn, but it was clean, and I felt safe.

I got up with the sun the next morning and went downstairs, thinking that maybe the neighborhood would look better in the light of day. But the first thing I saw as I stepped out was a grotesquely deformed beggar. He was wispy as a shadow at dusk, dressed in rags and sitting lopsided on a pile of cardboard. He swayed back and forth in time to some rhythm only he could hear.

His gnarled hands were held out in a beseeching gesture, his eyes were closed, and a peaceful smile played across his weathered face.

Directly across the narrow alley from my hotel's entrance were the ruins of what had once been a large, brick building. The walls had collapsed long ago, leaving only a few crumbling ramparts protruding from the rubble. The place reminded me of photos I'd seen of Dresden after it had been saturation-bombed during World War II. The street was strewn with litter; bone-thin stray dogs scrounged for food among the trash. The air was thick with smoke, and the sickly-sweet stench of rot seemed to permeate the very fiber of the place.

Once out of the alley, I found myself on a side street lined on both sides with busy shops of all kinds — food stalls, machine shops, even a tailor's with tuxedo jackets on hangers displayed behind plate glass. Throngs of people crowded the narrow lane. Bicycle rickshaws and tuk tuks plied the river of humanity, the people flowing around the vehicles like water around rocks in a stream. As the only Westerner, I received my share of odd glances and curious stares. This was not a neighborhood frequented by tourists.

I made my way to the neighborhood's main street. Rickety trolleys trundled by, overflowing with riders, some hanging out of the doors. This street, too, was packed with people, and I had to wade through the throng, getting bumped and jostled as I made my way along the sidewalk. I passed groups of men, women and children bathing at water stations placed every few blocks. Their brightly colored saris, Kameez salwars, and dohti kurtas, still wet from the morning's laundering, were strung on every available space, giving the place an almost festive air as their owners lathered, combed and shaved. As I passed one alley, I saw a street barber shaving a customer with a straight razor. The man sat statue-still on a wooden box.

Boys and men hurried past, toting metal cans or leather sacks of drinking water. At one intersection, a group of men were slaughtering chickens, butchering and plucking them right on the sidewalk. I saw goats tied up with ropes or steel cables or rusty chains, standing or lying under rickety makeshift mangers constructed of scraps of building materials. Sheets of tin, cardboard, plastic, old doors, roofing material, and worn wooden planks kludged precariously together with wire and tucked into doorways and alleys served as homes for animals as well as people. Sacred cows meandered down the middle of the street.

All the buildings looked ancient and in advanced states of decay. Made mostly of dull red clay brick, some were so far gone that wooden beams propped up the walls, while others had collapsed completely. Plastic sheets and tarps among the ruins marked the spots where squatters lived.

I had no context for the sights that met my eyes that first morning in Kolkata. I was shocked, amazed, and oddly mesmerized by the strangeness of it all. I just didn't know how to process what I was seeing, and it left me dazed. But maybe the most amazing thing about the tableau was the attitude of the people. Even among all that poverty and rot, the people went about their business no differently than would the citizens of Chicago or Paris. Even the street people, the lowest of the low, seemed to be engaged in the fabric of the community. It was amazing to see how life had adapted to such harsh conditions. Talk about resiliency of the human spirit!

The Phone Card

I'd chatted with the desk clerk that morning, picking his brain about where I might find a SIM card for my phone. I'd purchased new chips in Vietnam, Cambodia and Thailand with no problem. I would pop into a store, pay a few bucks, and bang! I had service. But as I was soon to discover, India was a whole different kind of deal. As near as I could figure, it had something to do with terrorism coming out of neighboring Pakistan. Terrorists have nefarious uses for cell phones, so the Indian government makes it very difficult for a foreigner to obtain service. I had to fill out a sheaf of forms and get the hotel manager to vouch for me, and still, it took two days for approval.

I had not intended to stay in Kolkata very long, a few days at most. My plan was to ride west from there through north-central India and then up to Nepal and south to Delhi, and I was anxious to get back on the road. I'd been sitting around too long, and the idleness was starting to get to me. It took several days to get my bike assembled and everything up and running, but soon I was ready to leave Kolkata. Almost.

I have asthma and need to take daily medications. My supply would run out in ten days, so I had my daughter, Maren, ship a three-month supply to my hotel in Kolkata. It was due to arrive the same day I did, but now, two days later, it still hadn't shown up. I traced it to Delhi, where the medications now sat. FedEx kept assuring me that the package would arrive tomorrow, but after three "tomorrows," I was still without my meds.

I was finally able to contact the office in Delhi and was told that I would have to provide something called a Form 50 before they could forward the package to Kolkata. "I'm sorry, sir," the woman on the phone said, "it is the law!" After some back and forth, I discovered that I could pick up the package in person in Delhi. "Oh yes," the lady on the other end said, "we will gladly hold the package for you until you arrive."

"I don't need a Form 50?" I inquired.

"No, you need that only if you are shipping it to Kolkata. No other documentation will be necessary if you come pick up your package. We will hold it here for you."

Now I'm getting somewhere, I thought, *at least I have a plan.* I'd been looking forward to riding across India, but I didn't have enough medication to make it all the way. I looked into flying to Delhi and then back to Kolkata the same day, but the logistics were tight, so I gave up the idea of a trans-India tour and instead made plans to take the train. I would ride my bike to the train station and book passage the first thing in the morning. I'd be in Delhi soon.

Across India

Indian Railways

I would often awake with a start and think, *where am I?* I might be in a tent in Fargo or on a stranger's couch in London or in bunk in a hostel in Rome. This time I was on the floor of the Howrah Train Station in Kolkata. People were crowding around me. Occasionally, someone would step over me. I sat up and looked around. My back was killing me. I tried to rub the sleep out of my eyes. I had arrived at the station early, only to be told I'd have to ride back across the Hooghly River to a different building to book passage. After filling out more forms, and with my ticket finally in hand, I rode back to the station, where it took another couple of hours to book my bike and equipment as baggage. With all arrangements made and no place to sit, I'd settled down on the floor against a column to rest. *I'll just close my eyes for a few seconds*, I thought. That had been twenty minutes ago. Now I got up and walked around. All the chairs were taken, and people clustered in little camps on the floor all around the huge, barn-like structure, their baggage piled up in mounds.

I'd decided to send an e-mail to Maren to let her know I was okay, but as soon as I switched on my phone there was a call from her. "Dad, did you get my e-mail?" She sounded grim.

"What's wrong?"

"I got a message from FedEx. They've delivered your package to the hotel in Kolkata."

"Cornbread hell," I said, "are you sure?"

"That's what they're telling me."

I looked at my watch. My train would be pulling out in a few hours. *Would I have time to get back to the hotel, pick up the box, and get back to the station? Maybe. Or could I call and have the manager send it to me in a cab? Possible, but risky.* Different plans of action raced through my brain. Whatever I was going to do, I'd have to do it fast. "Okay, Honey," I said, "I'll let you know."

He who hesitates is lost. But it's also true that haste makes waste. Then again, my dad used to say, "If you want something done right, do it yourself." I decided to go with Dad, and jumped in a cab. The fifty-minute ride to the hotel through the gathering Kolkata rush-hour traffic kept me on tenterhooks. When we arrived, I told the cabby to wait and dashed into the hotel. The manager greeted me with a huge grin and my FedEx box. I gave the cabby an extra hundred rupees to make time, and man, did that cat drive! Back at the station, I jumped out of the car while it was still rolling and hoofed it over to Track 9. I needn't have rushed. I made it with time to spare, but the solution of one problem had led to the creation of another.

Now that I had my asthma medicine, I no longer needed to get to Delhi in a hurry. I could take my time and make the trip on my bike as I'd originally planned. The problem was that I didn't have my bike or my bags; they were checked into the Indian railway system, slowly making their way through that Byzantine, post-colonial organization, and I had no idea how to retrieve them. I'd had to go across town just to buy tickets, and it had taken me additional hours of schlepping everything from one department to another to arrange shipment of my gear as cargo. I had a stack of documents that I would have to present at the other end to claim my stuff. There was no telling what bureaucratic hoops I'd have to jump through to cancel that contract and get everything back now. My bike and all my camping gear were going to Delhi whether I was on that train or not.

Passengers were starting to mill around the doors of the train now, preparing to board. I heaved a sigh and gave in to my fate. I would take the train across India after all. I found my compartment and stretched out on the upper berth.

The Backpack

Back in Kolkata, where I'd bought my train tickets, I'd struck up a conversation with a couple from Australia. They, too, were hoping to get a ticket to Delhi. "Have you ridden the Indian trains much?" I'd asked, as we sat in the lobby waiting for our numbers to be called.

They traded looks. "Oh, brother," the young man said, "it's a real pain."

"How so?"

"Well, first, there's only a slim chance you'll get a ticket today. The way it works, you have to make an application. Then it has to be approved. If you're lucky, you might get your ticket in a couple of days."

"You might have to wait a week or more," added the young woman.

"No," I said, "that can't be."

She shrugged. "Well, this is India . . ."

I'd sat in stunned silence. After all I'd been through, it now looked as though I would still be stuck in Kolkata. Then I had an idea, and I turned to the young man. "You guys are going to Delhi, right?"

"Uh-huh."

"What if we rented a car and drove there together?"

They broke out in laughter. "You want to drive in India?" the woman said.

"Well, I'm riding a bike in India, could driving be much worse?"

"Wait," said the man, "you plan to ride a bike to Delhi?"

I began to feel a little foolish. "Well, I was *going* to..."

They both shook their heads. "Good luck," the woman said.

"You'll sure as hell need it!" chimed the man.

"Hey, I've ridden in some pretty tough parts of the world . . ." I began, but their number was called before I could make my case and they got up and went to bargain for their passage. As it turned out, the gods of travel were smiling on me that day, and I was able to buy tickets for my bike and me. And now here I was on the Trans-India Flyer, dozing to the gentle swaying as it slowly made its way westward out of the station.

It's a twenty-five-hour trip across India by train. I don't think the locomotive ever went faster than thirty miles an hour. I had a sleeper car in the Deluxe-First-Class Section, and it wasn't too bad. The carriage was old and shabby, but I had my own berth equipped with a fan, a reading light, and an electric outlet. There was no dining car, but every few hours a porter would pass by with a cart of pre-packaged meals. I had stocked up on enough food to get me though dinner, and the next morning, I purchased an aluminum foil-wrapped packet for breakfast. The rice and vegetables weren't bad.

The train stopped often, and during the trip four very nice Indians cycled through my compartment. It was a good chance to talk to the locals and gather information and advice. My bike-riding experience in India was limited so far. I'd puttered around Kolkata, but I'd yet to experience rural India, and that's where the bulk of my riding would be.

The hours dragged by, and to ease the boredom I strolled up and down the train, watching the scenery drift slowly past. It was March now, late winter, the crops had not yet begun to sprout, and the fallow fields were still a dull and endless brown. Off in the distance through the ever-present haze of smoke, I'd occasionally glimpse a line of trees. It was the only green in sight.

It's common in India for passengers to hang out of the open windows and doors of moving trains to cool off in the breeze. I adopted a similar practice, though instead of leaning out, I would stand back well inside the vestibule. The buildings in the villages we passed were one- and two-story rectangles of white-painted cement, with metal roofs. Most of the villages had only a few buildings, while others looked to be bustling centers of commerce. The train would occasionally stop at these larger villages, and rattle past the smaller ones. I often saw crowds at crossings waiting for the train to pass.

We had slowed at one such gathering, and as we crept past, a young man emerged from the throng and began running alongside. He threw his backpack toward the open door where we stood, and one of my fellow passengers deftly caught it by the strap. The boy, who was maybe fifteen, ran as hard as he could to keep up, making for our door with the intention of hopping on and securing a free ride. At first it looked as if he might make it, but the train was gaining momentum, and it was getting to be a race.

The fellow who'd caught the pack handed it to me and leaned out even farther, hanging on by his fingertips and reaching for the boy's outstretched hand, now only a foot away. There were three or four of us in the vestibule all yelling encouragement, but alas, after a few moments of hell-bent sprinting, the lad began to fade. He was running out of energy, stumbling and almost falling.

Finally, he gave up. I was so caught up in the action that I nearly forgot about his backpack. Coming to my senses, I quickly gave it a sling out the open door. All eyes were on it as it arced through the air, hit the ground, and tumbled a few times, coming to rest in the dirt. The boy was walking now, and he looked my way, picked up his dusty bundle, smiled, gave a wave, and turned around and walked back to the crossing.

"Wow, that's not something you see every day," I said to the man standing next to me. But no one else seemed alarmed or even surprised at the drama that had unfolded. I suppose that sort of thing is commonplace in India.

Delhi

I arrived in Old Delhi about 10:00 p.m., collected my bicycle and gear, and hired a tuk tuk in front of the station. I'd picked a hotel from the Web back in Kolkata and had written the address down on a scrap of paper that I showed to the driver. He first asked for 1,000 rupees, which is twenty dollars U.S., and I told him no. The street outside the station was a sea of humanity, and as we stood there haggling, others began to gather around. One of the onlookers, a gentleman probably in his fifties, asked me how much the driver wanted. When I told him, he began shouting at the man, telling him that he should be ashamed of himself. "Two hundred only!" he growled. "You are trying to cheat this poor fellow!"

Now the crowd was getting heated, and others joined in berating the tuk tuk driver. The air was charged with tense vibrations. People crowded in close, pushing and shoving and shouting. For a moment, it looked like a riot might break out. The driver argued for a while, but finally gave in.

"He will take you for 200 rupees," another person told me. "Do not give this scoundrel a penny more!" With the price settled, the crowd began piling my belongings into the tuk tuk. My bike and panniers took up the whole passenger compartment, so I had to ride up front with the driver on a seat made for one. As we raced out of the train station and onto the street, I hung out one side of the tuk tuk and the driver hung out the other. We careened through heavy traffic, narrowly missing pedestrians, cars, other tuk tuks, busses, and the occasional sacred cow. Several times I closed my eyes, sure we were about to die in a fiery, head-on collision with a ten-ton truck. As we rounded one corner the front tire hit a pothole and the whole rig tipped dangerously. Instinctively, I put a foot out to try to stabilize the thing, and nearly fell out. A last-second grab for the mirror mount was all that saved me. It was a crazy twenty minutes, but I have to admit, it was fun in a twisted, oh-my-god-I'm-going-to-die kind of way. I admire the skill of the Indian drivers. They are true masters of the art of motorized ballet.

I checked into my hotel, got a good night's rest, and rose the next morning anxious to hit the road. I had been in India for ten days, and at last I was going to ride. But getting out of Old Delhi was an ordeal; I had technical problems from the start. First, the hotel card reader wouldn't recognize my MasterCard, so I had to hunt up an ATM. That didn't work either, so I dug into my emergency funds to pay the hotel bill. Then the GPS on my smart phone went wacky and sent me down sketchy streets. I had a pretty good idea where I wanted to go, so I ignored the phone and went with my gut. An hour later, I was in a dead-end alley in the middle of a wild dogfight.

Yeah, I know, it was pretty cool.

The Faint

I rode north all day on Highway AH2, which is a freeway with a big shoulder for scooters, bicycles, horse- and cow-drawn wagons and tuk tuks — basically all the slow-moving traffic you see everywhere in India. I rode past scarecrow-thin young men pedaling large, three-wheeled truck-like contraptions loaded down with all sorts of cargo. I saw one poor fellow hauling two full-sized refrigerators. And I thought I was carrying a heavy load! For the first few hours it was bumper-to-bumper. The air in India is foul, and even worse in heavy traffic. Sometimes I could wiggle past the cars and trucks, but most of the time I crawled along choking on the exhaust fumes with everyone else. After a while, the heat and bad air started getting to me. I was sweating like crazy; it seemed I couldn't drink fast enough to keep up with all the fluid I was losing. Then, about 2:30, during the hottest part of the day, I started feeling sick and getting dizzy. I had trouble keeping my balance, and I felt as if I needed to vomit. Then my right leg cramped up. I was in a place where I couldn't pull over, and I cried out with pain every time I made a pedal stroke. Then my other leg cramped up, too. I was howling like a coyote, but I had to endure the pain and keep going until I could find a safe place to get out of traffic and off this cursed road.

Fortunately, an off-ramp appeared, and I took it and pulled into one of the ubiquitous roadside food stands, bought a cold Coke, and guzzled it down in about three seconds. Then I got a bottle of cold water and poured it over my head. That made me even dizzier, so I plopped down in a chair in the shade. I was so exhausted, sick and demoralized that I could hardly move. It seemed like my body was in revolt and that my biosystems were shutting down one by one. I rose unsteadily to my feet and stumbled to the squat-toilet in back.

When I returned, the men hanging around the place took pity on me and led me outside to a hand pump, where they doused my head with cool water for a few minutes. They helped me back to my chair and sat with me until I regained enough strength to get back on my bike. They suggested that I ride no farther than the village of Hapur, about ten minutes away, where they assured me I'd find a room. I was off the freeway now and on a secondary road. When I reached Hapur, I stopped to ask some locals about a hotel, but none of them spoke English. As I was about to ride on, a well-dressed man approached. The locals, I suppose, were of a lower caste and were deferential toward him, parting to let him pass. He hardly acknowledged their presence. "Yes, sir," he said when he got close, "are these ruffians bothering you?"

I smiled. "No, not at all, I was just asking about a hotel."

He nodded. "Yes, there is a place just up the block."

I still wasn't feeling good, and when I got to the hotel, I crashed. Waking up hours later with a terrible headache, I drank about a gallon of water and then collapsed. I suppose I'd picked up a bug along the way and my body needed rest to fight it, because when I got up the next morning, though I was weak, I felt pretty good otherwise. It was the only time I got sick in India, and considering the exotic foods I'd been eating, I felt lucky to be struck only once.

Road Monkey

The ride from Hapur to the Nepal border turned out to be some of the toughest touring I'd ever done. The roads were flat, but the heat, humidity and bad air made it a grueling ride. One bright spot, though, was the monkeys that live in the jungle beside the road. Motorists pull over and throw bananas to them, and the creatures peel the fruit and scarf it down just like little people. They would come right up to me and give me a look that said, "So what do you have for me?"

It's said that India is a country of contrast and contradiction. The economic gap is huge, and often wealth and poverty are close neighbors. I was three or four days northeast of Delhi, riding through an impoverished section of rural India where the conditions were squalid. At one point, I rode alongside an open sewer for several kilometers. It was next to the road, and the stench on that hot, humid day was overpowering. I couldn't imagine what it was like for the people who lived in the rows of shacks that bordered the sewer on the other side. I rode through that little village holding my nose, but just a few kilometers farther on I came upon an upscale restaurant where waiters with bow ties served me a tall glass of iced tea at a table with a white linen tablecloth.

As I got closer to Nepal, the country became more rural. Eventually, I had to leave the secondary road and found myself riding on a narrow lane through dense jungle. The road started out pleasant and smooth, but before long it turned into a broken mess. I had to navigate through sections of crumbling pavement jutting up like ragged little islands out of an ocean of dry, red clay. Traffic was total madness, and a curtain of red dust hung in the air. I dodged farm tractors hauling overloaded wagons of god-knows-what, speeding busses and trucks, and of course the ever-present tuk tuks, all slaloming through the ruts trying to find the sweet spot, whether it was on their side of the road or not. There was more jungle, too. The farmers' fields were cut out of dense growth and up close to the road. Motorized pumps drew columns of water out of the earth. It was hot, as usual, and as I rode past the geysers I was tempted to stop, clamber down into a field, and stand for a while in the cool water.

Later that same day, I pulled over and lay down on a patch of grass under a tree to rest. A gentle breeze blew, and it felt so good that I dozed off. When I awoke, a group of peasants stood around looking at me; they pointed and giggled when I sat up and wanted to know all about my bicycle and me. One wizened old fellow, around whom several younger men gathered, was holding a seminar on my bike's rear derailleur. Though I doubt he'd ever seen one before, he seemed to have an intuitive understanding of its workings.

These humble folks were poor in material wealth but rich in spirit. I had watched them toiling in the fields and had seen where they lived. It was a subsistence existence, yet their natural curiosity and enthusiasm shone through. Even though they lived in what we Westerners would think of as squalor, it seemed they had found a kind of harmony in it all. It was more than a simple resignation to fate, I could see it in their eyes.

Freedom From, Freedom To

For some time I had been wrestling with the idea of harmony, too: the challenge of balancing the trade-offs between security and freedom. At what point did security become a prison and freedom chaos? I remembered a philosophy course I'd taken in college and a section on the philosopher Emanuel Kant. I recalled Kant's idea of negative and positive liberty, or Freedom From and Freedom To. As I recalled, Kant's theory applied to big social structures such as religion and government, but I was beginning to see a different take on the idea. Freedom From, I reasoned, would be the more basic of the two. Examples that came to mind were freedom from hunger, freedom from confinement, freedom from disease, freedom from . . . well, you get the idea. Freedom From, it seemed, was really just another way to think about security. Freedom To would be more liberating and complex and elusive: freedom to love, freedom to dream, freedom to seek the unknowable. The second kind of freedom, I reasoned, could be had only after the first was achieved, at least to some degree. After all, it wouldn't be possible to travel the world if I were locked in a cage. Though they conflicted, Freedom From and Freedom To were related. I had come to suspect that security and freedom weren't opposing forces at all. Maybe they were just the extreme ends of the same continuum.

Life on the road had made me more flexible and adaptable and less judgmental, and that made me free-er. Sure, I still had to get up in the morning and do the things one does every day to sustain body and soul. But I was less a slave to the hands of the clock and more in touch with my natural rhythms. I ate when I was hungry, not when mealtime rolled around. I rested when I was tired, not when the five o'clock whistle blew. There was no one to tell me where to be or when to be there. There was no job to go to, no monthly bills to pay, no lawn to mow. I was a stranger in a strange land, and with no image to live up to, I could be whoever I chose to be.

I had achieved a measure of freedom I'd never known. The downside was that I sometimes felt adrift and purposeless and vulnerable. I was on my own, with no one to guide or advise me. I had no home other than my tent and no protection other than my own cunning. When I got sick or depressed or things went wrong, I couldn't turn to a friend or family member for help.

I had traded the Freedom From of my domestic life for the Freedom To of the road. But the question now was, *had I gone too far?* I had no answers, only more questions, but as I pedaled through the jungle toward Nepal, I had the sense that I was moving in the right direction.

Chapter Twenty-Four: Nepal

From Delhi it took six days to reach the Sarda River, which runs roughly along the border between India and Nepal. The road had been getting rougher and rougher until it deteriorated into little more than a crude, rocky footpath. There's a massive dam on the river, and I rode my bike across the narrow causeway that runs along the top. The footpath took up again on the other side, so ruggedly that I had to get off and push. Now I was finally in Nepal.

Nepali couple, Mahendra Highway

The jungle wasn't as thick here, and the path led me along the banks of a shallow, slow-flowing stream for a kilometer to a bridge. Once across, I climbed the opposite bank and emerged from the bush into a small village of tin-roofed huts. A dirt path wound through the settlement, and as I traversed it, the inhabitants came out of their homes or took breaks from their chores to watch me pass. Chickens and goats fled at the sight of me, but the children gathered around and followed me to the outskirts. "Bye bye!" they called as we walked along together, "Bye bye!" It seemed that that was the only English word they knew, and they used it for hello as well as goodbye.

The path now gave way to a gravel road good enough to ride on, and the jungle receded, replaced now by expansive, cultivated fields. I pedaled a few kilometers, then came to the official Nepal border crossing, where I encountered a barrier similar to those at railroad crossings, except this one's counterbalance was a basket filled with rocks. Next to the barricade was a stone hut that housed Customs. I got my passport stamped, and the lone official raised the barrier and let me cross. I had reversed directions and was heading east now. A few kilometers farther on I saw a uniformed man standing at the side of the road. He waved and signaled for me to stop. Off the road in a clearing was another cement building with a sign in English that said "Immigration." I went in and bought a visa good for a month.

As I continued, the road got better and better, until I was riding on a real, paved surface. I'd seen signs advertising The Hotel Opera, and when I reached the town of Mahendranengar, six kilometers farther on, I checked in for two nights. Based on my experience in Kolkata, I supposed it would take at least an extra day to get a SIM card for my phone. Besides, the ride through northern India had worn me out, and I wanted to take a rest day. It was late afternoon, and I took a nap. I awoke in the evening and went out to explore Mahendranengar. I discovered a dusty little border town. I passed by barbershops, dry goods stores, restaurants and a hardware store, where I picked up kerosene for my stove. The proprietor asked what I was going to do with it, and instead of simply explaining, I decided to put on a show; I would dazzle him with my Amazing Western Technology. I assembled my stove on the sidewalk, primed it, then struck a match. Nothing happened. I struck another match, and then another. Still no flame, and I started to worry that my show was going to be a dud. My stove can run on a lot of different fuels, but I'd never tried kerosene. It looked like I was going to have egg on my face. I could tell by the expressions on the faces of the half-dozen people who had stopped to watch that they were beginning to doubt that my fancy American contraption was going to work. I tried a third time, and the stove came to life with a roar and a round of applause.

Later, as I waited for my stove to cool off, I quizzed the group about my proposed route to Butwal. "You'll have no problem," one young fellow assured me, "the road is good and there are lots of places to eat and sleep. There are some hills, but other than that, you should not worry, there are no robbers, lots of police, and you will have a fine trip."

I had dinner that evening in the hotel restaurant, where I had my first Nepalese beer, Everest. It came in a one-liter bottle, and though I drank it with a big dinner, I got buzzed. I went back to my room, turned on the fan, and fell into a deep, dreamless sleep.

The next day, one of the hotel clerks went with me to the Nepal Cellular store, where I was happy to discover that, unlike in India, signing up for a prepaid plan was as simple as in the U.S. I had my phone up and running in a few minutes, and they even threw in a free t-shirt.

I visited an ATM and withdrew some Nepali rupees, got to bed early, and rose the next morning before sunup. It was still dark when I started out on the Mehandra Highway headed east. Half an hour into my ride, it got light enough to see, and I stopped and stowed my lights. Though it wasn't yet 6:00 a.m., it was already getting warm. I'd not had breakfast, so when I spotted a group of people gathered around a food stall in a little village, I rolled up and got in line. As I sat at the rough-hewn table eating eggs and rice, I watched the little village come to life. Merchants readied their shops, farmers brought their produce to market in horse-drawn carts, and neatly dressed school children hurried to their classes. Chickens scratched in the dust at my feet, and a goat wandered by. After breakfast, I bought a bottle of warm Coca Cola and cookies and got back on the highway.

The Mahendra Highway runs the length of Nepal, connecting India in the west to India in the east. It is a modern, two-lane road built by the Indian government and roughly parallels the Nepal-India border for 1,000 kilometers. I started at the far western end but would take it only as far east as Butwal, which is at the midway point. I found the Mahendra to be in good shape, with decent shoulders. The traffic was as crazy as it is everywhere in Nepal, but I was used to that, and I was happy to have a good road to ride on.

The Village Brahmin

I was traveling through rural farm country now. It was early April, and green shoots were pushing up through the soil of the furrowed fields. I would pass through several villages and cross four or five rivers in the course of a day. The rivers, called kholas, run down out of the Himalaya by the score. The water was low this time of year, the rivers forming small channels through a broader flood plain.

By afternoon, the heat and humidity became unbearable. The first few days I toughed it out and pushed on, but each night I'd be sick. I realized I wasn't having fun. So I got in the habit of starting out in the cool, predawn hours and calling it a day when it got too hot to ride. If I was near a village with a hotel, I'd check in and lie under the fan. If midday found me out in the bush, I'd flag down a bus and hitch a ride to the nearest town with a hotel.

One day, I found myself in a small, dirt-street village at quitting time. There was an arch at the entrance to town, and displayed along the top were pictures of Mao, Marx, Lenin and Ho Chi Minh. I knew there had been a Maoist revolt in Nepal a few years before and that the dispute had been settled when the government granted the Maoists recognition and representation. This village, evidently, was one that had been in on the revolt and still maintained a strong Maoist identity. As I pedaled slowly under the arch, I spied a group of policemen and soldiers gathered under an awning near the side of the road. Addressing one of the cops, I asked, "Is there a hotel?"

The policeman nodded. "Hotel," he said with a broad grin, and pointed across the dusty street. "Hotel is there."

I pushed my bike down the dirt road that served as the village's main street and stopped at a shop. "Hotel?" I asked the proprietor.

"Yes, yes, very fine hotel!" He pointed to a dilapidated building across the road.

Just then another man approached. "Yes, sir," he said, "you are looking for a room?"

"Just for the night . . ."

"Very good, sir, please to follow me." He was about forty, well dressed, and his English wasn't bad. We walked into what looked like a restaurant and he bid me sit down at one of the tables. "Soft drink?" he asked.

"If it's cold," I replied. My head was swimming from the heat.

He said something to the man running the place, and in a flash, two ice-cold Pepsi Colas appeared. We sat and chatted. I kept asking if there was a hotel in town, but he kept deflecting my questions. "I have a brother in Chicago," he said. "Have you to been to Chicago?"

We'd talk about Chicago and the USA for a while, then I'd steer the conversation back to the subject of hotel rooms. "Is this the hotel?" I asked. He shrugged and wagged his head coyly in the way many Nepalese do. I saw this gesture often but was never able to decipher its meaning. It seemed to serve many purposes.

Soon the little place began to fill up with people. They sat at every table, and those who couldn't find a seat stood watching. Evidently, the word had gone out about the American and his bicycle, and no one wanted to miss the show. I felt uneasy being the main attraction. The crowd seemed to hang on my every word; they would nod or shake their heads at my slightest utterance. There was a steady, low murmur, and the crowd now spilled out of the restaurant and into the street. People jostled for position, parents holding their children up so they could see. Then I sensed a commotion by the entrance. Now it was suddenly quiet, and the crowd began to part like the Red Sea for Moses. A young man, who looked to be in his mid-thirties, emerged from the milling throng. He approached our table and smiled. "May I join you?" he asked. His English was perfect. It was clear from his demeanor, and by the deference the others showed him, that this fellow was a big man in town; he was clearly the village Brahmin.

I smiled back. "Sure," I said, "take a seat." We exchanged introductions, and he got down to business.

"First, let me say 'welcome to our village' and that I am honored to meet you, sir," he said, holding his hands together in that Nepalese gesture that is like praying.

I nodded and returned the greeting. "Namaste," I said.

"I understand you are looking for a place to spend the night," he said after a few pleasantries.

"That's right," I replied.

The Brahmin smiled and nodded and motioned to the proprietor. He said something to him in Nepalese, and the fellow hurried off as though on a mission from God. We sat and talked, and I answered the usual questions about my trip; then the proprietor returned and spoke briefly with the Brahmin. The Brahmin listened, nodded, and the proprietor backed away respectfully.

"Your room is ready," he said. "When you are finished with your refreshment, this fine gentleman will show you to your quarters." He made a casual gesture toward the proprietor, who nodded in agreement. "And if you are in need of anything, tell this man, and he will come and get me. I will see to it. Also be assured that you and your belongings are secure. You are under my protection."

Later, the proprietor led me up a narrow stairway and down a hall to a small room with pink walls. There were stuffed animals on the single bed, and on the window were pink, frilly curtains. It looked as if I had been given the owner's daughter's room, for which I paid the whopping sum of three dollars U.S.

A Tiger in the Eye

"If rhino charges, you must run zigzag pattern," Bishnu whispered, making short, choppy motions with his hands, "not like the snake, not smooth. And remember, rhino always attacks down like this, then up." He put his hand on his forehead, made a horn of his finger, and mimicked the rhino's goring movement. "Run zigzag. Not straight and not like snake."

"Right," I whispered. "What if . . ." But there was no one to hear me. Bishnu, my trusty Nepali guide, was gone. He'd disappeared into the tall grass to find the Bengal tiger we'd heard roar a few minutes earlier. I bent down and re-tied my soggy sneaker, which was wet from the river we'd waded across, dirty from the mud bank we'd scrambled up, and now filled with sand from the high grass plain of this Nepali jungle where I now crouched. I pulled my water bottle out of my pack and took a long drink. The water was tepid, the temperature of old tea, and while it slaked my thirst it did little to refresh. It was late afternoon, and we'd been in the Bardia National Park since 6:00 that morning. The sun beat down mercilessly. I took off my hat and wiped my brow.

It seemed that Bishnu had been gone a long time. I checked my watch. Had it been ten minutes or twenty? In this jungle, it was hard to gauge the passage of time. The sun hung motionless in the sky. I was tempted to sit down, but Bishnu had been pretty serious about the rhino thing, and I decided to stay in my semi-sprinter's stance instead. I kept my head on a swivel, on guard for the slightest sound, but there was only stillness. Stillness and heat.

Bishnu

It had been one of those happenstance occurrences. I'd been riding through the jungle and hadn't thought about seeing tigers, but I learned later that they had probably been seeing me. I was stopped at one of the many military checkpoints along the Mahendra Highway when Bishnu, a young Nepali man, approached. "Good afternoon, sir," he said, "may I ask if you have booked a hotel room for this evening?"

"I'm just going up the road a few kilometers to the next village."

He smiled. "I have a very fine place of lodging not far from here where you may see elephants, rhinos, crocodiles, and perhaps, if you are very lucky, a Bengal tiger."

"Uh-huh," I said. "How much and how far?"

"Only 400 rupees and only thirteen kilometers."

Four hundred rupees was four dollars U.S., and thirteen klicks wasn't much farther than the next village, plus, there was the wildlife. I'm a sucker for wildlife. "Okay," I said, "let's go see the tiger." Later, I learned that a walking safari in the Bardia National Park with Bishnu cost forty dollars, but I figured I would never have another chance to see a man-eating beast in the wild, so I signed up. I spent the night in a thatch-roofed mud hut furnished with a mosquito-net-draped bed, like something out of an old Tarzan movie.

At 5:30 the next morning, we started out from the Jungle Basecamp Safari Resort. It took an hour to reach the Bardia River. Finding a shady overlook on the bank, we took up our positions. I was propped against a tree; Bishnu was fifteen feet up another tree perched on a branch, scanning the jungle with his binoculars. I dozed most of the morning and early afternoon, and by 2:30, I was thinking the whole thing was a bust and was about to say so. That's when we heard the roar. Bishnu knew where to look, and shortly he had the big cat spotted. He scrambled down the tree and grabbed me by my arm, hustling me down the riverbank and through the water. And now, I crouched here alone in the tall grass, waiting for Bishnu to return with news of the tiger . . . or to be gored by a rhino.

Soon I heard the grass rustle off to my right, and I spun in that direction. Bishnu appeared, a wide, excited grin on his face. He bared his teeth and made his hands claw-like, the sign I suppose for "tiger." Wheeling back around, he signaled for me to follow. We hurried through the grass in a low crouch, arriving in a few minutes at a high point. We belly-crawled the last few meters, and then Bishnu pointed toward the far bank. A pool had formed in the river thirty meters away, and standing chest-deep in the water was a full-grown, 600-pound adult male Bengal tiger.

All my senses went to DEFCON 1. The jungle suddenly seemed more real. The sky looked bluer, the scent of the river was more pungent, and I could now hear subtle jungle sounds that until that moment had gone unperceived. It's amazing how quickly reality re-orders itself when you realize that you're no longer at the top of the food chain. We lay in the tall grass for a while watching the tiger, until Bishnu said it was time to leave. We scrambled back across the river, making it to the road after dark. On the way out, we saw tiger claw marks on tree trunks and a six-inch-wide snake track. As we passed a log on the riverbank, it suddenly came to life and slithered into the water. The crocodile startled us both.

The Bus With No Windshield

My plan was to ride to Butwal in central Nepal and then leave the Mahendra Highway to head north on the Siddhartha Highway, which winds up through the foothills of the Himalaya to Pokhara. I'd yet to ride in the Himalaya; I'd heard that it was dangerous, but I figured I'd gather information along the way and then decide if I wanted to try it. I rode east for several days, passing through the villages of Kohalpur, Chaulahi and Mourighat, where I crossed the Arjun Khola on a modern bridge and climbed over the Sivalik Mountain Range. After taking the best part of a day to make it back down to the flatlands, I was looking forward to some easy riding. The countryside didn't change much. There were lots of dusty little towns and farms. I'd be riding through dense jungle one moment and past farmers' fields the next. Invariably, my presence caused a stir, especially among the kids. As soon as they spotted me they'd drop what they were doing and head out at a dead run.

"Bye bye!" They would shout as they ran, "Bye bye!" I'd slow so they could catch up. They'd swarm around, touching my bicycle and me and smiling and laughing. It was as if the circus had come to town. I kept cookies or fruit in my handlebar bag and handed goodies out at these impromptu roadside gatherings.

Nepali public transit

One day, west of Butwal, the late afternoon sun caught me. I flagged down a bus, and half a dozen riders piled out to help me get my gear on board. One fellow scampered up the ladder to the roof while others threw him my panniers. When my luggage had been secured, they grabbed my bike and hauled it to the top of the bus, too. Then we all scrambled back on board, the driver gunned the engine, and the old tub slowly accelerated. As we rattled down the road, Indian music blaring on the stereo, a passing bus tossed a rock that came through our bus's windshield. Luckily, no one was hurt, but the glass was destroyed. Several men jumped out and removed the broken shards so that now there was no windshield at all. The broken glass was simply left at the side of the road.

I got off in Butwal and found a hotel, had dinner in the restaurant, and got to talking with the owner's son, who spoke English. I told him of my plan to ride up through the Himalaya to Pokhara and asked his advice. He shook his head. "That road is narrow, winding and steep. There are no shoulders, and what pavement there is is in bad condition. There's a lot of bus and truck traffic, and they hang over the edge of the road! I do not recommend trying to ride a bicycle to Pokhara."

I took his advice, and the next morning, I packed up and rode to the bus terminal. After buying a ticket to Pokhara, I loaded my gear on the bus. As I secured my bike to the roof rack, I saw the old bucket that I'd come to town in the day before. I'd assumed they would take it out of service long enough to replace the windshield, but no, they had no intention of putting new glass in that old beater. From now on, it would simply be known as "The Bus with No Windshield."

It was a six-hour ride through the foothills of the Himalaya to Pokhara, and what a ride it was! Just as I'd been warned, the road was narrow, winding, steep and scary. Precipitous drop-offs of hundreds, if not thousands, of feet yawned at the edge of the road. The drivers sped along leaning on their horns each time they careened around a blind corner. All this madness took place to a score of Indian music blaring over an old, tinny-sounding stereo. These maniacs would pass at the most inopportune moments, and more than once I was sure we were about to meet a fiery death. But somehow we reached Pokhara safe and sound. It was dusk by the time I got my gear together and my bike on the road. I stopped at several hotels along the main strip, but they were all full. Because it was Nepal New Year, the city was filled with celebrants, and I'd been told that I wouldn't find a room at any price. So I got back on my bike and coasted down the hill toward Phewa Lake, where the last rays of the sun glinted off the water. I had no idea where I would sleep, but I wasn't worried. Something would turn up.

In Pokhara

Phewa Lake

I awoke to the crowing of a rooster. I could tell by the way the room felt that it was late. The place was already heating up. I could sense the fan turning lazily above the bed. I lay still with my eyes closed. *Let's see,* I thought, *where am I?* I sat up and looked around. The room was nice by Nepal standards, even luxurious. There was a big-screen TV over there on the wall and lots of natural light. In the corner was the open door to the bathroom, and through it, I could see the edge of a bathtub. Fluffy white towels hung on a rack. Ah yes, it was all coming back to me now. I'd ridden along the lake stopping at every hotel until I found this place a few blocks from the shore. They'd had a room for only eight dollars a night. I'd been so worn out that I'd fallen asleep as soon as my head hit the pillow, and had slept soundly through the night, and now it was . . . I checked my watch . . . almost 8:30! I hadn't slept that late for a long time, and it felt good. I got out of bed, grabbed a quick shower, put on my cleanest dirty clothes, and went downstairs to find breakfast.

On one level, Pokhara is as rustic as every other town and village in Nepal, with its share of shanties, dirt streets and old cars. But Pokhara is also a city with a Western facet. It's the jumping-off point for expeditions to Annapurna and other big Himalayan mountains, and there is a guide and porter service on every street corner. A thriving trekking industry offers plane and helicopter sightseeing trips, and you can sign up at storefronts for a day of hang gliding, mountain biking, and river rafting. Counterfeit, brand-name outdoor equipment is for sale at countless shops. When I asked one shop owner why the North Face label on a shirt I was looking at was wrong, he shrugged. "How much would you care to pay?" was his response.

Annapurna Basecamp

I grabbed breakfast at a restaurant and passed the rest of the morning wandering around town, returning in the early afternoon to my hotel where I asked the clerk about hiring a guide to take me to the Annapurna Basecamp. "Ah yes, I know a very good guide and only fifteen dollars a day!"

"Great," I said, "when can I leave?"

I made arrangements to store my bike and gear at the hotel, and early the next morning, my guide, Prem, arrived. We jumped in a cab and drove a few kilometers out of town to a little village where our five-day hike to Basecamp would begin. I wrote the following account of the trek as it happened.

Day One

My Nepali guide, Prem, and I leave the highway at the village of Phedi at 8:30 in the morning, heading for the Annapurna Basecamp, or ABC, as the locals call it. The first half hour is a climb up the side of a steep grade, but the stone steps help a lot. When we reach a small hotel at the top of the first knoll at the village of Dhampis, we stop for a brief rest. It's hot, and I am moving slow and sweating, so when we re-shoulder our packs, Prem insists we load most of our gear into the bigger of the two sacks that he then carries. I am given the lighter pack that holds little more than a bottle of water.

I appreciate his offer to act as porter as well as guide, but I suspect his motives are something less than wholly altruistic. He's young, just twenty-three, and climbs at a much faster pace than my sixty-three-year-old body can manage; I think he'd just as soon I pick up the pace, even if it means a greater burden for himself. "I am young and strong," he tells me. "You enjoy hike much better with small pack . . . Yes, I think so."

The rest of the day is up and down: climb, descend, repeat. Up one ridge, then down into a river valley, then up the next hill. The Nepali villages we pass are tucked up against steep mountainsides on small terraces. The buildings look like they've been put together from the parts of other buildings. Windows and doors don't match; walls are made from rock, timber and poured concrete. The roofs might be clad in metal, fiberglass, native slate or some combination of all three. They're eclectic looking, and none seem to be very old. I suspect that when hit with an earthquake or avalanche, the villagers simply construct the new village from the fragments of the old one.

At 4:00 p.m. we reach Pothana, where we will stop for the night. The accommodations are basic: a small, cement chamber with bare walls and one window. There are two wooden platforms raised two feet off the stone floor, with six-inch-thick mattresses.

A single compact fluorescent bulb dangles by its wire. Dinner is served in a common dining room, where I join a group of Brits coming down from ABC. They are sunburned and grizzled and happy. My guide takes my dinner order and disappears into the kitchen. In a half hour, I'm enjoying a plate of fried noodles with vegetables in a spicy red sauce. I wash it down with a bottle of Everest beer and stumble off to bed.

Day Two

Annapurna, the tenth highest mountain in the world, was first climbed in 1950 by a French team led by legendary mountaineer Maurice Herzog. It was the first of the 8,000-meter Himalayan giants to be conquered. My goal is more modest; I'll be happy just to make it to Basecamp.

I am awake before sunrise and lie beneath the blanket urging the dawn. As the first weak rays stream in through the small window, I'm up and packing. Prem is still asleep, so I tiptoe out, find the washroom, brush my teeth, and splash cold water on my face. I glance at my watch and see that it's barely 6:30. I'm the first of the trekkers up, and I wander over to the dining room where I rouse a sleepy cook and order pancakes and milk tea. As I'm finishing my meal, Prem comes in and sits down beside me.

"You up early," he says. "I think maybe I stay here a while and you start out." He points toward the trail winding out of sight around a ridge. "Stay, stay on trail and I catch up after."

That's okay with me, I thought. *I prefer to hike alone.* It gives me the opportunity to drift along at my own slow pace and stop to take in the view when the spirit moves me. I start out with a group of porters, each of whom carries two or three huge climber's packs tied together and supported by a headband. The men look like they're struggling under the heavy loads, and I feel bad for them.

Before I start, I take a few minutes to appreciate the view. The sky is clear and in the far distance I can see huge, snow clad peaks. I don't know their names, and there's no one around to ask, so I snap a few photos and hit the trail. Most of the walking this morning will be on the flat or downhill. It's nice not to have to climb so much, but I resent losing all the hard-gained altitude of Day One. By late morning, Prem has caught up, and we descend again to the Modi Khola, a raging torrent hurrying down through a tortuous gorge from the glaciers far above. With my heart in my throat, I cross a swinging cable bridge strung precariously thirty feet above the Khola's boiling waters and jumbled boulders. Immediately on the other side, we begin to climb again. This one is steep, and I use the rest step taught to me by the Mt. Rainier guides to make the thirty-minute ascent to the top of the ridge. My heart sinks when I spy our goal for the day: the ridge-top village of Jhinu. I can see from my airy perch that I'll have to drop down hundreds of feet to a tributary, then re-ascend those hundreds of feet, plus a hundred more before this day is done. Jhinu is renowned for the curative powers of its hot springs. When we reach the village, Prem insists we hike the fifteen minutes to the springs for a good soak, but that last climb has left me exhausted, and when I see that it involves descending back down to the Modi, I stop, turn, and head for my room, where I take a nap.

Day Three

I'm awakened in the middle of the night by a dull ache. It takes me a moment to pinpoint it, and finally I realize that it's my old knee injury kicking up again. I reach down to massage it and discover, to my horror, that the knee is swollen to half again its normal size. I can move it, but it hurts. I take some ibuprofen and fall back into a fitful sleep.

Jhinu is at 1,780 meters — hardly high enough to qualify as High Altitude, at least not for the company that Maurice Herzog and his teammates kept. They were the first to reach a height of over 8,000 meters under their own steam, but they paid a dear price. As I stand outside the guesthouse this morning, I get my first good view of Machhapuchhre, or "Fishtail," a companion peak of Annapurna. It's not nearly as high as Annapurna, but etched vividly against an impossibly blue sky, it looks imposing as hell.

Village, Himalaya

I gently stretch to work the stiffness out of my bum knee and try to imagine what it had been like for Herzog when he and Louis Lachenal finally stood on Annapurna's summit. And when, during the descent in a hypoxic daze, Herzog made the tragic mistake that nearly cost him his life. But it's best to put such grim thoughts out of my mind for now. It's a fine, clear morning, I've had a big breakfast, my pack is light, and my knee is usable if not quite in sprinting condition. If I baby it, and use my walking stick, I'm certain I can make it to Basecamp just three days from now. Prem and I have fallen into a comfortable routine. I'm out of bed and on the trail by 7:00 a.m.; Prem likes to sleep in, and usually doesn't get going until later. Today, he catches up with me midmorning, and we take a break at Kuldhigar. "Do you want to eat, Father?" He asks. He's taken to calling me by this name, and by "Ba," which he tells me is Nepali for dad.

"Nah," I say, "I'm not hungry." The truth is, I find it uncomfortable to eat in front of Prem. The fifteen bucks a day I'm paying his agent back in Pokhara is supposed to cover his room and board. He waits on me hand and foot and sits patiently while I pack in the calories. I assume he gets food from the kitchens of the tea houses where we stop, but I never see him eat. Food is expensive this far up the trail, and I can't afford to buy his meals, so I've been skipping lunch. Prem is engaged in conversation with the other guides, and I shoulder my pack, grab my walking stick, and, with a wave to Prem, start out from Kuldhigar. As I pass the next guesthouse, I buy a candy bar and eat it as I hike out of the village.

The goal for today is the village of Bamboo. We gained a lot of altitude yesterday, and this afternoon I lose some of it in my descent to the village. As I go lower toward the khola, the jungle thickens, the trail winding past giant ferns and tall palms. Through a break in the canopy overhead, a huge bird wheels across the sky and disappears. Near a jumble of boulders on a steep cliff side, I pass an ancient, gnarled rhododendron tree with beautiful red blooms. Some of the blossoms have fallen onto the trail and form a scarlet carpet. For the first time, I fully realize what a strange and exotic place this is. With its weird sights, sounds and scents, the idea hits me just how far from home I am.

At 3:00 p.m. I reach Bamboo, and as I step into the shelter of the tea house, the rain begins to fall lightly and sporadically, then in full force. I collapse on my bed and drift off into a light sleep. But soon, the pounding of hail on the metal roof awakens me. I get up and dash through the deluge to the restaurant just in time to see Prem walking up the trail. I give him a wave and a shout and point to our room; he runs over and disappears inside.

I sit down at the table next to a young trekker, and we introduce ourselves. His name is Alastair, a Brit, and like me, he's in the marketing game. We hit it off right away and talk shop over dinner.

Day Four

I get an early start out of Bamboo this morning, heading for the village of Deurali, where we'll spend the last night before the push to ABC. The trail hugs the bank of the Modi Khola now, and the sight and sound of the river is never far away. It's a steady, uphill grind from here, and the canyon narrows as I get closer to the river's source. Machhapuchhre dominates the skyline over there to the right, and I stop often to snap pictures. I walk in faint, predawn light, but the sky is a deep blue beyond Machhapuchhre. Soon the sun will be up. It's still cold, though, and I'm wearing a thin pair of fleece gloves and the orange counterfeit North Face fleece hat I bought at a trekking shop in Pokhara. The chill hasn't done anything to help the stiffness in my knee, and I stop to stretch. It's a pleasant feeling being cold, though. There's a sharpness in the air that's exhilarating, and I take in a deep breath and blow out a cloud of steam for the sheer joy of it.

It was cold, too, that day on Annapurna sixty-three years ago. Herzog and Lachenal had made the summit and were descending when, just below the top, Herzog paused to get something out of his pack. Because he was without bottled oxygen, Herzog was severely hypoxic, and he forgot why he'd stopped. As he tried to remember, he watched in horror as his gloves, which he'd removed to undo his pack, slid along the icy slope and out of sight. Even in his compromised state, he understood the dangers of exposed flesh at 26,000 feet. He did the only thing he could: he started down, hoping to reach high camp before frostbite set in. By the time he reached the tents, his hands and feet were frozen. Luckily, two other climbers had ascended to the high camp to act as a support team. If not for them and the emergency first aid they administered, Lachenal and Herzog would have perished that night.

Though the two summiteers were still alive the next morning, getting them down the treacherous slopes of Annapurna in their now-crippled condition would prove an epic ordeal. The worst was yet to come.

There's an axiom in mountain climbing that says, "By the time you realize something is wrong, it's too late to do anything about it." I've been on the business end of that axiom, so I survey my surroundings to try to spot potential dangers, and I realize the place is full of them. I'm standing on a narrow path carved out of a steep cliff. A misstep could send me tumbling into the river, or I could be crushed by a rock falling from the mountain above. I shrug, take up my walking stick, and continue along the trail with a light heart.

The first village I come to is Dobhan, but I'm clicking along at a decent pace; my leg is limbering up, and I truck right on through without stopping. I've got summit fever now. I'm itching to get to ABC, and I pick up the pace, though speed at this point doesn't matter. I won't get to Basecamp until tomorrow no matter how fast I go today, so I force myself to slow down. No point risking that knee. Prem has caught up; he's walking behind singing snatches of *Oh Suzie Q*. We stop at the next village, Himalaya, where I buy us Cokes for $5.80. The sun has climbed over the peaks; it's warm now, and I stretch out on the ground and soak up some rays. I doze, then awake with a start. I look around, not certain at first where I am. It takes a few minutes to gather my gear and get going. My head feels as if it's stuffed with cotton; I don't know if it's a residual effect of my nap or the altitude. We're at nearly 10,000 feet, and I've always been susceptible to mountain sickness.

I reach Deurali just as it begins to rain. Prem has arrived first and tells me that the guesthouse is full. He asks if I mind sharing a room with another trekker. It turns out my roommate is none other than my new pal, Alastair. We have dinner together, and during our conversation I find that he is finishing the Annapurna Circuit: a grueling, twenty-six-day trip that winds through the

Annapurna Sanctuary and has taken him as high as 15,000 feet. His trip makes me feel wimpy, so I don't mention that I'm starting to feel the altitude at this paltry height of 10,000 feet.

Day Five

Today is the day! I'm up before dawn, packed and ready to go by 6:30. As usual, I start out by myself and set a quick pace for MBC, Machhapuchhre Basecamp. As I hike out of the village, the trail begins to angle down toward the Modi Khola. The jungle is behind me now, and the landscape has changed from lush green to shades of gray and brown. The place is nearly barren, with short, wiry grass and stunted trees dotting the rocky landscape. It reminds me of the Alpine regions in the mountains back in Washington, and I feel right at home. I cross the khola on a rickety bridge made from a rusty steel ladder supported by stacks of rocks. The water foams and boils and splashes between the rungs of the ladder, and I give a sigh of relief when I reach the other side. I don't even realize that I've been holding my breath.

Machhapuchhre still dominates. Annapurna is blocked from view by a high ridge on my left. I won't get to see it until I reach MBC and take a hard left turn up the glacier-carved valley that leads the last few thousand feet to ABC. But I don't have to wait long. In an hour and a half, I see ahead and above me the welcome green roof of the guesthouse at MBC. Prem is up ahead somewhere, and I hurry along the rocky path. I take a rest break at MBC and sit at a table in the sun, marveling at my first view of the Annapurna Massif. Prem has to keep pointing out the peak to me; it looks like one continuous ridge from here. Annapurna is big and impressive, but not the singular peak I had imagined.

The afternoon weather gets worse the higher we go. The clouds have been moving in earlier and earlier. Down below, the rains held off until two in the afternoon, but now we can see the wispy white clouds forming that signal a coming storm, and it's only 10:00 a.m. Prem and I scurry up the valley toward ABC. We can see the guesthouse perched on a plateau; it seems maddeningly close, but I restrain myself. High in the mountains, distances can be deceptive. As we climb higher, even the hearty little trees that struggle along the banks of the Modi Khola are absent. The grass is only a few inches high and tough as steel wool. Patches of snow linger in the shade of mammoth boulders that lie jumbled along the slopes. High, snow-capped ridges rise out of the valley on either side.

I keep my head down and try to keep my breathing steady, but I can't seem to get a full breath. The air is thin up this high. I'm in running shoes, and my feet are wet from the small streams I've waded through. My knee hasn't been feeling good today; I've been leaning on my walking stick. But none of that matters now. I'm on the last rock stairway to the Annapurna Basecamp. Three steps, then two, then . . . I pause before the last step. I want to savor this moment, and I take off my sunglasses, wipe the sweat from my face, and look up toward the mountain. Everything beyond a few dozen yards is cloaked in thick, impenetrable clouds. I can't see a thing, but I don't care. I mount the last step and I'm there.

Tonight

I'm in the dining room, and I've struck up a conversation with a young couple, Jade and Chris. Jade is an up-and-coming designer from New Zealand. Chris is a master gardener from Australia. They arrived at Basecamp shortly after I did. We order Everest beers and toast our achievement. It's warm and cheery in this low-ceilinged room, and we all bask in the glow of good fellowship. Outside, the wind is howling, and the snow is coming down in earnest. Although I'm safe and warm, I can't help thinking about Herzog's ordeal. Though we're separated by more than half a century, his epic struggle occurred in similar weather on the treacherous slopes not far from where I'm sitting.

Herzog and Lachenal had badly frostbitten limbs and at sunrise had to be helped into their boots by fellow climbers Gaston

Rébuffat and Lionel Terray. They emerged from the tents and began the descent to Camp IV, only to become hopelessly lost in a storm. Without protection from the elements, they were forced to bivouac in a crevasse at 23,000 feet, where they spent a miserable night. Then, in the morning, they were buried by an avalanche. It looked like the end, but through a superhuman effort they dug themselves out and continued the descent. They didn't make it very far. Exhausted, and with Rébuffat and Terray snowblind, the climbers began arguing about which way to go. In an advanced state of delirium, Herzog sat down in the snow to wait for that long, slow slide into eternity. Miraculously, climbers from a lower camp made it to the lost party and helped them hobble down the mountain. Lachenal and Herzog survived the descent, and though they lost fingers and toes, both went on to live long, full lives.

Sunrise, Annapurna Basecamp

Even though Prem has gotten me an extra blanket, it's too cold to sleep. I can hear the storm raging outside, and I am worried that descending in my running shoes will be a problem. In addition, there's the whole thing with my knee. "To hell with it," I finally mumble, and pull the blankets over my head. "I'll worry about it tomorrow."

Namaste

On the way down the next morning, I stopped at Machhapuchhre Basecamp for breakfast and was stunned to learn that the camp had WiFi. I purchased thirty minutes and pinged my eldest daughter, Brittney. I was sitting outside with the mountain in the background when I made the call. "Holy cow, Dad," she said, "where are you?!"

I laughed. "I'm in the Himalaya at about 11,000 feet!"

"No way," Brittney exclaimed, a broad smile on her face. "Is that Mt. Everest?"

"Almost," I said. "It's called Machhapuchhre; they also call it Fishtail." I flipped the iPad screen around and panned from the base of the mountain to the top.

"I see why. It kind of looks like one." She gave me a sidelong glance. "Are you really in the mountains, or are you in some kind of trick photo booth?"

"I'm really in the Himalaya," I said. "Crazy, huh?"

"Are you clinging to the side of a cliff? It looks pretty scary."

"There's a tea house and a restaurant. I just had breakfast and couldn't resist giving you a call."

"Well, I'm sure glad you did. It looks like a fantastic place, all right."

We talked a while longer, and when it was time to resume the descent, we said goodbye. Gathering up my gear, I headed down the khola.

It took three days to get back to Pokhara. The night after I returned, I got together with some of the people I'd met at Annapurna Basecamp for a night on the town. Jade, Chris, Alastair and I had dinner and then went to a few bars. At one place, I ran into a German woman I'd met at ABC, Linda, who was out on the town with a group of her friends.

We were all heading to Katmandu, so we vowed to meet there. But first, I wanted to go for a motorcycle ride. There's an Indian-made cycle called the Royal Enfield that is an old, British single-cylinder design of 500 cc's that hasn't changed much since the original model. It's got classic 1950's lines, a single, big headlight, and a soulful exhaust note that was music to my ears. I'd seen them all over India and Nepal, where the police and army use them, and I was dying to get my hands on one. Alastair had never ridden a motorcycle, but he was game to try, so we found a place that rented the classic old machines and arranged to pick a pair of them up the following morning. We met for an early breakfast and then hurried to the shop. When we got there, the English woman who ran the place gave us a quick lesson in the intricacies of starting and operating the bikes, and we were off.

The one I was on was fifty years old, while Alastair had a newer model. We made it almost to the end of the block when the wiring on Alastair's ride caught fire. Batting out the flames, we turned around and made a beeline back to the shop, where the owner jury-rigged a work-around of the burnt electrical system. Soon, we were off again. This time we made it only as far as the end of the driveway when a Pokhara cop pulled us over and, after examining our rental agreements, confiscated our keys. The owner of the shop, who had been watching, hurried out. After a heated discussion with the cop, she got our keys back and sent us on our way. On the outskirts of town, though, Alastair waved and shouted: in all the confusion, he'd left his camera at the shop, so once again we returned to town.

With everything sorted out, and feeling like biker outlaws, we headed up into the foothills of the Himalaya. My machine kept slipping out of fourth gear, and Alastair's engine would suddenly quit at the most inopportune times, but we had a ball despite the mechanical problems. We motored up through the mountains, passing through small villages and terraced fields where farmers toiled in the unrelenting heat. The road wound along through deep canyons and beside raging torrents, climbing precariously up the sides of steep jungle ridges and over rickety bridges. As we climbed higher, the jungle closed in tighter. We sped past locals walking alongside the road who would wave and whoop and holler as we rumbled by.

We rode as far as the road would allow, the pavement soon turning to gravel, then dirt, then a rutted, single track where we decided discretion was the better part of valor and turned around. Stopping at a small village for lunch, we were approached by a man trying to sell us pearls that he assured us were genuine. Being many hundreds of miles from the nearest ocean, of course we were skeptical, but I guess the price was right, because Alastair picked up some for a pittance. I think he made the purchase more out of sympathy for the ragged fellow than in expectation of a killer deal. We made it back to Pokhara just as the sun was setting, which was fortunate because we discovered that the lights didn't work on either bike.

Katmandu

Jade and Chris flew to Katmandu, while Alastair and I took the bus. Alastair met two American women on the trip whom we hung out with for several nights in Katmandu. Alastair had his eye on one of them, and they went out on a date or two; he told me later that he'd given her the pearls he'd bought at lunch outside Pokhara.

Kathmandu is everything that is good and bad about Nepal. It's a polite, friendly town, the prices are cheap, the food is not bad, and of course there's the Himalaya. It's safer than a lot of places I've been in the USA, and a good place to kick back. On the flip side, you can't walk ten paces without someone trying to sell you something. Tiger Balm is a popular item; the streets are full of pitchmen pushing the stuff, along with Gurka knives, costume jewelry, and the occasional ounce of marijuana.

And then there's the air. You don't notice the pollution until you get out of town and look back. The brown haze that hangs over the city would rival a bad day in Los Angeles fifty years ago.

I was staying in Thamel, the tourist district of Kathmandu, where the round-eyes outnumber the natives. Nepal, and Katmandu especially, has a mystical attraction for Westerners. In a five-minute stroll down one of Thamel's narrow streets, you'll see a wide cross-section of humanity — everyone from dreadlocked hippies to middle-class families that look like they just got off the plane from Kansas City. There are upscale bars with names like "The Electric Pagoda" and "The Funky Buddha," where a bottle of Extra-Strong Everest Beer will run you a buck and a quarter and the menus offer everything from chicken burritos to cheeseburgers to something called American Chop Suey.

But to focus on the shuck and jive is to miss the bigger picture, or, should I say, the deeper vibe that permeates Nepal. Nepal is incredibly poor, and the suffering of its people is never far from sight, even here in Thamel. But the people take it in stride. It's not simply a dignified resignation to an unkind fate but a type of happy wisdom drawn from some inexplicable source.

After a few days hanging out in Katmandu, Chris and Jade left for Thailand and Alastair headed off to Everest Basecamp. I had booked passage on a Nepal Air flight to Istanbul, and the sun was not yet up when the cab let me off at the airport. The jet took off under a clear sky just as day broke. I had a seat on the Himalayan side and watched the sun come up on Everest from 30,000 feet, just about eye level with the summit. It was a fitting farewell to Asia.

I had been sitting in Katmandu for several days, and I was restless. It seemed that the only time I felt really centered was when I was on the move. But I would have to wait. The trip from Katmandu to Delhi to Dubai and finally to Istanbul would last almost twenty-four hours. The next time I rode my bike, I would be back in Europe.

Chapter Twenty-Five: Turkey

Fishermen, Galata Bridge, Istanbul

I arrived at the hotel midday, but my room wasn't ready, so I killed some hours wandering around Istanbul. My neighborhood was touristy, with cafes and bookstores lining its narrow, hilly streets. Just a few blocks away was the Bosphorus Strait, where tour boats, ferries, and deep-water ocean liners vied for space at the crowded docks. On the far hill sat the Blue Mosque; a few blocks west was the Grand Bazaar, and down the street the Galata Bridge. Yeah, it was a very cool place to be, and I was looking forward to exploring it, but I hadn't slept in thirty-three hours, so I went back to the hotel and crashed.

When I had checked in a few hours earlier, I had to think a minute when the clerk asked where I was coming from. "Dubai," I said, then, "Uh, no, check that, I'm coming from uh . . ." I launched into a long explanation about how I'd spent last month banging around Nepal and had flown from Katmandu to layovers in Delhi and Dubai, and finally, here to Istanbul. I get chatty when I'm tired. The whole thing was pointless, of course, given the circumstances; he didn't care, he just needed something to put in his book. I showed him my passport and retrieved the box my buddy, Mike, had sent from the USA. I'd called him from Katmandu when some of my bike parts failed and I'd been unable to find replacements. He'd been kind enough to rustle up the needed components and ship them to my hotel here in Turkey. My plan was to spend a few days playing tourist and bike mechanic, and then head north toward the Black Sea.

When most people visit a city like Istanbul, they take the tour bus or go for a ride on a boat; they see the local sights. But when I landed in one of these exotic ports, I was more likely to be found inside a camping store or bike shop than seeing a historic landmark. I'd be so busy taking care of business that I rarely got to do those neat, touristy things. The day after I reached Istanbul, I got up early to assemble my bike, and I promptly broke the stem that had been repaired in Vietnam. Luckily, I'd suspected the repair might not last and had bought a new stem online, having Mike send it to me in Turkey along with a new Brooks saddle. I'd also replaced the seat post in Katmandu and needed a special clamp to complete the fix; I scurried around from bike shop to bike shop scaring up the part, and it wasn't until the afternoon that I had my bike in working order.

Next on my agenda was plotting a route to Greece. I'd been surfing the Net, reading of others' experiences cycling in that part of the world, so I had a rough idea of the route I wanted to take. I had to restock my larder, buy fuel for my stove, and locate maps. Besides all that, there was laundry to do. But this was Istanbul, one of the most interesting cities in the world, and even with all those chores, I still managed to do a little sightseeing. I walked the two or three kilometers to the Grand Bazaar and was amazed by the variety of goods for sale there — everything from exotic spices to gold and diamonds to colorful pottery to lamps with elaborate designs. The crowds were massive; we were packed together so tightly that I simply let myself be moved along by the throng. Later, I pedaled over the Galata Bridge to scout out the route, riding along the banks of the Bosphorus, the narrow body of water connecting the Black Sea with the Sea of Marmara. I was on the European side, but just a few hundred yards over the water lay Asia. There aren't many places in the world where things like the ends and beginnings of continents are so close and clear-cut.

The Bosphorus

By the third day, I was ready to set out. I visited a grocery store and stocked up on food, and a local sporting goods shop provided me with fuel for my stove. Rising early, I paid my hotel bill and headed north toward the Black Sea. Though this part of the Strait of Bosphorus lies within Turkish sovereign territory, because of its strategic importance it is considered international territory. Russia uses it to move its navy between its ports on the Black Sea and the Mediterranean Sea, and I was told that the U.S. keeps tabs on the Russians from a spy station looking down on the Strait.

It was a Saturday, and traffic was light as I rode along the Bosphorus. The sun was just breaking through a gang of clouds across the water over in Asia; the fishermen were out, the pavement was smooth, and a sweeter introduction to cycling in Turkey I couldn't imagine. After twenty kilometers, I left the water and headed up into the mountains. The first kilometer or so was steep, and I had to get off and push a few times, but after an hour I reached the top and sailed happily through a series of winding rollers. I was enjoying the riding so much that I neglected to check my map, and soon I discovered I had made a wrong turn a few klicks back.

One Degree of Separation

I was consulting my GPS when a fellow on a mountain bike stopped to help. We got to talking, and he asked where I was from. "Oh, Seattle," he said after I told him, "I know Seattle."

"Have you been there?" I asked.

"Sure," he replied, "I spent some time there."

"Crazy."

"Yeah," he said, "I work for Phillips Medical Systems."

"Get out," I said, "my best buddy works for Phillips."

"Yeah? What's his name?"

"Mike Mann."

His jaw dropped and his eyes went wide. "Sure," my new friend said without a moment's hesitation, "I know Mike! I've worked with him for years!"

His name was Maarten, and he told me that he and his wife, Janneke, were also long-distance bike tourers. "Listen," he said, "why don't you come spend the night with us? We'd love to hear about your travels.

I jumped at the chance. We loaded our bikes on Maarten's car and drove to his house a few kilometers away. Janneke made dinner, and we sat around the table and drank wine and talked until late. The next morning, which happened to be Mother's Day, we sat on the patio and had a leisurely breakfast, after which Maarten drove me back near the place where we'd met the day before and helped me load my panniers on my bike. We chatted for a few minutes, and then I was off.

Dog Camp

I pedaled through small towns and wild countryside. I climbed uphill and down and sped along the flats, propelled by a ferocious tailwind. Making a hundred kilometers by afternoon, I decided to camp early. I had been passing places that looked something like campgrounds, but not quite; they were more like the big day-use parks we have in the USA. Most were located in wooded areas and had snack shacks, playground equipment and large parking lots usually crammed full of cars. I hadn't seen an According-to-Hoyle campground anywhere, so I pulled into one of the day-use areas and asked if I could camp there. Though she spoke no English, the woman who ran the concession stand and I were able to communicate, and she indicated a spot where I could set up my tent. The park was in a dense forest; all that shade made for a nice, cool camp.

I made dinner and then went to the concession stand and bought a beer. Sitting on a bench, I watched kids play until dusk, when things began to wind down. The woman I'd spoken to earlier closed up shop and bid me goodnight. Now the last few cars left, and I was alone . . . almost.

Sometime during the night, I was awakened by the sound of dogs fighting. It sounded close. I grabbed my flashlight and peeked out. There were feral dogs everywhere! There must have been ten or fifteen of them, and they circled my tent. Evidently, the trash from the day-campers drew the beasts from miles around; the place became a regular canine supermarket after dark. I yelled and threw pebbles to scare them off, but a few minutes later they were back. They kept up a racket all night that kept me from getting much sleep. When the first rays of sun broke through the trees, I was up and on the road.

I think it was the cool, damp weather that made the riding so pleasant that day. After the hot, dry dust of Asia, the little rain that fell was a welcome respite, and I took my time, stopped a lot, and reached Kirklaerli by 4:15 p.m.

Turkish motorists were some of the most considerate I'd encountered in all the sixteen countries I'd biked through so far. They would slow down to pass me, and a lot of the oncoming cars would blink their lights and wave or give me the thumbs up. It was a small thing, I suppose, but when I was feeling beat at the end of a long day, it did wonders for my morale. Friendly people and courteous drivers weren't the only reasons I loved riding in Turkey, though. The only big hills I encountered were the ones out of Istanbul on the first day. A few low mountain passes aside, the rest of the pedaling was on the flat, or on small, rolling hills, on roads that were generally in good shape. They had little traffic and were free of trash, and the countryside was lush and green. It was mid-May now, and the fields would soon be in full production. Off in the distance were low, wooded hills and lines of tall trees. I had stopped at one picturesque spot to snap a photo when my camera broke. The lens refused to deploy, and I had to partially disassemble it to find the switch that activates the servomotor. From then on, I had to fool with the broken switch every time I wanted to take a picture. I couldn't complain, though; I'd bought my little Olympus ten years before and it had served me well.

A Very Good Day

A few klicks past Kirklaerli, I noticed that my bike's bottom bracket, the part that the pedals attach to, was loose. I'd passed a little bicycle/motorcycle shop earlier, so I turned around and made my way back. It turned out that the shop was a gathering spot for locals, and they deemed my arrival something of an event. While the owner fixed my bike, five or six of them gathered around and chatted with me. One, a young man who spoke English, translated for us. Soon someone from across the street showed up with a round of Turkish tea, and we all sat and drank and talked some more. Then it was time for breakfast. Another neighbor came by with sliced tomatoes, three different kinds of cheeses, more tea, bread, jam and butter, olives, more tea . . . Well, you get the idea; it was quite a feast. Finally, the work was completed and I went to pay, but the owner would have none of it. "You are a guest in my country, and I am happy to help you," he told me through our interpreter.

D020

Since leaving the Bosphorus, I had been riding in a northwest direction on Highway D020. After Kirklaerli, the road curved toward the south, so that now I was traveling in an almost due west direction. On the morning of the fourth day out of Istanbul, I reached the city of Edirne, just a few kilometers from the borders with Greece and Bulgaria. Now I had a choice to make. I could continue west through Bulgaria and Serbia to the port city of Bar, where I could catch a ferry across the Adriatic Sea to Italy, or I could head south through Greece to Athens and get a boat there. Both options appealed to me, and as I sat in a café pondering my dilemma, it occurred to me that I was less than a month from completing my 'round the world trip. I'd invested more than a year in this trip, and now it was coming to an end. What would I do when I reached Rome? I couldn't imagine going back to a normal life; I was just too changed for that.

I had seen the Roman ruins of central Europe, but not the Greek ruins of southern Europe. So it was settled; I'd go see Athens. My plan was to cross the border into Greece and head south to Alexandroupoli, ride west along the Adriatic coast to Thessaloniki, then head south again to Athens. That would be a trip of a little more than 600 miles and would take me two weeks. I'd spend a few days in Athens and then catch a ferry to Acana in north-central Italy. From there, it would be a stone's throw to Rome, and I would have gone around the Earth. It had always seemed that the road stretched out ahead forever. Now, I could see the finish line, and I found the thought troubling.

I had embarked on this trip to satisfy a vague longing. Something was missing from my life, and I'd set out in search of it. But lately, as my journey was drawing to a close, I was starting to get an inkling that something deeper and more basic was driving me, though I couldn't yet put my finger on exactly what that might be.

Chapter Twenty-Six: Greece

I rolled into Alexandroupoli after nine hours on the bike, sunburned, windblown and tired. Finding a hotel on a side street, I checked in and collapsed on the bed; I was asleep in minutes and didn't wake up until well after dark. I'd eaten little all day, stopping only to grab an occasional Coke and an orange or a banana, and my stomach was growling. So I made a trip to an all-night grocery, where I filled my basket with cheese, croissants and a liter of orange juice. I stumbled back to my room and made a hasty meal, then crashed. It was quite the end to a crazy day.

I was way ahead of schedule. It had taken just two days to make the trip south from near Edirne, where I'd crossed the border into Greece, to Alexandroupoli, on the Adriatic Sea. I had spent the first night in the village of Orestias. After that, I'd intended to take my time getting to the coast, but I'd gotten carried away and had ridden the whole remaining 130 kilometers on the second day and arrived exhausted.

My hotel in Alexandroupoli was on a quiet street a few blocks from the beach. I had a room on the third floor, with a window that caught the morning sun. The scent of the Aegean Sea filled the little suite. The room was dominated by a highboy bed and matching bureau of oak. At some point, a water closet with a western toilet, instead of the more common Turkish, or squat, toilet, had been added to the room. The building was old and had been meticulously maintained. The lobby floor and walls and reception desk were dark-veined marble. Gold trim adorned the doors and windows, and a gold-accented banister curved up a winding staircase.

I felt tired and lazy the next morning, so I decided it would be a rest day, and I slept in late. But by 9:30, I was restless and went looking for something to do. I hadn't given my bike much attention since Istanbul, and there were a few things that needed attending to. One problem in particular had me on tenterhooks since the bad tumble I'd taken while riding along the Bosphorus.

The accident had occurred as I sped down a broad waterfront promenade. The road was narrow and busy, so I rode on the sidewalk. As I pedaled along, I suddenly realized that the sidewalk was getting very narrow. A guardrail bordered one side and an industrial-sized trashcan the other. I was heading straight for the gap and at the last second judged that I wouldn't fit. I hit my brakes and swerved, sailing off the curb and striking the pavement with my front wheel. I'd performed similar emergency moves countless times before and was braced for the jolt, but I wasn't ready for what happened next.

The Path That Can be Named

When I'd reassembled my bike in Istanbul, I'd found that some bolts had been lost during shipment. I decided to replace them with plastic zip ties instead of the usual steel fasteners. I doubled up on zip ties just to make sure, but when the front wheel banged into the roadbed, the impact produced more stress than the zip ties could stand. The whole front rack broke loose from its upper moorings and fell forward, rotating around the bottom brace, which was bolted on. This caused the rack, panniers and all, to flip over the front tire and dig into the pavement like the blade of a bulldozer. The bike cartwheeled and threw me head over heels onto the ground. I survived the fall with only a few scrapes and bruises and was able to make my bike rideable again through the judicious use of zip ties and electrical tape. But after the spill, I distrusted that front rack; I wanted to get it attached solidly, and that meant using the right fasteners. I'd babied it and tried to find replacement bolts in the small towns I'd been passing through, but with no luck. Alexandroupoli looked to be a good-sized city, and maybe I could finally get what I needed. I wandered around until I found a hardware store, where I bought the bolts, washers and nuts I needed to secure the rack properly. Then I spent a few hours giving my bike a general going-over, cleaning it up and making it ready for the trip up the coast.

I left Alexandroupoli early and headed west along the Aegean. I had come to rely on the mapping feature of my smart phone so much that I hardly looked at my paper maps anymore. I tried to avoid the main highways, and I found the electronic maps superior for smaller roads because they were more up-to-date and had better detail.

Greek ruins, Aegean Sea

So I checked Google Maps on my phone, and sure enough, it showed me to be on a thick yellow line of a sort that had always in the past indicated a nicely paved secondary road. But the image on the little screen didn't jibe with what I was experiencing on the ground. Yeah, there was the blue Aegean to my left, and mountains to my right, and I'd just passed an archeological site, but that's where the similarity ended. The road had been good up until now, but things had changed rapidly once the pavement petered out. I got back on my bike and pedaled another kilometer up the road, dodging huge rocks, dismounting and pushing through hopeless sand pits, and generally having a tough time. I thought about turning around, but I'd come so far already . . .

I'd plotted a route the night before that hugged the coast, and for the first twenty-five kilometers, things had gone according to plan. I'd pedaled through the quaint coastal villages of Makri, Panorama and Kimisi. I rode past vineyards and orchards and the occasional ancient ruin. The road was narrow, but there wasn't much traffic, and the scenery was fantastic. The road had been playing tag with the beach most of the way, curving close, then heading up a draw into the mountains. But now, the pavement ran parallel to the beach, and then became the beach. The asphalt turned into sand and rocks, and riding my bike proved impossible; I would have to push. The only hope was that this was a temporary washout and the pavement would pick up again just over the next rise. I wiped the sweat from my brow. It was late morning now, and getting hot.

Hope is a hard thing to kill, and I couldn't get it out of my head that if I just pushed on a little farther, this crude path would turn into a smooth two-lane with clear sailing to the next little town. But I knew better, and after 300 meters I turned around and headed back the way I'd come. Soon I was back on pavement. It would be a ride of more than 20 kilometers to the next village where I might find the right route. It was frustrating to have to backtrack, but a reality of bicycle touring that I had come to grudgingly accept.

The situation brought to mind something I'd once read in the Tao that had stuck with me: "The path that can be named is not the true path." Was I on the true path? I was hot and sweaty and frustrated, and I really didn't care what path I was on as long as it led someplace shady where I could lie down and take a nap.

Cherries for Breakfast

I'd spent the best part of the day climbing over a mountain range and onto a high, windy inland plateau. I was now three days out of Alexandroupoli and well on my way to Thessaloniki. The riding was good, though I was eventually forced onto a main highway and had to contend with a lot of traffic, as well as a ferocious headwind. I headed for the coast on side roads as soon as I could, and spent the night at a campground on the beach. There was a bar there, and over a few beers I watched the day grow dark. The next morning, I had a great ride along a narrow road hugging the beach. A hint of a breeze came in off the Adriatic, and the air had that slightly briny chill you sometimes get near the water even when the night has been warm. As I rounded a corner, an old fellow who was helping build a fence around an archeological dig flagged me down. He motioned that I should wait, and then he hurried around to the back of his car, opened the trunk, and pulled out a paper bag. Coming over to where I stood, he handed it to me; it was full of ripe, red cherries. He motioned that I should have some, so I grabbed a handful and started munching away. They were delicious! We stood there for the better part of a half hour while talking and having cherries for breakfast. He spoke no English and I no Greek, but we understood each other. He told me about the ruins he was working near and about the people who had lived there over the ages. I could tell by the reverent way he spoke that he held this place in high regard.

Headwind Blues

There was no doubt about it: the road had definitely dead-ended. I'd climbed the hill only to find that my lane was closed off with Jersey barriers. I had already ridden ninety kilometers in a day-long headwind, and I was beat. I hurried across the oncoming lane and took the first side road I came to. Stopping in a park, I pulled out my phone and checked Google Maps. It looked as if there might be another road I could take, but all the twists and turns indicated a lot of climbing. I took off my helmet and stretched out on the bench; I'd rest my brain a few moments before tackling the problem.

When I woke up and looked at my watch, I saw that I'd been out for nearly fifteen minutes. Precious time had been wasted, time that I'd have to make up if I wanted to get to Thessaloniki before dark. I scanned my phone's little screen, got on my bike, and with one hand on the handlebar and the other holding the phone, I navigated through the residential neighborhood to the main road. In a few minutes, I was on top of a hill overlooking Thessaloniki. It had taken me five days to make the trip from Alexandroupoli. I'd ridden along the Adriatic, across mountain ranges, and past innumerable ancient archeological sites. I'd pedaled through rural areas and small villages, but as I got closer to the big seaport, the surroundings began to take on an industrial/urban flavor. I had become used to the country, but now that I was in the city, the hustle and bustle and dense traffic put me on edge. No more riding for hours in a delightful daze; now, I had to stay alert and on my toes, my head on a swivel.

It was a high-speed, downhill run into Thessaloniki, and I arrived at the city center in less than an hour. I rode around looking for a cheap hotel, but found nothing in my price range. Finally giving up, I checked into an upscale hotel, went to my room, and plopped down on the bed.

An hour later, my growling stomach awakened me. I checked my watch and saw that the restaurant was open, so I went downstairs. The restaurant was first class, with white tablecloths and uniformed waiters. The menu was in Greek, but one of the waitresses spoke English and helped me order. I guess they eat late in Greece, because even though it was past 7:00 p.m., the restaurant was nearly empty.

Athens

It was a short ride from the Athens train station to my hostel, where I checked in and locked my bike in the basement. It wasn't bad, as hostels go; I shared a room with two other travelers who seemed like nice enough guys. Michael, the fellow who ran the place, was quite a character. He looked to be in his mid-sixties, thin, with deep-set, dark eyes and a weathered complexion. His face looked like a catcher's mitt. I suspected Michael was bald, but I couldn't be sure because he wore a fright wig that sat crookedly on his head. He walked with such a severe stoop that his gaze was perpetually downcast; he would cock his head and look up at me when he spoke. But though he looked weird, he was a nice guy and had helped me wrestle my bike downstairs, where it now sat locked to a pipe.

I had decided to take the train from Thessaloniki and had reached Athens about noon. It had been my first experience riding Greek trains, and I was pleasantly surprised at how clean, modern, efficient and, most important, cheap they turned out to be. In some of the countries it had been a hassle to arrange passage for my bike. In India, getting all my stuff and myself on the same train had been a day-long job. But here in Greece, I simply handed my bike, panniers and all, to an attendant who took care of everything. And it all cost just a few euros. When I reached Athens a few hours later, my bike was waiting for me at baggage claim.

I had reserved a bed in this budget hostel near the station, and now I had nothing to do except relax and take in Athens. It would be my last European capital before I reached Rome, and I planned to make the most of it. I spent the first afternoon wandering around, getting to know my neighborhood; I'd gotten good at navigating these big, ancient cities. At first, it had been frustrating. The nightmare ride from Heathrow Airport through London had really put the fear in me. The second day had been even worse, and by the time I'd reached Antwerp, I was living in dread of the Big, Old European City. Just making it from one side of town to the other had often taken the better part of a morning or afternoon. The streets were a maze of winding lanes and dead ends. One afternoon in England, I circled the same roundabout three times before I could get off.

But by the time I'd reached Prague, I had mastered the art of finding my way around old urban environments. I had scurried around the Czech capital like a native. And now, here I was in one of the most ancient cities, with just my maps and a whole afternoon to kill. First, I walked the 2.4 kilometers to the base of the Acropolis. The sun was setting and I felt like unwinding, so I stopped into a bar and had an ouzo. There was a bar menu, but nothing looked good, so I finished my drink and took a roundabout path to my hostel.

I got up early the next morning and retraced my route to the ruins. I paid twelve euros, and they turned me loose inside. I'd studied these ancient Greek temples in art history as well as in architecture and design classes, and now here I was, walking among them! Restoration work is ongoing, and the Parthenon was clad in scaffolding. The area around the temple was roped off so that I could get to within only a few dozen meters of it, but it was a real treat just to be so close and to watch the play of light on the ancient stone. I spent the better part of the day wandering around the ruins, and stopped to overhear a tour guide telling a story about the Peloponnesian War.

I got back to my hostel in the early evening, made dinner in the communal kitchen, and hit the hay. I would leave for Italy in the morning.

The Last Dog

I was stopped at a light near the Athens bus station when the dog attacked. I was looking at my map and didn't see him come up from behind. At the last moment I caught a flash of brown fur out of the corner of my eye, and I jerked my leg out of the way just in time. Even though I escaped injury, the dog managed to take a bite out of my pants leg. There was a group of policemen standing nearby, and they all laughed. I had remounted and was pedaling like mad, but the dog kept up with me, nipping and growling. I reached down and grabbed a plastic water bottle out of the cage and squirted it in the dog's direction. He dodged and skidded to a halt, and I made good my escape.

I'd ridden the dozen or so kilometers from my hostel to the bus station through mostly empty streets. It was early still, and there were a few stray cabs and delivery trucks on the road, but not much else. As I pedaled down the narrow lanes, the only sound was the hum of my tires on damp pavement. Arriving at the bus station, I arranged passage to Patras, where I would catch the evening ferry across the Adriatic. At first the bus driver wasn't going to let me put my bike in the baggage compartment, but I waved my bike's ticket at him and he relented.

When we reached Patras, the bus let me off across the street from the docks where the ferries tie up. I found a ticket agent and booked passage on the next sailing aboard the Palermo, scheduled to leave around 8:00 that evening; it would be pulling out of port just at sundown. I made my way to the pier and found a place where I could get a drink. It was early yet, and the place was nearly deserted. I struck up a conversation with one of the security guards, who offered to keep an eye on my bike while I went upstairs to the bar. The ocean side was all glass, and as I sat sipping a beer, I watched a giant, red-and-white oceangoing ship slowly sidle up to the dock. I learned later that it was the Palermo, the ship I'd be taking to Italy.

A Voyage by Sea

Imagine a small movie theater without the screen and you have a rough idea of the compartment I shared with ten or fifteen other thrift-minded travelers on board the Palermo. With twelve decks, a swimming pool, and a casino, the Palermo more closely resembled a luxury cruise ship than a ferry, but our quarters were anything but first class.

I'd boarded a few hours earlier and parked my bike among the scores of semi trucks below on the car deck. I'd spent the first few hours wandering from deck to deck and finally wound up at the outdoor bar, sipping ouzo, as the coast of Greece receded in our wake. I'd always wanted to take a long ocean voyage, and now I had my chance. It would take twenty-four hours to reach Ancona, in northern Italy. I stood at the rail and marveled at the wonder of it all until it got too dark to see.

Back in the compartment, some people were sleeping on the floor while others dozed fitfully in their chairs. Once in a while, someone would get up to go to the bathroom or to wander out on deck for fresh air. I had folded up the chair arms and was stretched out on three seats, with my sleeping bag tossed over me like a blanket. Our quarters were on one of the lower decks, and the rhythmic vibrations from the engines seemed almost like the heartbeat of some living creature.

I didn't sleep very well and was up before sunrise. Upstairs in the cafeteria, I bought a meager breakfast. I was shocked at the high cost of food onboard and was glad I'd stocked up before leaving land. The weather was fine but windy, so I spent most of the crossing inside. We steamed into port just before nightfall, and it took half an hour to get the big ship tied up. But soon, I was riding through the dark streets of Ancona. I had reserved a place in a hostel near the pier, and as I lay in bed, I decided to take the train to Rome the next day instead of riding. I was now just a few hours from the end of my trip, and I guess I was getting anxious.

Chapter Twenty-Seven: Italy Again

The trip from Ancona to Civitavecchia was a happy blur. I passed the time thinking about all the places I'd been: London, Amsterdam, Prague, Saigon, Bangkok, Katmandu . . . and about the many adventures I'd had. I thought about how Bishnu had taught me to stalk a Bengal tiger, and how Chad had rescued me from that Montana blizzard, and how I'd gotten out of bed at 0-dark-30 to watch the sun rise on Annapurna.

I asked a passerby to take my picture.

In all, I had visited seventeen countries and crossed three continents. I couldn't count the number of new friends I'd made or the many acts of kindness shown me by complete strangers. Though I didn't keep count, I estimated that I'd ridden about 12,000 miles, and now, just a few more and I'd have gone around the world.

I reached Civitavecchia, Italy, midday on May 29, 2013. There was no brass band, no welcoming committee, no media present to record the historic moment. I asked a passerby to take my photo, and then I bought a bottle of red wine and a baguette to take down to the beach. As I sat watching the sunset over the Mediterranean, I began to ponder the meaning of this strange adventure. What had it been about? Certainly the months of rugged living had left their mark on my body. I had lost more than thirty pounds and had to use a length of twine to hold my pants up.

Life on the road had forced me to confront many harsh truths. I'd hit rock bottom a time or two, and had been humbled in ways I'd never imagined. Still, there were incredible highs, and they more than made up for the hardships I endured.

But had I learned anything new? Or had I just rediscovered what I'd already known — the tried and true lessons about focus, determination, resilience, ingenuity, patience, perspective, confidence, empathy? All those noble principles we're taught as kids, but too often lose sight of as we age.

Nothing I'd seen or done or felt had triggered an epiphany. I had a greater sense of my place in the scheme of things, but I felt no wiser. I'd been to The Edge, but I'd had no profound vision of what lay beyond the veil. I was now a changed person, but so what?

Over the course of the last eighteen months, I had come to embrace my longing. After all, it had led me to so many strange and wondrous places! It had been gradually dawning on me that perhaps the true objective of my quest wasn't something you could *find* at all — not a place or a philosophy or a person, but rather the act of searching itself.

I had made many new friends, and seen the great capitals of the world, but each time I alighted somewhere, I soon became restless and would succumb to the road's siren call. I'd discovered that I was at my best — my truest and most genuine self — when I was on the move, my handlebars pointed toward some distant horizon.

The question was no longer *'What's missing?'* The question now was, *'What has greater meaning, seeking or finding?'*

It was dark now. A ferry pulled away from the dock, and I watched as its lights slowly disappeared over the horizon. *Maybe I'll take that boat to Spain*, I thought idly, *or what about Africa?... go see the Pyramids.*

I ate what was left of the baguette and washed it down with the last of the wine. Then I went looking for a place to sleep.

The End

Made in the USA
San Bernardino, CA
15 November 2017